Diverse Teams:
Rediscovering an Ancient Approach to Urban Mission

Stephen Stallard

Urban Loft Publishers | Skyforest, CA

Diverse Teams:
Rediscovering an Ancient Approach to Urban Mission
Copyright © 2022 Stephen Stallard

All rights reserved. Except for brief quotations in critical publications or reviews, no part of this book may be reproduced in any manner without prior written permission from the publisher.

Urban Loft Publishers
P.O. Box 6
Skyforest, CA 92385
www.urbanloftpublishers.com

Senior Editors: Stephen Burris & Kendi Howells Douglas
Copy Editor: Christian Arnold
Cover Design & Interior Typesetting: Amber McKinley Craft

All Scripture quotations, unless otherwise noted, been taken from the Christian Standard Bible®, Copyright © 2017 by Holman Bible Publishers. Used by permission. Christian Standard Bible® and CSB® are federally registered trademarks of Holman Bible Publishers.

ISBN-13: 978-1-949625-18-9
Made in the U.S.

ACKNOWLEDGEMENTS

It takes a village to write a book. Over the last five years, I have been mentored by Mike Dodson, Manuel Sosa, and Ken Davis. I have been pastored by Taylor Field, who ably built upon the legacy of my first pastor, my deceased Father, Jimmy Stallard. While writing about multicultural teams, I have had the privilege of being a part of such a team in Brooklyn. I am grateful to Woodley, Shawn, Tze, Emily, Salome, Kevin, and Chris for showing me the beautiful potential of multicultural teams. Thanks are due to my friend Damon Horton for the gracious foreword and to Stephen Burris for bringing this manuscript to life.

My family stood behind me every step of the way. My children came into the office at just the right time, to encourage me to rest and play with them. Malia, Xavier, Darius, and Cyrus, thank you for reminding me what is important in life: you.

Sonya, without you this book would have never been written. Thank you for encouraging me and for believing in me every day of this journey. I love you, and I'm thrilled to follow Jesus hand-in-hand with you.

This book is offered up as an act of worship to the eternal God: Father, Son, and Spirit. You are the one who is worthy of study and worship, and this work is only possible because of you.

ABBREVIATIONS

ACCS	Ancient Christian Commentary on Scripture
IJFM	*International Journal of Frontier Missiology*
BDAG	*A Greek-English Lexicon of the New Testament and Other Early Christian Literature*
CBQ	*The Catholic Biblical Quarterly*
DACB	*Dictionary of African Christian Biography*
JBL	*Journal of Biblical Literature*
ICJ	*International Congregational Journal*
NAC	*New American Commentary*
NICNT	*New International Commentary on the New Testament*
NTS	*New Testament Studies*
JSNT	*Journal for the Study of the New Testament*
IJUT	*International Journal of Urban Transformation*
JofUM	*Journal of Urban Mission*
MOR	*Management and Organization Review*
ZECNT	*Zondervan Exegetical Commentary on the New Testament*

TABLE OF CONTENTS

FOREWORD 7

PREFACE: BUILDING A BRIDGE TO BROOKLYN 11

CHAPTER ONE: INTRODUCTION 15

CHAPTER TWO: READING THE BOOK OF ACTS LIKE A FIRST CENTURY CHRISTIAN 31

CHAPTER THREE: UNDERSTANDING CULTURE LIKE A TWENTY-FIRST CENTURY HUMAN 67

CHAPTER FOUR: MAPPING CULTURE FROM JERUSALEM TO ANTIOCH 107

CHAPTER FIVE: MAPPING CULTURE ON PAUL'S TEAMS 137

CHAPTER SIX: DIVERSE URBAN TEAMS IN ACTS AND IN THE MODERN WORLD 173

APPENDIX: CULTURAL MAP OF THE MINISTRY TEAMS IN THE BOOK OF ACTS 213

BIBLIOGRAPHY 214

FOREWORD

Over the years I've been privileged to know Stephen we have shared many things in common. A common love for our Lord Jesus, the riches of God's Word, great food, and a love for bringing all of these together in sync with our love for the city. Stephen and I have had many conversations regarding the complexities of biblical contextualization and fidelity in multi-cultural, multi-ethnic, multi-generational, and multi-linguistic settings. I have drunk deeply from his well of wisdom regarding the work Jesus had done through he and his family in Brooklyn. In Diverse Teams: Rediscovering an Ancient Approach to Urban Mission you will see how Stephen masterfully brings Scripture, the voices of Church Fathers and Mothers, into dialogue with the challenges often faced in urban settings. Stephen aptly proves how God's calling of His children to live on Jesus' mission is not one of isolation rather, a call into living as God's family together. The beauty of living as God's family is the inclusion of both genders, Jesus followers a diversity of ethnicities, cultures, and generations as well as social classes. Although on the outside, our spiritual family's diversity may look similar to the montage of our communities in the cities we live, our internal rhythms of togetherness should be comforting to all those inside of our team while appealing to those on the outside, compelling them to inquire more about us, so prayerfully the Lord would draw them into our family by embracing Jesus as Lord and Savior. No matter what unique challenges you are facing in your setting of ministry, I pray the Holy Spirit brings comfort to your heart as you read

Diverse Teams and discover Jesus' church has been where you are before. Stephen's research pulls from both Scripture and the corridors of Church History in order to surface how our family in Christ over the past three millennia have responded to similar challenges. Stephen's placement of the "cultural map" is beneficial for readers today when assessing how followers of Jesus during the church's infancy were figuring it out, without the full revelation of God's Word that we're in possession of today. As Paul mentions in Acts 17:26, what a joy it is to rest in the fact God has allowed us to be born with the ethnicity we have, but also has determined the times in which we were born and where He has planted us to live on Jesus' mission. I'm appreciative of how Stephen provides each of his readers with definitions to the terms in which he uses throughout Diverse Teams as this allows each of us to track with his research and thoughts throughout the book. Stephen is a true Missiologist, meaning he has considered not only the reader but also the nuances of the diverse frameworks of the overarching life rhythms of each readers context. He has gone to great lengths to shape his thoughts through the lens of Scripture (specifically through the book of Acts), all the while connecting us with the necessary bridges to understand application for life in the 21st Century.

As you read Diverse Teams, I invite you to pay attention to his footnotes, read the texts of his bibliography, and ask the Holy Spirit to provide you with illumination from God's Word so that you too will be able to apply the content in your immediate missional context. The world around us is lost and in need of direction as they search for truth. My prayer is the readers of Diverse Teams would glean from Stephens' insights and mobilize to meet truth seekers in their proximity where they are, so together they may lead them further into their search for truth, so they may find truth personified in the God-man Jesus Christ (c.f. John 14:6). In addition, I ask Jesus to draw His followers together, that they may form teams that embody the truthfulness of God's Word and live it out in front of the world that is watching them, so gospel proclamation would become necessary due to their commitment to gospel demonstration in their community. I cheer you on in your journey, as I remain committed to partnering with the Diverse Team our Lord has called me to join in Southern California.

On the frontline with you,

D.A. Horton

Program Director of Intercultural Studies at California Baptist University
Associate Teaching Pastor at the Grove Community Church

PREFACE: BUILDING A BRIDGE TO BROOKLYN

My favorite vantage point in my adopted hometown is the Brooklyn Promenade. On countless occasions I have descended from this Promenade with my family to play in the beautiful Brooklyn Bridge Park. We typically finish our adventures by sampling ice cream on the waterfront, or perhaps by meeting friends for Grimaldi's legendary pizza. But my favorite part is up above, in the heights. On this nearly 2,000-foot walkway, I can peer below at the busy highway, teeming with traffic. Or I can sit on a bench and gaze at the stunning view.

What I see from the Promenade never fails to inspire me. To the south, out in the Harbor, I see a Lady with a torch, lighting the way to all who will come to these shores. Across the East River, I take in the Manhattan skyline, including the elegant Freedom Tower, erected in the aftermath of 9/11. To the north stands my favorite building in all of NYC. The Empire State Building was where I asked Sonya to marry me (and where she said yes!). It is a building that houses memories, but it also inspires me to dream, and I follow its contours as they disappear into the clouds. And yet, the most impressive structure that I view from the Promenade might not be a building at all, but a bridge.

The Brooklyn Bridge stretches across the East River, linking Manhattan and Brooklyn. It stands as an extraordinary testament to human ingenuity and determination. The project cost millions of dollars, resulted in the death of several construction workers, and took fourteen years to finish. Since people were understandably nervous to traverse the world's longest suspension bridge, the publicity-hungry P. T. Barnum sent twenty-one circus elephants over the bridge to demonstrate its safety (and market his business). The new bridge connected the cities of Brooklyn and New York. It made possible the connection between various parts of New York and established a foundation for a booming city.

Today, the Bridge's granite and limestone towers still stand strong. Its Gothic revival arches still capture the imagination. And its pathways still serve as conduits for cars, trains, and pedestrians going about their lives, probably barely aware of the marvel upon which they stand. The Brooklyn Bridge is functional and beautiful. It gets a person across the East River, but it is not just about moving from point A to point B. The journey is made more enjoyable by the experience offered by the Bridge.

This book is about building a bridge to Brooklyn. It is about learning an ancient approach to urban mission, one found in the Book of Acts. It is a book about how that old model can best be used in the cities of today, so that urban churches and ministries can flourish. The book you are holding in your hands is not about Brooklyn, or even about cities, per se. But it is an attempt to build a bridge from the ancient world of the early Church to modern cities, like Brooklyn.

Building this bridge will require us to explore three primary fields: New Testament studies, Anthropology, and Urban Studies. This book seeks to demonstrate that diverse teams are an ancient and still viable approach to urban mission. In our chaotic, post-pandemic world, perhaps diverse teams can even operate like the Brooklyn Bridge. They are both functional and beautiful. It is that combination that still inspires me as I stand upon the Promenade and gaze upon the Brooklyn Bridge. And it is the beauty, power, and potential of diverse teams that inspires this book.

To My Love.

CHAPTER ONE: Introduction

The complex urban environments of the twenty-first century are challenging, and yet fertile, ministry settings. Those who live and minister in dense urban neighborhoods know that a dizzying array of methods can be required. One increasingly popular strategy is the embrace of diverse ministry teams. For instance, Mark DeYmaz states that those who lead diverse churches should "safeguard the diversity of your staff and therefore the credibility of your church, mindful that no one people group should become so dominant in number as to undermine the vision."[1] DeYmaz notes that, this spirit of intentionality "is the middle ground between quotas and wishful thinking."[2]

In a similar fashion, Rodney Woo chronicles his difficult but determined journey towards a more inclusive leadership team at the church he pastored. He notes, "The church needed to raise spiritually effective leadership from each racial group" of the congregation.[3] This commitment to diverse leadership teams was modeled for Douglas Brouwer when he became the pastor of the International Protestant Church in Zurich, Switzerland. He observes, "When I first arrived at IPC, only one member of the board was from the U.S. The other board members were from Switzerland, the U.K., the Netherlands, Hong Kong, Kenya, and India. That diversity, I learned later, did not occur by accident. It occurred by design."[4]

Daniel Hill also argues that diverse leadership teams are essential to those who wish to engage in diverse ministry.[5] He proposes ten prin-

---

[1] Mark DeYmaz, *Building a Healthy Multi-Ethnic Church* (San Francisco: Jossey-Bass, 2007), 72.
[2] DeYmaz, *Building a Healthy Multi-Ethnic Church*, 72.
[3] Rodney Woo, *The Color of Church: A Biblical and Practical Paradigm for Multiracial Churches* (Nashville: B&H, 2009), 203.
[4] Douglas J. Brouwer, *How to Become a Multicultural Church* (Grand Rapids: Eerdmans, 2017), 53–54.
[5] Daniel Hill, "Just Power: Ten Principles for Building Intercultural Leadership Teams," in *Intercultural Ministry: Hope for a Changing World,* ed. Grace Ji-Sun Kim and Jann Aldredge-Clanton (Valley Forge, PA: Judson Press, 2017), 111–123.

ciples that he believes can produce more inclusive teams that share power in an equitable fashion, as he notes that "the locus of intercultural transformation revolves around the navigation of power. Each congregation needs to develop a plan for how it will explore historical power dynamics and implement a system for sharing power across diverse constituencies."[6] For Hill, it is not enough to have a diverse team. Instead, he advocates for power shared equitably on leadership teams (the issue of power sharing will be explored in more detail in Chapter Six).

DeYmaz, Woo, Brouwer and Hill all represent an increasingly popular approach to church mission. They all believe that inclusive teams are a best practice for diverse congregations. In fact, their writings exemplify what sociologists in one study have discovered to be true about the emerging movement. Michael Emerson, George Yancey and Karen Chai Kim interviewed nearly two hundred members of multiethnic churches and noted that "Most of the churches included in our study have racially diverse clergy and lay leadership, which reflects some of the racial makeup of the church members."[7]

Advocates of diverse ministry teams usually note that this is a best practice. Sometimes, they also point to the Book of Acts as their inspiration for designing such teams. For instance, Mark DeYmaz believes that "the leadership at the church in Antioch (Acts 11:19 – 25; 13:1) serves as a model for enlisting diverse leadership within a local church setting."[8] This book is an attempt to determine if that is a correct reading of the text, as well as an appropriate application to contemporary contexts. This book seeks to explore a straightforward but complex set of questions: Is there an ancient approach to urban mission? Are diverse teams an element of that ancient approach? And how can we build a bridge from the

---

[6] Hill, "Just Power: Ten Principles for Building Intercultural Leadership Teams," 123.

[7] Curtiss Paul DeYoung, et al., *United By Faith: The Multiracial Congregation as an Answer to the Problem of Race* (Oxford: Oxford University Press, 2003), 177.

[8] DeYmaz, *Building a Healthy Multi-Ethnic Church,* 71.

patterns established in the Book of Acts to the cities of the twenty-first century?

It will not suffice merely to observe that diverse teams are a best practice for many urban ministries. It is important to grapple with the origin story of diverse teams in the inspired record of the Book of Acts. After all, when exploring an ancient approach to urban mission, there is no better place to start than in the Book of Acts. In this book we will explore cultural data and patterns from the Book of Acts and attempt to fashion a relevant application to contextually similar urban contexts.

The Big Idea

There is a *big idea* that animates this book. It is the idea that diverse teams were a crucial element of the ancient approach to urban mission that was pioneered in the Book of Acts. Additionally, in this book I will contend that the ancient method of employing diverse teams is worth retrieving by those who are engaged in contemporary urban mission.

Three different streams of evidence will converge to support the *big idea*. First, we will examine clues regarding the genre of the Book of Acts. We will discover that some forms of ancient historiography were designed to provide a pattern for imitation. This points in the direction of a "representative patterns" approach to applying the Book of Acts.

Second, in the heart of the book, we will create a "cultural map," produced from a study of the various teams throughout the Book of Acts. Patterns will emerge in the church at Jerusalem, the church at Antioch, and in the Pauline teams. Third, we will learn that there is a high level of similarity between contemporary major cities and the settings described in the Book of Acts. Consequently, we will be able to build a bridge from the ancient cities of Acts to contemporary cities, such as Brooklyn. We will be able to make application from the ancient urban context to the postmodern urban context.

Where to Go and How to Get There

In order to investigate an ancient approach to urban mission, we will engage in a careful, four-step process. First, we will examine the Book of Acts to discover the proper method(s) for application. Second, we will examine models of culture and then contrast these with how culture "worked" in antiquity. Third, we will use our newly developed model to construct a "cultural map" of ministry teams in the Book of Acts. This will include teams in the churches at Jerusalem and Antioch, as well as the Pauline Teams. Fourth, we will make application for those who minister on teams in contemporary cities.

In the pages that follow, we will embark upon a whirlwind tour through the fields of Anthropology, New Testament Studies, and Urban Studies. Chapter Two will examine the Book of Acts to determine an appropriate methodology for application of this narrative. Descriptive and prescriptive approaches to Acts will be contrasted, and various genre classifications for this book will be examined. After exploring these various methods, I will argue for a *representative patterns* approach to reading and applying the Book of Acts.

This approach will focus upon discovering repeatable patterns throughout the Book of Acts. These patterns, when discovered, could provide a guide for missionary methods. This chapter will attempt to ground the representative patterns approach in the genre of the Book of Acts, the speeches of the Book of Acts, and in the words of Paul. The argument of this chapter is introductory in nature, but it is a crucial step in the overall journey of discovery. If repeatable patterns of multicultural teams are discovered in Acts, and if the events of Acts are meant to show the reader how to conduct missions, then one should utilize this model in contextually similar urban contexts.

Chapter Three will engage another introductory question, that of culture. This study is, at its heart, a quest for traces of diversity on ministry teams in the Book of Acts.[9] Consequently, it is important to define terms such as culture, multicultural, and multiculturalism. To facilitate this discussion, Chapter Three will engage social science conversation partners to hear from modern, postmodern, and postcolonial theorists. After comparing these various approaches to culture, a model will be constructed, and then tested against the way that culture actually "worked" in antiquity. If the model is viable in the world of Josephus and Herodotus, then one might reasonably conclude that it is a legitimate way to understand culture in the Book of Acts.

The heart of our exploration commences in Chapter Four. This is the first of two chapters devoted to producing a "cultural map" of the first Christian ministry teams. The churches and ministry teams in Jerusalem and Antioch will be examined for traces of multiculturalism. This study will seek to culturally map these two churches, and the individuals that feature prominently on their ministry teams. At Jerusalem, this will involve examining the Hebraic Apostles, the Hellenistic Six Proto-Deacons, and Nicolaus the Proselyte. At Antioch, this will involve examining Barnabas, Simeon called Niger, Lucius of Cyrene, Manaen, and Saul of Tarsus.

Chapter Five will continue the cultural map by examining the Pauline teams on Paul's first, second, and third missionary journeys. Again, the goal will be to culturally map individuals who joined Paul to serve on mission with him. This study will not only examine those who might be deemed pastor-elders but will also include all noteworthy team members. This effort will focus primarily on the Book of Acts but will necessarily involve some correlation from the Pauline epistles.

---

[9] The present volume focuses on cultural diversity, leaving aside the question of gender diversity on ministry teams in the Book of Acts. The scope of the book requires a narrower focus, hence the emphasis upon culturally diverse teams as an approach to urban mission. However, the astute reader will note that there was a significant percentage of gender diversity on some of the Pauline teams.

Finally, we will build a bridge to Brooklyn. Chapter Six will transition to the 21st century, where we will discover how contemporary cities are, in many ways, similar to the settings of the Book of Acts. This will mean patterns of multicultural ministry teams discovered in the Book of Acts can be used as a model that can legitimately be applied to urban contexts. We will take initial steps towards suggesting how to apply such a model, discussing opportunities and challenges that will be involved when one attempts to implement such a model. These opportunities and challenges include cultural equity, cultural intelligence, and cultural tension.

Before we begin our exploration, it is crucial to define a few key terms. In this book, what do we mean by the words race, ethnicity, culture, multiculturalism, and diversity?

Defining Key Terms

A Working Definition of Race

I will not use the term "race" extensively in this volume. Legitimate concerns exist over whether it is a helpful concept for studies such as this. These critiques can be boiled down to two basic concerns. First, some wonder if race in antiquity was the same as race today. Second, some are wary of the term because of historical, ethical, or religious reasons. Both concerns will be briefly discussed, and a reason will be presented for a focus upon culture, instead of race.

Race is a complicated term. In the past, it was linked with scientific understandings of biology. These ideas were rooted in distinct "phenotypes," such as hair texture and eye shape. Most notably, skin color was used as the primary criteria for sorting various "races." Yet this approach has fallen out of favor as the sciences have continued to develop. Michael Rynkiewich notes that "race is a socially constructed category but it no longer has any scientific standing in human biology or anthropology."[10] Rynkiewich is correct in his observation of the academic guild's interest in race as a social category. In the past, discussions of race centered upon the human body. Now, those discussions focus upon the intersection of the body and society. Denise Eileen McCoskey asserts, "Race ... does not derive passively from human anatomy, but is dependent on social intervention, on the formulation of theories that designate the surface of the human body as the primary vehicle of race and also determine exactly *which* physical features 'matter' in determining racial groups."[11]

One of the challenges of using race as a rubric in this study would be in identifying how race "functioned" in the ancient world. The scientific theories that once grounded understandings of race had not even been invented when the Book of Acts was written. So, modern readers must ask themselves if discussions of race in the Book of Acts are anachronistic. In response to this query, it is important to acknowledge that racial difference was real in the ancient world, but it was not identical to our contemporary understandings of race. Shelley Haley summarizes the complexities of this topic and issues a warning: "Do not read our construct of race into ancient cultures. Did the Romans conceptualize a phenomenon such as 'racial difference'? Yes. Did the Romans notice skin-color difference? Yes. Did they attach a value to skin-color differences? That question is not answered so easily."[12]

A common method for assigning difference in the ancient world was the practice of physiognomy. As Mikeal Parsons observes, "In the ancient Greek and Roman world it was commonplace to associate outer

---

[10] Michael Rynkiewich, *Soul, Self, and Society: A Postmodern Anthropology for Mission in a Postcolonial World* (Eugene, OR: Cascade Books, 2001), 175.

[11] Denise Eileen McCoskey, *Race: Antiquity and its Legacy* (Oxford: Oxford University Press, 2012), 2.

[12] Shelley Haley, "Be Not Afraid of the Dark: Critical Race Theory and Classical Studies," in *Prejudice and Christian Beginnings: Investigating Race, Gender and Ethnicity in Early Christian Studies,* ed. Laura Nasrallah and Elisabeth Schüssler Fiorenza (Minneapolis: Fortress Press, 2010), 30.

physical characteristics with inner qualities. The study of the relationship between the physical and the moral was known as *physiognomics* and was widely practiced in late antiquity by philosophers, astrologers, and physicians."[13] This sounds much like the pseudo-scientific racial theories that birthed some forms of modern racism. In fact, Parsons notes, "The underlying conviction that the body of the Roman male free citizen was the normative body, physically and politically, is critical to understanding the bias against slaves, women, and 'inferior' men and races that permeates so much of physiognomic thinking in the ancient world."[14]

It seems that race was a concept of the ancient world, albeit one that functioned differently than contemporary understandings of race. Therefore, it would not automatically be anachronistic to discuss race in the Book of Acts. However, discussions of race in a book like Acts must proceed with caution, recognizing the divergence between the ancient and modern worlds.

A second set of ethical, historical, and religious concerns have also been lodged against the usage of the term "race" in studies such as this. Some wonder if there is simply too much baggage associated with this term. Given the horrors of the Holocaust, in which racialized thinking was employed by Adolph Hitler, many academics have shied away from discussions of race. Some prefer to use newer terms, such as ethnicity (see below).[15]

Although the term race has some value in these types of discussions, I do not plan to use it as a rubric in this study. I have made this decision for two reasons. First, better terms and concepts exist. For instance, subsequent sections will explore ethnicity and culture, both of

---

[13] Mikeal C. Parsons, *Body and Character in Luke and Acts: The Subversion of Physiognomy in Early Christianity* (Grand Rapids: Baker, 2006), 17.
[14] Parsons, *Body and Character in Luke and Acts*, 25.
[15] Denise Kimber Buell insightfully summarizes and weighs these concerns. Denise Kimber Buell, *Why This New Race: Ethnic Reasoning in Early Christianity* (New York: Columbia University Press, 2005), 13–21.

which are better positioned to answer some of the questions posed by this book.

Second, and most crucially, this book is focused upon unearthing historical details from the Book of Acts. Many of the figures listed in this document are enigmatic. Modern researchers cannot always identify the race of these men and women from antiquity (if race is constructed, at least in part, by a societal taxonomy of phenotypes). Researchers can, however, unearth information about the ethnicity and culture of far more individuals in the Book of Acts. This data is still accessible to the modern reader. Yet racial data would be much more elusive. For instance, what was the skin color of the physician Luke? It is difficult to know. However, one can reasonably conclude that he was a Gentile, possibly from Syrian Antioch (see the discussion of Luke in chapter five). For these reasons, I will not use the term "race" as a significant heuristic concept in our study of teams throughout the Book of Acts.

A Working Definition of Ethnicity

Many contemporary scholars prefer the term ethnicity over race. As Barreto notes, this is due, in part, to the legacy of racially driven violence. He observes, "The Shoah discredited the scholarly endeavor to map the biological roots of 'race' as did the conquest of the Americas by casting their native inhabitants as less than human."[16] He recounts, "Hoping to escape this legacy, scholars opted for a new term, 'ethnicity,' in which culture, not biology, was the primary determinant in the distinguishing of groups of people."[17] Within this statement, the reader can see a preference for a term not yet defined in this study: "culture." Indeed, any detailed exploration of ethnicity must necessarily involve

---

[16] Eric Barreto, *Ethnic Negotiations: The Function of Race and Ethnicity in Acts 16* (Tübingen: Mohr Siebeck, 2010), 29.
[17] Barreto, *Ethnic Negotiations,* 29.

defining a cluster of key concepts. Therefore, some caution is needed when approaching this complicated term.[18]

In popular terms ethnicity often refers to a person's national background. Examples include Jamaican, Jewish, and Irish ethnicities. People often think that they possess an "essence" that makes them part of an ethnic group. In scholarly circles, defining ethnicity is more complex. Jonathan Hall lists three "core elements" of ethnicity. He notes that these are "a putative subscription to a myth of common descent and kinship, an association with a specific territory and a sense of shared history."[19] These core elements are biological (myth of common descent), geographical (association with territory), and historical (shared history).

To a certain extent, one can see the correlation between the popular and scholarly understandings of ethnicity. For instance, if a person views her ethnic identity as Jamaican, it is likely she believes she can trace her "bloodline" to Jamaica. This "biological" connection to the Caribbean island somehow links her to other people through shared geography and history. At this point, it is important to acknowledge that a myth of common descent can be true or false. Sometimes ethnicity can be constructed based on a fictive bloodline. Some biblical scholars have even identified traces of this approach in the writings of Paul, who crafted a common ancestry when he linked Gentile Christians to their "Father Abraham."[20] From Paul the Apostle to Tiger Woods, a person's ethnic identity is shaped in part by a person's real or fictive myth of common ancestry.

In this book, Eric Barreto's definition of ethnicity will be followed: "Race or ethnicity is a socially constructed, discursive, pliable claim to be

---

[18] Rynkiewich, *Soul, Self, and Society,* 163–167, includes a helpful discussion of ethnicity, one that frames different approaches to the concept. Rynkiewich's missiological methodology is informed by the latest developments in anthropology.

[19] Jonathan Hall, *Hellenicity: Between Ethnicity and Culture* (Chicago: University of Chicago Press, 2002), 9.

[20] Caroline Johnson Hodge, *If Sons, Then Heirs: A Study of Kinship and Ethnicity in the Letters of Paul* (Oxford: Oxford University Press, 2007).

a group of people defined around myths of putative commonality of kinship or ancestry including origins, language, culture, religion, geography, and other organizing principles."[21] This definition is helpful because it recognizes ethnicity as both fixed and fluid. It is something that can be negotiated as it is socially constructed. This definition, while rejecting the idea that a person possesses an ethnic essence, does ground ethnicity in certain core elements. This is like the previously mentioned work of Jonathan Hall, who recognized that ethnicity can shift, can be based upon fictive claims, and is also grounded in certain commonalities.

The term ethnicity will be used throughout this book. When it is used, Barreto's above definition will control its usage and meaning. However, ethnicity is not the primary focus of study in this volume. This is due, in part, to the previously mentioned historical difficulties that plague the ancient study of race. One cannot always identify the ethnicity of an individual in the Book of Acts. For instance, would Lucius of Cyrene have identified as an ethnic African? Or was he Jewish? These questions are difficult to answer. However, what is clear is that Lucius was, at least partially, culturally African (see discussion of Lucius in chapter four).

This study is an investigation of the patterns of culturally diverse teams in the Book of Acts. This means that the terms most relevant to our discussion are "culture" and "multicultural." It is to a definition of these terms that we now turn.

A Working Definition of Culture and Multicultural

Culture is a notoriously slippery concept to grasp, as well as a difficult term to define.[22] I will only briefly engage this issue here, since building a model of culture will be the task of Chapter Three.

---

[21] Barreto, *Ethnic Negotiations*, 27.
[22] Wrogemann lists six different models of culture. Clearly, this a difficult subject, and answers are elusive. Henning Wrogemann, *Intercultural Theology, Volume One: Intercultural Hermeneutics* (Downers Grove, IL: IVP, 2016), 112–134.

In the field of missiology, Paul's Hiebert's classic definition has been widely embraced. He asserts that culture is "the more or less integrated systems of ideas, feelings, and values and their associated patterns of behavior and products shared by a group of people who organize and regulate what they think, feel, and do."[23] Howell and Paris present a more succinct and contemporary definition of culture, when they assert, "Culture is the total way of life of a group of people that is learned, dynamic, shared, power laden, and integrated."[24]

It seems from this definition that Howell and Paris built upon, and moved beyond, Hiebert's original model of culture. This newer definition of culture (which will be assessed in Chapter Three) will be utilized throughout this study because it incorporates the latest insights from the social sciences. As James and Lillian Breckenridge observe, "By whatever standard we measure, culture will be expressive of a holistic social testimony in which an entire society identifies itself by its political, social, and religious/philosophical beliefs."[25] Consequently, this study will explore the teams in Acts, searching for evidence of various "total ways of life" (cultures).

Ethnicity, as defined in the previous section, is a subset of culture. If ethnicity corresponds to how people self-identify, culture corresponds to that web of symbols and artifacts that is continually negotiated (and

---

[23] Paul Hiebert, *Anthropological Insights for Missionaries* (Grand Rapids: Baker, 1985), 30. Interestingly, Hiebert's final book, published twenty-four years later, includes a similar, but not identical, definition of culture. He defines culture as " ... the more or less integrated system of beliefs, feelings, and values created and shared by a group of people that enable them to live together socially and that are communicated by means of their systems of symbols and rituals, patterns of behavior, and the material products they make." Paul Hiebert, *Constants in Human Context: Anthropological Explorations for Contemporary Missions* (Grand Rapids: Baker, 2009), 150. The subtle differences in the two definitions are, perhaps, a window into the changing nature of the social sciences, and of their impact upon missiology. This evolving model of culture will be discussed in greater depth in Chapter Three.

[24] Brian M. Howell and Jenell Paris, *Introducing Cultural Anthropology: A Christian Perspective,* 2nd edition (Grand Rapids: Baker, 2019), 40.

[25] James Breckenridge and Lillian Breckenridge, *What Color Is Your God? Multicultural Education in the Church* (Grand Rapids: Baker, 1995), 24.

renegotiated) in the public sphere. Overlap exists between these two concepts, in part because culture is not unidimensional. Ashford and Thomas helpfully remind us that "on the one hand, culture appears to be something that we make, while on the other hand, culture appears to be something that makes us."[26]

A person could be ethnically Jamaican and culturally British. Their ethnicity would stem from their biological connections (real or fictive), geographical connections, and historical connections, all of which tie them to the Caribbean island. Yet their culture could conceivably be British, since they could adopt the posture, customs, accent, food, politics, and religion of their former colonizers. These artifacts and symbols would always be negotiated in public, producing an ever-changing, ethnically Jamaican, culturally British individual. This dynamic interplay between ethnicity and culture can lead to shifting identities, ones characterized by hybridity or biculturalism. In Chapter Three, we will explore how the ancient phenomenon of Hellenization might lend itself to bicultural models of identity.

If culture is a "system" as Hiebert argued (or a "total way of life," as Howell and Paris posited), then how should one define the term "multicultural?" In this book, the term multicultural will be used to refer to the presence of multiple cultural systems, whether in one person, in one church, or on one team. It should be noted that the term multiculturalism will not be employed in a philosophical sense, akin to contemporary ideas regarding the validity of pluralism.[27] Instead, this research project will explore teams that might be multicultural. A multicultural team would be one in which multiple cultural systems (or "total ways of life") are present

---

[26] Bruce Riley Ashford and Heath A. Thomas, *The Gospel of Our King: Bible, Worldview, and the Mission of Every Christian* (Grand Rapids: Baker, 2019), 157. This concept will be discussed further in Chapter Three.

[27] See D. A. Carson's trenchant critique of philosophical pluralism in contemporary society. D. A. Carson, *The Gagging of God: Christianity Confronts Pluralism* (Grand Rapids: Zondervan, 1996), 19–37.

within the team. For the sake of clarity and variety, I will use the terms "diverse" and "multicultural" interchangeably.

Understanding our Limits

This volume is focused on discovering patterns of multicultural teams in the Book of Acts and applying them to ministry teams in urban contexts. As a result of the unique focus of the present study, related issues will be left unexplored.

Although the Pauline epistles will be consulted (in order to correlate the identities of members of the Pauline teams), I will not present any theories regarding Paul's theology of culture, or multiculturalism. The focus will remain on Paul's actions in the Book of Acts. Additionally, Paul's cultural identity will be briefly explored, but only in a cursory fashion. Much recent research has been conducted on Paul's status as a Jew. While this is noteworthy and significant, we cannot delve deeply into Paul's background. In this book, Paul is merely one person to be examined, among many. A similar limitation applies to all the ministry team members surveyed in this study. Our goal is to ascertain the cultural identity of various individuals, and not to produce an exhaustive biography of each person.

Hermeneutical issues will be raised in an exploratory fashion. At times, this will produce questions that will need to be answered by future research. For instance, although possible genres for Acts are considered, the present study cannot engage in an exhaustive analysis of the topic of genre. Theological issues will also be engaged on an introductory level. These will, at times, raise further questions beyond the scope of this volume. For instance, is there a link between Charismatic theology and a heightened sense of the normativity of the Book of Acts? This is an important question, one that, hopefully, will be taken up by other researchers.

The biggest limitations have already been described in the section on pertinent definitions. Although issues of race and ethnicity are salient and worthy of study, this volume is focused upon culture. Consequently, I will leave questions of race and ethnicity to other, more able, writers.

CHAPTER TWO: Reading the Book of Acts like a First Century Christian

What is the proper method for applying the Book of Acts? Is there only one, or are there multiple legitimate approaches? Does the appropriate method depend upon one's era in history or one's location on the map? These (and related) questions are complex, defying easy answers. In this chapter, it will be impossible to exhaustively resolve all these issues. To do so would require writing perhaps dozens of books!

However, it is necessary to engage two advanced issues in the study of the Book of Acts. Consequently, I will examine both descriptive and prescriptive approaches to applying the Book of Acts. I will also explore potential classifications for the genre of Acts. Emerging from this review, we will be able to construct a representative patterns approach to applying Acts. This will include a case study of the connection between Pauline doctrine and method.

This chapter is preliminary in nature, but still important to the overall direction of our journey. If, in later chapters, patterns of multicultural teams are discerned, then we will have a framework for knowing what to "do" with that data. The representative patterns model (traced in this chapter) will be employed in later chapters to produce a "cultural map" of various teams throughout the Book of Acts and apply it to contemporary cities. In the meantime, this chapter will explore methodologies for reading and applying Acts. The goal is to develop a usable approach that will enable the reader to spot patterns of diverse teams in Acts and apply them to ministry settings in urban contexts.

Methodology

For biblical interpreters and expositors, the task of applying imperatives is often (but not always) straightforward.[28] For instance, Paul's admonition to "Flee sexual immorality" (1 Cor 6:18 CSB) is direct, and relatable to our contemporary contexts. Yet a story possesses a different structure, one that challenges us to discern its intent.[29] For instance, in Acts 4–5, we read that the Christians in Jerusalem shared their possessions, and that Ananias and Sapphira died because they lied about sharing their possessions. The puzzled reader could be forgiven for asking, "What is the story telling me to do?" Perhaps the reader is being instructed not to lie, or to share her possessions. Or perhaps the text is simply informational, and therefore it "stops" after describing what happened in the 1st century.

This brings us to the question that lies at the crux of the debate: how should Christians read the Book of Acts? Wright and Bird assert, "Luke-Acts is partly a manual for discipleship and partly a blueprint for operating a church."[30] Many agree, and yet quibble over the details. Yuckman notes, "There are many possible ways to learn mission from Acts. Some have used Luke-Acts as a grab-bag of timeless commissioning statements or as a 'casebook' of mission principles. Others have looked back to Acts as the golden age of missionary triumph in an attempt to recreate

---

[28] One set of exceptions is commands issued in the Old Testament. Are Christians bound by these instructions? This raises multiple layers of questions surrounding the relationship and continuity (or lack thereof) between the two testaments. See John Feinberg, *Continuity and Discontinuity: Perspectives on the Relationship Between the Old and New Testaments* (Westchester, IL: Crossway, 1988).

[29] Meir Sternberg, *The Poetics of Biblical Narrative: Ideological Literature and the Drama of Reading* (Bloomington, IN: Indiana University Press, 1987).

[30] N. T. Wright and Michael Bird, *The New Testament in Its World: An Introduction to the History, Literature, and Theology of the First Christians* (Grand Rapids: Zondervan, 2019), 644.

it."[31] Which approach is correct? Or is there even one right approach to reading and applying the Book of Acts?

The Anglican missionary Roland Allen argued for what seems to be a prescriptive approach, because he believed that Acts was more than a history book.[32] Regarding the record of some of Paul's journeys in Acts,[33] Allen declares, "It is impossible but that the account so carefully given by St. Luke of the planting of the churches in the Four Provinces should have something more than a mere archeological and historical interest. Like the rest of the Holy Scriptures it was 'written for our learning.'"[34] Allen never articulated a theoretical rationale for this position (at least, he did not do so in his famous book *Missionary Methods*). He merely assumed it to be true, and then he urged missionaries to follow the example of the Apostle Paul. However, not everyone agrees with Allen. New Testament scholars, theologians, and missiologists have all grappled with this issue.[35]

In the pages that follow, we will explore the strengths and weaknesses of both the descriptive and prescriptive approaches.[36] This discussion is relevant to our overall quest because it frames the issue and helps us to understand what role the patterns of Acts might play in con-

---

[31] Colin Yuckman, "Mission and the Book of Acts in a Pluralist Society," *Missiology* 47, no. 2 (April 2019): 104–105.

[32] Roland Allen, *Missionary Methods: St. Paul's or Ours?* (Grand Rapids: Eerdmans, 1962).

[33] Gallagher has noted that Allen did not necessarily believe that all of Acts was prescriptive. Instead, he notes, "Allen formed his theory of Paul's missionary tactics based largely on Paul's second journey …" See Robert Gallagher, "Missionary Methods: St. Paul's, St. Roland's, or Ours?" in *Missionary Methods: Research, Reflections, and Realities*, ed. Craig Ott and J. D. Payne (Pasadena: William Carey, 2013), 4.

[34] Allen, *Missionary Methods*, 4.

[35] See two excellent centennial reflections on Allen's influential volume, one authored by Robert Plummer and John Mark Terry, *Paul's Missionary Methods: In His Time and Ours* (Downers Grove, IL: IVP, 2012), and the other by Craig Ott and J. D. Payne, *Missionary Methods: Research, Reflections, and Realities* (Pasadena: William Carey, 2013).

[36] A descriptive approach reads a biblical narrative as informational; these texts describe what happened. A prescriptive approach reads a biblical narrative as a prescription for contemporary Christian living. Of course, as will be noted in this chapter's discussion, both views allow for nuance.

temporary missiological models. For instance, in later chapters, data will be explored on the cultural composition of various ministry teams in Acts. The aim will be to explore our big idea about diverse teams. However, even if we find ancient traces of diversity, we will still be left with another question: what relevance does this data have to contemporary ministry settings? Are the patterns that might emerge from Acts merely descriptive in nature, or do they call for replication? In other words, if multicultural teams are found in the Book of Acts, is that a prescriptive pattern that Christians should imitate in the 21st century?

Reading Acts Descriptively

New Testament scholar Dean Flemming boldly declares that "Martin Hengel is right. For Luke, Paul is the model missionary."[37] This is a sentiment with which many might concur. However, Flemming did not believe that Paul's status as Luke's "model missionary" meant that Pauline methods were normative for contemporary missionaries. He went on to say, "For us, the value of Paul's preaching in Acts is not in slavishly imitating either its specific content or method."[38] The missiologically focused New Testament scholar believed that Paul need not be imitated, but that contemporary readers could still learn from Luke's description of Paul's ministry. This is a descriptive approach, one that Flemming would probably apply to the entire Book of Acts.

In a similar fashion, missiologist Donald McGavran argues that Roland Allen's record of Paul's ministry is accurate, but that "we cannot blindly apply this summary of New Testament methods ... today."[39] McGavran believed much is left to be learned from New Testament methodology. However, he also believed that differences in context necessitate

---

[37] Dean Flemming, *Contextualization in the New Testament: Patterns for Theology and Mission* (Downers Grove, IL: IVP, 2005), 56.

[38] Flemming, *Contextualization in the New Testament*, 85–86.

[39] Donald McGavran, *The Bridges of God: A Study in the Strategy of Missions* (Eugene, OR: Wipf & Stock, 2005), 135.

different approaches. Consequently, he resisted a normative reading of Paul and (presumably) of the Book of Acts in general. Still, he was favorable to much of Allen's thinking, even recommending that all those working in people movements should be required to read Allen's books.[40]

Flemming represents the world of New Testament scholarship, while McGavran is an historically distinguished missiologist. They both appreciate the examples left to readers in the Book of Acts, yet they are also cautious about uncritical application. They might not use the terms prescriptive and descriptive, but they do both seem to favor a more descriptive approach.

This method is also borne out in the writings of New Testament scholar Eckhard Schnabel. In his magisterial work Early Christian Mission, he devoted fifteen hundred pages to describing the history of mission in the New Testament. Yet he spent only twenty pages on application to the present era. In that brief discussion, he argues, first, that the New Testament should be authoritative for missionary practice. He states, "Indeed, if the interpretation of New Testament texts no longer serves to authenticate missionary work, then scholars have capitulated to the often-controversial results and aporias of source, tradition and redaction criticism."[41]

Schnabel goes on to offer more nuance, when he argues, "It is naïve to think that historical experiences [from the Book of Acts] are normative and can or should be repeated."[42] Schnabel is concerned that contemporary readers might seek to replicate experiences from the Book of Acts that do not fit a given context or era. After all, he notes, "Historical experiences often have a complex nexus of historical causes that cannot be reproduced."[43] I believe this is an important point, and it is one I will

---

[40] McGavran, *Bridges of God,* 136.
[41] Eckhard Schnabel, *Early Christian Mission* (Downers Grove, IL: IVP, 2004), 1569.
[42] Schnabel, *Early Christian Mission,* 1570.
[43] Ibid.

return to as I construct a representative patterns model for applying the Book of Acts.

Even though Schnabel is wary about naïve and simplistic approaches to applying Acts, he still believes that the New Testament documents play an important role in guiding our missionary methods. Providing a dose of nuance and balance, he asserts, "This does not mean that the history of the early Christian mission does not provide lessons for missionary outreach …. However, before distilling 'principles' from the historical narratives of the New Testament, one needs to distinguish hermeneutically between what is descriptive and what is (possibly) prescriptive."[44]

Intriguingly, Schnabel seems to allow that there might be elements of the early Christian mission that are prescriptive, although he does not clarify what they might be. Overall, one sees in Schnabel the same concerns and basic approach that are clearly expressed by both Flemming and McGavran. All three scholars lean towards a selective application of the Book of Acts. This seems to be because they view Acts as a document that is primarily descriptive. Perhaps these various writers would all prefer to express different nuances. Still, they all seem to approach the text of Acts from a generally descriptive framework.

How should one assess the descriptive model for reading and applying the Book of Acts? As with almost any model, this one has its strengths and weaknesses. The first advantage of the descriptive approach is that it honors the text by focusing upon it, instead of upon the reader. Sometimes contemporary readers (including missiologists) can be too quick to derive missional principles from a biblical text like Acts. Advocates of the descriptive approach remind us to slow down and ensure that we are reading Acts as an ancient document. This is an important word of caution, regardless of one's interpretive system.

---

[44] Ibid.

The second advantage of the descriptive model is that it equips readers to grapple with certain difficult narratives. For instance, should modern Christians cast lots to select leaders, speak in tongues, and sell their land to give to those in need? All these practices are recorded in the first few chapters of the Book of Acts. A descriptive approach equips the reader to recognize the historical situatedness of the text, thereby freeing her from the demands of a rigidly literal application. Some might argue that this is a disadvantage, and not an advantage, because it could allow the reader to ignore whatever she does not want to obey.

Regardless of one's approach, it is important to remember Carson's word of caution: "Although it is right to recognize the occasional nature of Paul's letters, it is wrong to hide behind their occasional nature so that every time our practices do not square with them we attribute the difference to the occasional nature of the apostolic documents and thus leave unchanged whatever it is we are doing (or not doing)."[45] Carson's reminder about the epistolary literature of the New Testament is also applicable to its historical narratives. We must not rush to declare that a text is descriptive, simply so that we may avoid following its intent.

What are the disadvantages of the descriptive model? The chief disadvantage is that the descriptive approach could tend towards selectivity. Nearly all interpreters believe that Acts demands something from them. However, readers do not generally apply everything they read. Many believe that some things are binding, and some are not. What are the criteria for making those decisions? Some, like Fee and Stuart, have proposed guidelines.[46] Yet any approach can be subjective and might leave certain elements of the text unapplied. One must be careful about a

---

[45] Donald A. Carson, "Paul's Mission and Prayer," in *The Gospel to the Nations: Perspectives on Paul's Mission,* ed. Peter Bolt and Mark Thompson (Downers Grove, IL: IVP, 2000), 178.

[46] Gordon Fee and Douglas Stuart, *How to Read the Bible for All Its Worth,* 4th ed. (Grand Rapids: Zondervan, 2014), 112–131.

subjective approach that could lead to the elevation of the reader over the text.

Reading Acts Prescriptively

In contrast to the descriptive model for reading and applying Acts, some approach this New Testament text from a prescriptive framework. Craig Keener, in his monumental treatment of the Book of Acts, argues directly for prescription. He declares, "Luke's record and adaptation of Jesus's teachings in the Gospel should be enough to alert us to Luke's interest in praxis and not mere information for its own sake. Luke-Acts offers patterns that are prescriptive, not merely descriptive."[47] According to Keener, this means that "Jesus (in the Gospel) and the evangelizers and church planters (in Acts) provide a missiological model for Luke's audience as they continue the task."[48] Keener does not shy away from using the label "prescriptive." He boldly enters the theological fray by arguing that both the "natural" and "supernatural" activities of the Church in Acts are to serve as models for us today.[49]

Keener's colleague,[50] missiologist Timothy Tennent, seems to favor a prescriptive approach. He notes, "Increasingly, missions practice around the world understands the Book of Acts not only as an accurate description of the Holy Spirit's work through the early church, but also as

---

[47] Craig Keener, *Acts: An Exegetical Commentary,* vol. 1 (Grand Rapids: Baker, 2012), 440.

[48] Keener, *Acts*, 440.

[49] Keener, *Acts,* 440-441.

[50] Asbury Theological Seminary (a seminary in the Wesleyan tradition) is currently the professional home of both Keener and Tennent. This leads one to wonder if there is, indeed, a connection (as Tennent suggests) between Pentecostalism and a prescriptive approach to Acts. Furthermore, Asbury (and Tennent and Keener, in particular) has deep ties with global Christianity. This raises the question of whether the growth in prescriptive readings of Acts is linked with Majority World Christianity. Is there something about non-Western Christianity that leads readers to apply the Book of Acts in a prescriptive manner? This question is fascinating, and worthy of further research, but is outside of the scope of the present study.

a prescriptive paradigm that should guide the church's practice today."[51] According to Tennent, this shift in perspective has been facilitated, in part, by the global growth of Pentecostalism.[52]

For some, the prescriptive nature of Acts is merely assumed. For instance, in a footnote to a recent article, Colin Yuckman boldly asserts, "It goes without saying that practitioners of Christian mission take the canonical Acts as normative."[53] It is not apparent why this issue is so clear to Yuckman. However, he is probably expressing the perspective of many Christians who see themselves in the story of Acts, and who wish to renew their churches by returning to New Testament praxis.

How should one assess the prescriptive model for reading and applying the Book of Acts? As with the descriptive model, this one has its strengths and weaknesses. The primary advantage of the prescriptive approach is that it could lend itself towards consistency in application. Instead of constructing criteria by which some of Acts is normative, and some is not, prescriptive advocates are liberated to apply the entire book. While this internal consistency is an attractive feature, one wonders whether anyone has ever truly consistently lived and ministered in this way. The chief disadvantage of the prescriptive model is that it could allow the reader to gloss over history. At this point, it is necessary to remember Schnabel's earlier warning: historical events are unrepeatable. A historical text like Acts describes events that are oftentimes quite simply unrepeatable. This appears to be the weak link in the prescriptive model.

Is there a path out of this impasse? On the one hand are those who believe that Acts is descriptive, and merely provides a historical record. Others argue that Acts is prescriptive and therefore provides a paradigm

---

[51] Timothy Tennent, *Invitation to World Missions: A Trinitarian Missiology for the Twenty-first Century* (Grand Rapids: Kregel, 2010), 428.

[52] Tennent, *Invitation to World Missions,* 414–428.

[53] Yuckman, "Mission and the Book of Acts," 113. For a more nuanced, yet affirming perspective, see Stephen Voorwinde, "How Normative is Acts?" *Vox Reformata* 2010: 33–56.

for how Christians should live and minister. Yet the hermeneutical options are not limited to these two approaches. In fact, some advocates of the descriptive model nuance it to such a degree that they allow elements of prescription.[54] This leads one to wonder if there is, possibly, a via media, one which appropriates the best of both positions.

I want to advocate for such a third option for reading and applying the Book of Acts. First, however, we will need to engage an issue that is intertwined with a reader's hermeneutic for Acts. The issue of genre is inextricably linked to the way in which one reads and applies the Book of Acts. Therefore, before advocating for a "third way" approach to reading Acts, we must take a detour to explore possible genres for this ancient document.

What Kind of Book is This? The Genre of the Book of Acts

Over the course of this chapter strengths and weaknesses have been discovered in both the descriptive and prescriptive approaches to reading and applying Acts. Consequently, neither option is completely satisfactory. If we are going to find a way forward, it might be through a fresh examination of genre. This exploration will enable interpreters to grapple with ways in which the author might have meant for the book to be read (and applied). This in turn will feed into the potential discovery and discussion of patterns of diverse teams in Acts.

At least two prominent genre categories are frequently used to classify the Book of Acts:[55] historiography and biography (βιος).[56] We will

---

[54] See Schnabel's previously cited comments.

[55] In a previous generation of New Testament scholarship, more attention was given to the possibility that Acts was an apologetic to Theophilus (and the broader Greco-Roman power structures). However, in more recent times, attention has focused more often upon the historical monograph and the βιος. For an example of the older approach, see Bruce's discussion of the apologetic nature of Lukan historiography in F. F. Bruce, *The Book of the Acts* (Grand Rapids: Eerdmans, 1976), 20–21.

[56] Historiography is an ancient form of history writing and βιος is an ancient form of biography.

briefly explore both options.⁵⁷ Furthermore, we will devote special attention to the implications that the genre of Acts has upon the question of the application of the Book of Acts. In other words, does understanding the genre of Acts help us to chart a via media out of the descriptive/prescript-ive impasse?

Acts as Historiography

It is obvious that Luke was writing history when he penned the Book of Acts.⁵⁸ Yet the question remains, what does that mean? What kind of history was he writing? The Book of Acts certainly does not seem to fit into the mold of modern works of history. Instead, Luke-Acts seems to be history that is written with a theological agenda.⁵⁹ In fact, Todd Penner calls Luke "a theological or hagiographical historian."⁶⁰ Because Luke is clearly providing his readers (most notably, Theophilus) with a historical record (albeit a theologically driven one), many have classified Acts as an example of ancient historiography.

For example, classicist Daryl Palmer believes that Acts is an example of a specific form of historiography called the historical monograph. He notes, "In modern discussion the phrase [historical monograph] is commonly applied to ancient historical writings which deal with a limited issue or period without regard to the length of the books themselves."⁶¹ According to Palmer, Polybius (writing in the 2nd century B.C.) described ancient historians who wrote with a "particular" focus. In

---

⁵⁷ For a broader discussion that encompasses more than two options for classifying Acts, see Alan Bale, *Genre and Narrative Coherence in the Acts of the Apostles* (London: Bloomsbury, 2015), 48–69.

⁵⁸ Throughout this book I will assume that Luke wrote Luke–Acts.

⁵⁹ This does not mean that the historical veracity of Acts is then called into question. I accept the inerrancy of the Book of Acts, as well as that of the entire canon of Scripture.

⁶⁰ Todd Penner, *In Praise of Christian Origins: Stephen and the Hellenists in Lukan Apologetic Historiography* (New York: T&T Clark, 2004), 58.

⁶¹ Daryl Palmer, "Acts and the Ancient Historical Monograph," in *The Book of Acts in Its Ancient Literary Setting*, ed. Bruce Winter and Andrew Clarke (Grand Rapids: Eerdmans, 1993), 4.

contrast to his universal history, Polybius described their more focused works.[62] Palmer believes that Acts is an historical monograph because it has a narrow chronological, geographical and topical focus.[63] Additionally, one could note that the focus of Acts is highly selective, lending credence towards the historical monograph classification.

Osvaldo Padilla also opts for the classification of historical monograph. Yet, he nuances that designation when he declares, "It is my suggestion that Acts is a Hellenistic historical monograph in the Jewish tradition."[64] Padilla helpfully reminds his readers, "The term historical monograph did not exist in antiquity and as such is a modern label. Nevertheless, it is clear from Greco-Roman literature that such a type of historical genre did in fact exist."[65] Padilla notes that the historical monograph "has a more concentrated focus in terms of time period, subject and characters."[66] For Padilla, this helps to categorize the Book of Acts as a historical monograph.

Darrell Bock believes that Acts is a work of ancient historiography, but he does not employ the narrower model of historical monograph. Instead, he illustrates what he believes are the similarities between ancient historiography and the Book of Acts. In particular, he notes the speeches, the "we passages" and the dating methods demonstrate similarity with Greco-Roman historiography.[67] In addition, he also notes the storytelling of Acts draws heavily upon the Old Testament and is stylistically similar to the writings of the Maccabees.[68] For Bock, these similarities illustrate that the Book of Acts is historiography that is modeled after both Greco-Roman and Jewish historiography.

---

[62] Palmer, "Acts and the Ancient Historical Monograph," 5–8.
[63] Palmer, "Acts and the Ancient Historical Monograph," 28.
[64] Osvaldo Padilla, *The Acts of the Apostles: Interpretation, History and Theology* (Downers Grove, IL: IVP, 2016), 62.
[65] Padilla, *The Acts of the Apostles*, 62.
[66] Padilla, *The Acts of the Apostles*, 64.
[67] Darrell Bock, *Acts* (Grand Rapids: Baker, 2007), 11.
[68] Bock, *Acts*, 11–12.

Ben Witherington, after surveying the generic options for Acts, also opts for a historiographic model.[69] He is concerned to maintain a close connection between the Gospel of Luke and the Book of Acts.[70] This is one reason why he believes that Acts is ancient Hellenistic historiography.[71] He asserts that "Luke's Gospel must be evaluated in the light of its sequel, but more importantly, for our purposes Acts must be evaluated in light of its literary predecessor."[72] Those who write on Acts could become so focused upon Acts that they neglect its important connection with Luke. However, the two volumes are best understood together, and Witherington helpfully re-establishes the link between Luke and Acts.

Of the four scholars that have been surveyed, three operate within the field of the New Testament, and one operates in the field of the Classics. Each of them is convinced that the Book of Acts demonstrates clear affinities for some type of ancient historiography. They do not all agree on the details. For instance, Palmer and Padilla prefer to classify Acts as a historical monograph (a specific type of historiography), while Bock and Witherington are content to designate it at the broader level of historiography. All of them are agreed that Acts is an example of an ancient form of history, one that was (in this case) theologically shaped to teach Theophilus, and the early church.

Acts as βιος

---

[69] Ben Witherington III, *The Acts of the Apostles: A Socio-Rhetorical Commentary* (Grand Rapids: Eerdmans, 1998), 2–21.
[70] For a defense of the unity of Luke-Acts, see Joel B. Green, "Luke-Acts, or Luke and Acts?" in *Reading Acts Today: Essays in Honour of Loveday C. A. Alexander,* ed. Steve Walton, et al. (London: T & T Clark, 2011), 101–119.
[71] Ben Witherington III, *The Acts of the Apostles,* 39.
[72] Ben Witherington III, *The Acts of the Apostles,* 24.

In his introduction to the patristic interpretation of the Book of Acts, Francis Martin lodged a remarkable critique of the Church Fathers. He notes that "they sometimes comment on Acts as though it were a Hellenistic biography. In preaching this way, Chrysostom and others were employing techniques of persuasion they had learned in the pagan schools in which history was used to teach morals."[73] Martin's comments are a fascinating window into the debate over the approach to Acts. When we turn to the *imitatio Pauli* in a subsequent section, the specific approach of Chrysostom will be explored. For now, it is enough to acknowledge that some of the Church Fathers might have viewed Acts as a biography.

How have contemporary writers evaluated this approach? In recent times, several scholars have explored the potential similarities between the Book of Acts and the ancient βιος (biography). Charles Talbert pioneered a fresh approach to the Book of Acts when he argued that there were literary patterns and theological themes intertwined in Luke-Acts. Talbert asserted that Luke adapted the genre of βιος, when he declares that Luke's "cultural context presented him with a suitable mode of expression. In the philosophical schools this type of question about where the true tradition was to be found in the present had been answered by a type of biography of the group's founder which included within itself a list or short narrative of the founder's successors."[74] According to Talbert, the first volume of Luke-Acts recounts the story of Jesus, the founder of the Christian movement. The second volume, then, tells the continuing story of Jesus through the lives of some of his notable successors.[75]

---

[73] Francis Martin, *Acts,* ACCS (Downers Grove, IL: IVP, 2006), xxiii.

[74] Charles Talbert, *Literary Patterns, Theological Themes and the Genre of Luke-Acts* (Missoula, MT: Scholars Press, 1974), 142.

[75] Although he does not argue that Acts is a type of biography, David Balch also makes the salient point that Luke is concerned with establishing continuity between the Founder (Jesus, described in Luke) and the followers (Disciples, described in Acts). Furthermore, he argues that this continuity extends back into the Old Testament. "ΜΕΤΑΒΟΛΗ ΠΟΛΙΤΕΙΩΝ–Jesus as Founder of the Church in Luke-Acts: Form and Function," in *Contextualizing Acts: Lukan Narrative and Greco-Roman Discourse,* ed. Todd Penner and Caroline Vander Stichele (Leiden, The Netherlands: Brill, 2004), 139–188.

Talbert stresses the link between Luke and Acts, believing that patterns in the life of Christ (in Luke) are repeated in the lives of leaders of the early Church (in Acts). Indeed, for Talbert, this is how readers of Acts know that they ought to imitate apostolic praxis. He asserts, "Luke's theological perspective also dictated that he show that the apostolic deed and word were normative because they were a reflection of the word and deed of Jesus, the founder of the community."[76] If Talbert is correct in this claim,[77] the implications are significant. We will explore these implications in a later section.

Sean Adams has built upon Talbert's ideas by exploring the possibility that Acts is a "collected biography." He notes that, in the world of antiquity, "there appears to be a distinct emphasis on collected biography, as a large majority of extant biographies are not of individual people but consist of multiple human subjects."[78] This could potentially correspond to Luke's description of events from the lives of multiple figures in the early Church. Adams includes a chart that portrays the narrative diversity of the Book of Acts.[79] He asserts, "Here we see that Paul is indeed the dominant character of Acts receiving 56.4% of the narrative. The next major character is Peter who appears in 23.4% of the narrative, followed by Barnabas (10.3%), Stephen (7.2%), John (6.0%), Disciples (general) (5.4%), Philip (2.3%), and Apostles (2.0%)."[80]

Ultimately, the question of the genre of Acts hinges (at least in part) on structural issues.[81] After all, one step in determining genre is to

---

[76] Talbert, *Literary Patterns*, 142.

[77] See Parsons and Tyson, who have edited a volume that includes robust critique of Talbert's model, as well as a helpful rejoinder from Talbert. Mikeal Parson and Joseph Tyson, *Cadbury, Knox, and Talbert: American Contributions to the Study of Acts* (Atlanta: Scholars Press, 1992), 133–240.

[78] Sean Adams, *The Genre of Acts and Collected Biography* (Cambridge: Cambridge University Press, 2013), 114.

[79] Adams, *The Genre of Acts*, 130–131.

[80] Ibid.

[81] In a related vein, Richard Burridge has catalogued the verbal subjects of the Book of Acts. He did so because he noted that " ... around half the verbs in ancient biographies were given to the deeds and words of their subject, a concentration not seen in

discover certain textual markers that are common to all such types of literature.[82] Adams believes that Acts displays clear and unmistakable features of collected biography. He notes that it focuses upon multiple characters, focuses upon succession, and focuses upon the identity of the disciples.[83] Adams also acknowledges that "Acts' affiliation with collected biographies is not perfect," as evidenced by its geographic focus and narrative style.[84]

Genre and the Application of the Book of Acts

Thus far, we have heard two arguments for classifying the genre of the Book of Acts. Some have contended that Acts most closely corresponds to an ancient form of historiography (perhaps the historical monograph). Others have asserted that Luke-Acts is probably some type of ancient biography, focusing upon the succession from the founder (Jesus) to the followers (Disciples). It is difficult to select between these two genres. On the one hand, the Book of Acts has a narrow chronological,

---

other genres, and particularly useful for distinguishing *bioi* from neighboring genres, such as historical monograph where many different subjects would share the limelight." Richard Burridge, "The Genre of Acts–Revisited," in *Reading Acts Today: Essays in Honour of Loveday C. A. Alexander* (London: T & T Clark, 2011), 12. He concludes that "Unlike the Gospel of Luke, Acts is not a biography of one person, although it could be interpreted as a biography of the early church...." Burridge, "The Genre of Acts–Revisited," 28.

[82] David Peterson, *The Acts of the Apostles,* PCNT, (Grand Rapids: Eerdmans, 2009), 5, notes that "Genre can be defined in terms of content, form, and function of a particular text." Elizabeth Shively, "Recognizing Penguins: Audience Expectation, Cognitive Genre Theory, and the Ending of Mark's Gospel," *CBQ* 80, no. 2 (2018): 282, argues that cognitive theory, when applied to genre, helps us to reason from known literary prototypes. She declares, "A significant result of the cognitive model is the realization that we tend to recognize a category as a *gestalt* before we particularize its individual features. The consequence is that we do not decide that a text must have a standard list of features in order to justify its membership in a category. Rather, we recognize a text *as a whole* in relation to a central or "best" example (like the sparrow) and may see some as extensions (like the penguin) but members of the category nonetheless." Shively's admonition is important, for she reminds interpreters that identifying genre is not simply a matter of cataloguing textual markers. Instead, readers of Acts should look for internal textual markers and should identify a possible literary "family resemblance" based upon broad prototypes.

[83] Adams, *The Genre of Acts*, 171.

[84] Ibid.

geographical, and topical focus. This would seem to favor the genre of historiography (especially the monograph).

On the other hand, the Book of Acts (especially when paired with its preceding volume, Luke) demonstrates some affinities with the ancient βίος. These affinities would include the succession story of the Christian Movement, as the disciples of Volume Two imitated the praxis of Jesus from Volume One. Perhaps it is helpful at this point to remember the caution of Richard Burridge, who notes that "the borders between the genres of historiography, monograph and biography are blurred and flexible."[85] Indeed, it is possible that Luke employed one genre (biography, perhaps) while simultaneously incorporating elements from another genre (perhaps the historical monograph).[86]

At this point, it is necessary to step back and ask what relevance these findings have upon our overall journey of discovery. The pertinent issue is that of application: how should Acts be applied in a methodologically sound fashion? The discussion above demonstrated that this question cannot be separated from the topic of the genre of Acts. How one classifies the genre of the Book of Acts could potentially influence one's model of application. Consequently, it is important to briefly consider how each of the two genres (historiography and βίος) could affect various models of application. When we do, we will discover that implications emerge for those who wish to select between descriptive and prescriptive approaches to reading the Book of Acts.

The historiography classification could potentially lend itself more towards a descriptive framework for applying the Book of Acts. This is because the focus is on telling the historical story (this is especially the case for the historical monograph). However, one must be careful to

---

[85] Burridge, "The Genre of Acts–Revisited," 28.

[86] Bale's words are relevant: "While most scholars acknowledge flexibility within a genre, there is simply no way to tell whether a text is *Bios* containing elements of epic or epic containing elements of *Bios*. This is a matter of importance." Alan Bale, *Genre and Narrative Coherence*, 69.

acknowledge that ancient historiographers wrote with an end in mind. They were never simply telling the story; they were crafting a narrative that was designed to elicit a particular response.

Indeed, the actions of the characters are central to that story and purpose. Richard Thompson, who treats Acts as historiography, notes, "The importance of characters to historiography is related to the very essence of a narrative like Acts. If ancient historiography, like poetry, includes plot as a mimesis of human action (πραξις), then human beings and groups, the characters of the story, are critical to that presentation and its potential readings."[87]

Thompson believes that ancient readers would have employed a mimetic lens as they read the stories of these characters. In a similar vein, Witherington asserts that "it is hard to doubt that faithful witnesses like Peter and Paul are being seen as exemplary in a positive sense, as patterns to be followed by Theophilus and others."[88] He also opines that "the vast majority of the behavior of the Christian characters in the story are probably meant to be seen as exemplary."[89]

Osvaldo Padilla (who classifies Acts as a historical monograph) notes that the author of Acts employs syncrisis. He quotes Marguerat's definition of this term, when he observes, "It consists in modeling the presentation of a character on another in order to compare them, or at least to establish a correlation between the two."[90] According to Padilla, one of the reasons for the use of syncrisis in Acts is that it enables the reader to understand what is expected of her. As he notes, "Syncrisis is used to prod the readers to imitatio of Jesus and his apostles."[91]

---

[87] Richard Thompson, *Keeping the Church in Its Place: The Church as Narrative Character in Acts* (New York: T & T Clark, 2006), 17.
[88] Ben Witherington III, *The Acts of the Apostles*, 98.
[89] Ben Witherington III, *The Acts of the Apostles*, 99.
[90] Padilla, *The Acts of the Apostles*, 101.
[91] Padilla, *The Acts of the Apostles*, 102.

Thompson, Witherington, and Padilla all favor a historiographical classification for the Book of Acts. Yet they all believe that this type of literature would have called its readers to do something in response to the text. Once again, one can observe the complexity of the debate over whether Acts is descriptive or prescriptive. A genre classification of historiography (perhaps especially the historical monograph) would point in the direction of description. Yet it would not ultimately resolve the issue, since ancient historiography often provided the reader with patterns to imitate.

Conversely, the βιος classification could potentially lend itself more towards a prescriptive framework for applying the Book of Acts.[92] Loveday Alexander observes that ancient biographies often provided templates for the reader to follow. She notes, "Reading Acts along these lines would encourage us to explore ways in which Paul is presented as a pattern for imitation, a narrative extension of the process already visible in the epistolary corpus."[93] If this is, indeed, how the ancient βιος was meant to be read, then the implications for this project are significant. To explore these ideas further, it is necessary to briefly examine two writers of antiquity who provide some evidence of this approach. The first, Lucius, is brought to the attention of modern readers by the esteemed Loveday Alexander.

Lucius of Samosata was a second-century Syrian author who penned a biography entitled Life of Demonax. This work was an attempt to chronicle the life of his friend and teacher, the philosopher Demonax. Lucius wrote with two goals in mind. He notes, "First, to keep his memory

---

[92] Stanley Porter argues that Acts is probably a βιος. Intriguingly, he opines, "The Book of Acts, continuing not only the literary tradition (alluded to in the preface), but also the literary technique and method, depicts those select and significant followers who successively promulgate the message of the risen Jesus, serving as missional types." Unfortunately, he does not elaborate upon the way characters in Acts are missional types. Stanley Porter, "The Genre of Acts and the Ethics of Discourse," in *Acts and Ethics,* ed. Thomas Phillips (Sheffield, England: Sheffield Phoenix Press, 2005), 14.

[93] Loveday C. A. Alexander, *Acts in Its Ancient Literary Context: A Classicist Looks at the Acts of the Apostles* (London: T & T Clark, 2005), 47.

green among good men .... and secondly, to provide the most earnest of our rising generation, who aspire to philosophy, with a contemporary pattern, that they may not be forced back upon the ancients for worthy models, but imitate this best ... of all philosophers."[94]

One of the reasons that Lucius wrote a βιος of Demonax was because he wanted to draw attention to the patterns of the philosopher's life. In this way, Lucius could paint Demonax as a template worthy of his readers' imitation. This second-century work was written later than Acts, perhaps by as much as a century. Yet it demonstrates that the βιος was used to establish prescriptive models in antiquity.

Earlier I noted that Francis Martin critiqued some of the Church Fathers for reading the Book of Acts as if it were a Hellenistic biography.[95] In particular, he singled out Chrysostom as an example of this approach. When a reader turns to Chrysostom's first homily on Acts, she notes his understanding of the connection between method and teaching. He opines that "nothing is more frigid than a teacher who shows his philosophy only in words: this is to act the part not of a teacher, but of a hypocrite. Therefore, the Apostles first taught by their conduct, and then by their words; nay rather they had no need of words, when their deeds spoke so loud."[96] Chrysostom believed that the apostolic method (as described in Acts) was an essential element of apostolic pedagogy. This correlates well with a prescriptive approach to reading Acts, one that can be rooted in the genre of βιος.

Our evaluation of approaches to Acts demonstrates that the historiography classification lends itself more easily to a descriptive framework, and that a βιος classification lends itself more easily to a prescript-

---

[94] Lucius of Samosata, *Life of Demonax* (https://lucianofsamosata.info/Demonax.html).

[95] Martin, *Acts*, xxiii.

[96] St. John Chrysostom, *The Homilies on the Acts of the Apostles* (Rome: Veritatis Splendor Publications, 2012), 36.

tive framework. However, the issue is far more complex. Although the βιος classification would seem to favor prescription, ancient historiographic writing in general can also elevate exemplary characters in such a way that it tilts towards prescription. The overwhelmed reader might be left wondering, where exactly, that leaves her.

When seeking to missiologically apply the narrative of Acts, the reader must honor authorial intent, which is connected to the issue of genre.[97] That is why Colin Yuckman asserts that "the quest to read Acts 'normatively' is bound up with the quest to pay attention to the way it is written."[98] Whether one believes that Acts is a form of historiography (such as the historical monograph) or a form of βιος (such as collected biography), it seems that the authorial intent for Luke-Acts was to provide a template for mimesis (at least on some level).

However, this does not answer all the relevant questions. As we previously noted, descriptive advocates usually allow for some prescription, and prescriptive advocates do not necessarily imitate the entire narrative. So, where does this leave our study? Ultimately, this leaves me dissatisfied with either the descriptive or prescriptive approaches (even though there are benefits to both systems). That is why I search for a via media, a model that will enable contemporary readers to chart a path out of this impasse. What is necessary is the identification of an approach that will allow the reader to read and apply Acts in a missiologically balanced and judicious manner. We will now explore a possible "third way" model.

---

[97] Although authorial intent is a contested concept, it is still a hermeneutically responsible approach to any text. For a defense of authorial intent see Sternberg, *The Poetics of Biblical Narrative*, 1–2 and E. D. Hirsch, Jr., *Validity in Interpretation*, (New Haven, CT: Yale University Press, 1967), 1–24. When reading Luke-Acts, we can discern clues to authorial intent from the so-called prologues to each volume. Luke 1:1–4 and Acts 1:1–3 tie the two volumes together and demonstrate Luke's commitment to telling the story of Jesus and his followers to Theophilus. In and of themselves, these prologues do not conclusively resolve the issue of the genre of either volume of Luke-Acts.

[98] Yuckman, "Mission and the Book of Acts," 113.

If effective, this model can serve as our tool in later chapters for spotting and applying patterns of diverse teams in the Book of Acts.

A Representative Patterns Approach to Reading and Applying the Book of Acts

The attempt to establish a via media for applying Acts is rooted in two ideas that must be held in tension. First, as our previous discussion demonstrated, the characters in ancient works (whether historiography or βιος) were meant to be imitated, at least on some level. Second, as Schnabel has noted, historical events are, quite simply, unrepeatable.[99] This means that it might be humanly impossible to imitate all the actions of someone like the Apostle Paul.

Considering these two tension points, the reader might ask herself if it is possible to discover a nuanced approach to applying the Book of Acts. Is it possible to discover an approach that balances the tension between these two poles? In this book we will attempt to build upon the work of others to provide just such a model. This model will then be applied specifically to the issue of diverse teams in Acts, as well as their use in urban contexts.

In this volume I am proposing that an ancient approach to urban mission involved the use of diverse teams. This approach is revealed through the patterns of the Book of Acts. These patterns carry representative weight, and should, therefore, govern our methods in contextually similar settings. A few notes of clarification are in order. First, the goal is to discover patterns in Acts. This means that one must identify repeated instances of an event or action. For instance, the casting of lots in the first chapter of Acts would not qualify as a pattern, since this is the

---

[99] Schnabel, *Early Christian Mission*, 1570.

only example of this type of activity in Luke-Acts.[100] Conversely, Paul's practice of (usually) working in teams would establish a pattern,[101] one that even goes back to the "team" of disciples (whether the twelve or the seven-ty-two) that Jesus formed. Others have noted the pattern of the plurality of leadership that emerges in Acts as elders are appointed for the new churches.[102]

Second, I am arguing that these patterns should be replicated whenever possible in contextually similar settings. This caveat is important because Schnabel is right: history is unrepeatable. The patterns (if they exist) carry representative weight when there is a high level of similarity between the contexts of Acts and the contexts of contemporary society. In this book, those contextually similar settings are the major cities of the modern world. With these two notes of clarification, we can now commence our examination of the representative patterns model for reading and applying Acts.

What does it mean for patterns to exist, and how do they carry representative weight? New Testament scholar Ben Witherington is a-ware of the challenges and notes, "Distinguishing what Luke sees as norms and what he sees as merely historically interesting is difficult."[103] However, Witherington does not believe that the cause is hopeless. Instead, he proposes three ideas, when he urges his readers to "(1) look for positive repeated patterns in the text, or (2) look for when there is only one pattern, or (3) look for when there is clear divine approval or disapp-

---

[100] This would not automatically mean that the reader should not cast lots when making a spiritual decision. Instead, this study is simply asserting that we are on safer ground when we seek to imitate the patterns established in Luke-Acts.

[101] Kathy Ehrensperger, *Paul and the Dynamics of Power: Communication and Interaction in the Early Christ-Movement* (London: T & T Clark, 2007), 46–62.

[102] Benjamin Merkle, *40 Questions About Elders and Deacons* (Grand Rapids: Kregel, 2008), 161–165. Merkle believes that contemporary local churches would be wise to appoint a plurality of elders. He argues for this, in part, because of the pattern that he sees in the Book of Acts. Although this is certainly not the heart of his argument (there are other relevant New Testament passages that he discusses), it does demonstrate that some have adopted an approach that draws upon patterns found in Acts.

[103] Ben Witherington III, *The Acts of the Apostles*, 100.

roval in the text for some belief or behavior or experience or religious practice."[104]

Witherington analyzes various examples from Acts, seeking to discern if they should be viewed as "positive repeated patterns."[105] While not all will agree with his conclusions, his analysis is useful in helping contemporary readers to grapple with this issue. Witherington rightly notes the existence of positive repeated patterns. This means that Luke had a favorable disposition towards those patterns that he stressed through repetition. These patterns can function as ideal images for the reader to embrace.

In the field of missiology, Craig Ott and Gene Wilson have argued for a similar approach. Building upon the work of Fee and Stuart, they argue for a focus upon representative patterns when they note, "By the use of repetition, literary emphasis, and other devices the author makes them stand out as normal (customary, typical) practices, even if they are not given normative (absolute, authoritative) force."[106]

Like Witherington, Ott and Wilson propose three guidelines for determining what is normative within a narrative. They argue, "Patterns with representative force (1) are repeated consistently (thus only one pattern is found), (2) stand in harmony with the rest of Scripture, and (3) are not unique to a particular context or culture. In this chapter we will call them *church-planting patterns.*"[107] For Ott and Wilson, the goal is not imitation. They note that "we do not seek to imitate the events and methods of Acts, but we do seek to continue in the same trajectory, in continuity with the dynamic of mission as depicted in Acts."[108]

---

[104] Ibid.

[105] Ben Witherington III, *The Acts of the Apostles*, 100–102.

[106] Craig Ott and Gene Wilson, *Global Church Planting: Biblical Principles and Best Practices for Multiplication* (Grand Rapids: Baker, 2011), 45.

[107] Ott and Wilson, *Global Church Planting,* 45.

[108] Ott and Wilson, *Global Church Planting,* 45–46.

Commonality exists between the approaches of Witherington and Ott/Wilson. Both approaches emphasize positive repeated patterns in the text of Acts. Both writers believe Luke stressed the repetition of certain events to provide a pattern for mimesis. Craig Keener concurs that patterns exist in Acts that are meant to provide a pattern for imitation. However, he argues for a prescriptive approach, in part, based upon patterns that can be found stretching back into Luke's Gospel. Keener asserts, "Since patterns in Jesus's ministry are replicated in the ministry of the Jerusalem church and then in the Gentile mission (the latter still carried on in Diaspora churches of Luke's era), it is difficult to evade the conclusion that the repetitive features in Luke's portrayal of the early church are deliberate and paradigmatic."[109] He continues, "If the mission continues till the end of the age (see Acts 1:8), Luke's history of the positive prototypes for this mission suggests how the church should continue to carry it out."[110]

Keener rightly understands that our approach to Acts must make sense of Luke, and vice versa. Acts is the sequel in a two-volume work.[111] Thus, from a literary perspective, we would expect to find a tapestry of patterns stretching from the Gospel of Luke into the Book of Acts.[112] Unlike Keener, the casual reader might not spot this literary tapestry in Luke-Acts. However, many readers do assume that the baton has been passed to them, and that they (somehow) carry on in the spirit of the Book of Acts. In this way, the patterns are reproduced (at least in theory).

---

[109] Keener, *Acts* 1:440.

[110] Ibid.

[111] The link between the two volumes is established clearly through the two prologues, and through the ending of Luke. It is apparent from these texts that Luke intends for his readers to see the connection between the story of Jesus (volume one) and the story of Jesus' followers (volume two). This then leads to the enigmatic ending of Acts. The open-ended conclusion is probably intentionally designed to invite the reader into the story, as one who continues the continuing story of Jesus and his followers.

[112] See Talbert for a helpful discussion of potential patterns in Luke-Acts. Talbert, *Literary Patterns*.

For instance, in 1622, the English cleric John Donne preached to a group that was preparing to depart to settle in the colony of Virginia. He selected Acts 1:8 as his text. At the beginning of his exposition, he noted that his audience, like the Apostles, were to carry the gospel to distant lands. He said, "Beloved, you are actors upon the same stage too: the uttermost parts of the earth are your scene. Act over [or perhaps, act out] the Acts of the Apostles."[113] Donne viewed the members of the Virginia Plantation as an extension of the apostolic mission. They were to cross the ocean and colonize the "New World" in the spirit of the Apostles.[114]

Tom Wright has expressed an approach to Acts that sounds like Donne.[115] He has urged us to see the story of Scripture as unfolding in five acts: creation, fall, Israel, Jesus, and the Church.[116] Wright believes that Christians are acting out the fifth act, and that the first scene of that act is recorded in the New Testament. However, he does not believe that we must slavishly imitate what we read in the New Testament. Instead, he believes readers are called to "improvise." For Wright, this means that we should (among other things), pay "constant attention to the themes, rhythms, and harmonies of the complete performance so far, the performance which we are now called to continue."[117] Wright's terminology sounds like another way of referring to the patterns of the New Testament. For

---

[113] John Donne, *A Sermon Upon the Eighth Verse of the First Chapter of The Acts of the Apostles: Preached to the Honourable Company of the Virginia Plantation, November 30th, 1622* (https://www.biblestudytools.com/classics/the-works-of-john-donne-vol-6/sermon-clvi.html).

[114] Donne's methodology illustrates the way in which the Book of Acts can be abused. Although he urged the travelers to forsake greed, his sermon was designed to buttress the colonial enterprise. Surely "acting out the Acts of the Apostles" means carrying on their missionary venture, but not stealing Native lands. Sadly, Virginia colonists did both. See Willie Jennings for an insightful discussion of the nexus of colonialism, mission, and theology. Willie James Jennings, *The Christian Imagination: Theology and the Origins of Race* (New Haven, CT: Yale University Press, 2010).

[115] Similar, yet without the colonial baggage.

[116] N. T. Wright, *Scripture and the Authority of God: How to Read the Bible Today* (New York: HarperOne, 2011), 122.

[117] Wright, *Scripture and the Authority of God*, 127.

the purposes of this study, the patterns in question are found in Luke-Acts (and especially in Acts).

Both John Donne and Tom Wright (in very different eras and settings) have called the Church to (somehow) continue the story of the Book of Acts.[118] In this chapter I am arguing that the "positive repeated pat-terns" (to use Witherington's phrase) provide us with the best guide for continuing the story of Acts. As we take note of consistently repeated patterns (especially ones that seem to bear the narrator's stamp of favor), we will discern old ways to move forward in a new time.[119]

At this juncture, it is necessary to step back and review what we have discovered so far. First, strengths and weaknesses can be found in both the descriptive and prescriptive approaches to reading the Book of Acts. Second, ancient works of history (from a variety of genres) highlighted key figures and called their readers to a lifestyle of imitation. Third, certain patterns provide readers with a worthwhile template for discerning what, exactly, one should imitate from the lives of the characters described in Acts. As readers look for patterns that carry representative weight, they can cautiously chart a via media between the descriptive and prescriptive frameworks.

In a brief Pauline case study, we will now explore a possible supporting line of evidence. For this case study, it is necessary to examine the connection between Paul's doctrine and praxis. First, we will examine the link between Paul's deeds and theology. Second, we will explore what Paul himself said about his own method. This will center upon what some have termed the *imitatio Pauli*. This Pauline case study will not be

---

[118] See also Michael Goheen who builds upon Wright's analogy of a play. Michael Goheen, *Introducing Christian Mission Today: Scripture, History and Issues* (Downers Grove, IL: IVP, 2014), 69–70.

[119] Jennings argues (about Acts) that "we must always follow the repetitions of God in this drama of the Spirit. What God repeatedly does says something of the divine will." Willie James Jennings, *Acts*, BTCB (Louisville: Westminster John Knox Press, 2017), 122.

conclusive in and of itself. However, it will contribute to the overall picture of an ancient work that presents its heroes as worthy of emulation.

The Marriage of Theology and Praxis

It is obvious that Paul is one of the heroes of the Book of Acts. Indeed, he has been described as Luke's model missionary.[120] That is one reason that many readers (such as Roland Allen) have attempted to imitate the methods of Paul. This comports well with what has been gleaned from our study's comparison of ancient forms of history writing. It is reasonable to infer that this was Luke's goal. In fact, as Thomas Phillips notes, "Paul became the role model for Acts' post-apostolic readers."[121] Yet what would Paul have thought of such imitation? Would he have viewed it as the greatest form of flattery?

It is always a speculative attempt to get into the mind of the Apostle Paul (or any other biblical figure). Such speculations frequently have no biblical warrant and can result in far-fetched analysis. Therefore, we will eschew analysis that is not strictly textual. Fortunately, Paul himself, through both his life and (especially) his words left to contemporary readers clear evidence of his thinking on this topic. First, his deeds demonstrate a connection between his theology and praxis. Second, his words demonstrate reflective theologizing about his own praxis. Each of these areas will be examined in turn.

---

[120] This statement, attributed to Martin Hengel, is quoted by Dean Flemming, *Contextualization in the New Testament*, 56.

[121] Thomas Phillips, "Paul as a Role Model in Acts: The 'We'-Passages in Acts 16 and Beyond," in *Acts and Ethics,* ed. Thomas Phillips (Sheffield, England: Sheffield Phoenix Press, 2005), 54. While this statement seems almost axiomatic, the particular way in which Phillips applies this idea seems to stretch credulity. Phillips argues that we are to model ourselves after Paul, in contradistinction to characters that feature in the first fifteen chapters of Acts. The present writer believes that Paul is a role model for the reader, as are Philip, Lydia, Peter, and others.

Paul's Deeds Demonstrate a Connection Between His Theology and Praxis

Multiple writers have noted a link between what Paul said and what he did. For instance, Michael Bird asserts, "The doctrines that Paul taught emerged principally out of his missionary situation …. In fact, the more we learn about Paul's missionary methods, the more we might learn something about his theology too!"[122] Approaching the issue from the opposite angle, Merkle asserts, "Getting Paul's ecclesiology right will enable us to get his methodology right as well."[123] Both New Testament schol-ars, although writing from varied vantage points, and with different interests, understand an important, indissoluble link exists between Pauline doctrine and praxis.

Indeed, Paul might have had a difficult time understanding our contemporary arbitrary distinction between "theology" and "applied theology." For instance, when one examines Paul's view of the Church as the "One New Humanity," one discovers that Paul's missionary methods were intertwined with his theology. The following survey will quickly sketch this link.

Paul's understanding of the gospel was broader than simply the salvation of individual souls.[124] He saw in it the beginnings of God's move to restore the creation (Rom. 8:18–25),[125] including fractured human rela-

---

[122] Michael Bird, "Paul's Religious and Historical Milieu," in *Paul's Missionary Methods: In His Time and Ours,* ed. Robert Plummer and John Mark Terry (Downers Grove, IL: IVP, 2012), 17.

[123] Benjamin L. Merkle, "Paul's Ecclesiology," in *Paul's Missionary Methods: In His Time and Ours,* ed. Robert Plummer and John Mark Terry (Downers Grove, IL: IVP, 2012), 73.

[124] Scot McKnight declared that "the gospel for the apostle Paul is the salvation-unleashing Story of Jesus, Messiah-Lord-Son, that brings to completion the Story of Israel as found in the Scriptures of the Old Testament." Scot McKnight, *The King Jesus Gospel: The Original Good News Revisited* (Grand Rapids: Zondervan, 2011), 60.

[125] Kenneth Keathley declares that "As for creation, the death, burial, and resurrection of Jesus Christ have cosmic significance." Kenneth Keathley, "The Work of God: Salvation," in *A Theology For the Church,* ed. Daniel Akin (Nashville: B&H Academic, 2007), 763.

tionships (Eph. 2:11–22).[126] Regarding these broken relationships, Paul believed that Jews and Gentiles were one in Christ (Gal. 3:28). This formulaic statement (variations of which are repeated in 1 Cor. 12:13 and Col. 3:11) is an important way for Christians to understand Paul's theology of Gentile inclusion. As Hansen notes, "For Paul, the unity formula finds its bearings in reference to the story of God fashioning a new people on the basis of the stories of Israel and of Christ."[127] This new people constitute "a new social group in which members treat one another as siblings," since the cross has justified this new "social arrangement."[128] Paul understood that the atonement brought about reconciliation, both with God and with other humans (Ephesians 2). Therefore, Jarvis Williams declares that "Jesus' death shattered all ethnic boundary markers between the two groups [Jews and Gentiles], and then recreated them into one new man."[129]

For Paul, no dichotomy is evident between his doctrine and his missionary praxis. His method recorded in Acts emerged clearly from the doctrine which he penned in the epistles. His approach could be described using Paul's own words. He took the gospel "first to the Jew, and also to the Greek" (Rom. 1:16). As Paul the missionary engaged in missional endeavors, he did so with a firm commitment to reach both Jews and Gentiles. He maintained a dogged doctrinal conviction that Jews and Gentiles were reconciled into one body through the cross and that the resulting Church was the first fruits of the New Creation. One would therefore expect his methods to align with his convictions, and this is precisely what we read in the Book of Acts.

---

[126] Kenneth Matthews and M. Sydney Park, *The Post-Racial Church: A Biblical Framework for Multiethnic Reconciliation* (Grand Rapids: Kregel, 2011), 204.

[127] Bruce Hansen, *'All of You are One:' The Social Vision of Gal 3:28, 1 Cor 12:13 and Col 3:11* (New York: T&T Clark, 2010), 200–201.

[128] Hansen, *'All of You are One,'* 201.

[129] Jarvis Williams, *One New Man: The Cross and Racial Reconciliation in Pauline Theology* (Nashville: B&H Academic, 2010), 132.

Paul and his co-workers planted churches throughout the Greco-Roman world. These churches were frequently[130] (but not always) comprised of Jews and Gentiles. For instance, on Paul's second missionary journey his efforts led to the establishment of "mixed communities" of faith in Thessalonica (Acts 17:1–4), Berea (Acts 17:10–15) and Corinth (Acts 18:1–17).[131] This Pauline methodology is unsurprising, given Paul's theological convictions concerning the gospel, the church, Gentile inclusion, and the New Creation. Indeed, as René Padilla declares, the New Testament portrays an "apostolic practice whose aim was the formation of churches that would live out the unity of the new humanity in Jesus Christ."[132]

As a result of this brief sketch, we can see that Paul both wrote about the Church as One New Humanity and performed this reality. His theology was not simply an abstraction on papyrus; it was lived out on mission. Contemporary readers cannot draw a clear dividing line between Paul's doctrine and his missionary methods, for his theology (at least on some level) was performative. He operated holistically, with his methodology continually emerging from his doctrine.[133]

Paul's Words Demonstrate a Connection Between His Theology and Praxis

Paul did not just do theology, he also reflected theologically about his method. Christopher Little documents five instances of what he terms the *imitatio Pauli*: 1 Cor 11:1, 1 Cor 4:16–17, Phil 3:17, 1 Thess 1:6, and 2 Thess 3:7–9.[134] In each of these passages, Paul celebrates the concept of

---

[130] . Luther Copeland, "Church Growth in Acts," *Missiology: An International Review,* vol. 4 issue 1 (January 1976): 13–26.

[131] According to the Book of Acts there were Jews and Gentiles in each of these church plants.

[132] René Padilla, "The Unity of the Church and the Homogenous Unit Principle," *International Bulletin of Missionary Research,* vol. 6 issue 1 (January 1982): 27.

[133] It is also possible, perhaps even probable, that Paul's missionary contexts prompted the development of certain elements of his theology.

[134] Christopher Little, *Mission in the Way of Paul: Biblical Mission for the Church in the Twenty-First Century* (New York: Peter Lang, 2005), 110–115.

imitation (both of himself and of some of his co-workers). In some, he directly commands imitation: "Therefore I urge you to imitate me" (1 Cor 4:16). In order to facilitate this command, Paul sent Timothy his protégé to the Corinthian church so that he could remind them about Paul's ways (1 Cor 4:17). It was not merely an imitation of Paul; it was an imitation of Paul's imitation of Christ (1 Cor 11:1).[135]

Paul viewed his life as a Christian as something that was (at least overall) worthy of emulation. Furthermore, the Apostle did not shrink from asking people to imitate him. However, it is at this point that some might raise an objection. Everyone would no doubt agree that modern Christians should emulate Paul's godliness and zeal for the gospel. Yet what about his methods? Indeed, a careful reader might accurately observe that the five clear references to the *imitatio Pauli* do not necessarily refer to Paul's missional methods (one possible exception is 1 Cor 11:1). Instead, they could be viewed as mere exhortations to live a godly life, just like Paul.

Yet, in answering this objection, Little points to Paul's words to Timothy, when he declares, "But you have followed my teaching, conduct, purpose, faith, patience, love, and endurance, along with the persecutions and sufferings" (2 Tim 3:10–11). According to Little, the teacher and the teaching are intricately connected, and Timothy would not have separated them in his mind. Consequently, contemporary readers of Paul's life and letters should not exclude the methodological implications of the *imitatio Pauli*.

We previously observed that Chrysostom, in his first homily on Acts, opines that the apostles taught using their conduct and words. It is

---

[135] Intriguingly, this fits into (but does not prove) Talbert's originally groundbreaking idea that Luke-Acts was a succession biography. According to Talbert, volume one (Luke) focused upon Jesus, the founder of the Christian Movement. Volume two (Acts) focused upon how the apostles and disciples were continuing the story of Jesus. Talbert believed that this would have demonstrated to the readers of Acts how they should then live. They should imitate apostolic praxis, because apostolic praxis was an imitation of Jesus. Talbert, *Literary Patterns*, 142.

fitting, then, that some of the last words of his final homily on Acts are a return to this theme. He argues, "Let us emulate Paul, and imitate that noble, that adamantine soul: that, advancing in the steps of his life, we may be enabled to sail through the sea of this present life, and to come unto the haven wherein are no waves...."[136]

Like Little, Chrysostom believed that Christians should imitate the Apostle Paul. Some might argue that the learned church father was referring to Paul's character and doctrine, and not to his method. However, given Chrysostom's linkage in his first homily between apostolic conduct and words, it seems likely that he would side with Little, who notes that "Paul's conduct in mission is a method of instruction which rests on equal footing with his teaching."[137]

If Little is correct, then the so-called *imitatio Pauli* strengthens the case that I have built in this chapter. I have asserted that, based upon genre considerations and the repeated patterns of Acts, contemporary readers should view Acts as a document that calls for methodological imitation, whenever possible.[138] Some might be unconvinced, and might ar-gue that Little has not proven his claim beyond the shadow of a doubt. After all, Paul could simply be urging his readers to imitate his holy lifestyle, and not his methods. However, Little's contention that Paul's methods were a part of his pedagogy seems reasonable, especially given ancient rabbinic methods of discipleship and the methods employed by the Greco-Roman philosophical schools.

At the very least, one can view the *imitatio Pauli* as a supporting (if not conclusive) line of evidence for the overall assertion that the "positive repeated patterns" of Acts are meant to be imitated. As one of

---

[136] Chrysostom, *The Homilies on the Acts of the Apostles*, 720.

[137] Little, *Mission in the Way of Paul*, 116.

[138] As always, a caveat is needed: methodological imitation is only suggested when one's contextual situation is like that of Acts. In Chapter Six we will argue that major North American cities are contextually similar to many of the settings of the Book of Acts.

the primary actors upon the stage in the Book of Acts, Paul left Luke's readers with a few patterns for consideration. Our interest in this book is the pattern of the development of diverse ministry teams. The existence and composition of these teams (some of which preceded Paul) will be explored in detail in Chapters Four and Five.

Conclusion

It is now time to retrace and summarize the argument of this chapter. First, we considered the two dominant approaches to reading and applying the Book of Acts. When the descriptive model was examined, we found that it helpfully recognizes the unique nature and unrepeatability of historical events. When the prescriptive model was examined, we found that it can lend itself towards a consistency in application (even though it is doubtful that anyone has ever truly applied the entirety of Acts). Since both approaches have legitimate strengths, we decided that a third model was needed, one which combined the strengths and (hopefully) avoided some of the weaknesses of each approach.

Before exploring this model, we delved into two prominent genre classifications for the Book of Acts: historiography and βιος. This step was necessary to buttress the claim that Acts is more than descriptive, and that contemporary Christians should (in some fashion) build their missionary methods upon its patterns. We discovered that forms of historiography (like the historical monograph) lend themselves more towards a descriptive reading of Acts, while the βιος lends itself more towards a prescriptive reading. I did not argue conclusively for one of the two suggested genres for Acts. Instead, I merely observed that some styles of ancient history writing (including the βιος and the historical monograph) provide patterns for imitation.

Having seen that the Book of Acts was likely crafted by Luke to provide patterns for mimesis, we were then able to explore an approach to reading Acts that we labeled the representative patterns approach. This model seeks out repeated patterns in Acts that seem to have the "blessing" of the narrator, and then calls for replication, whenever possible. This approach is not novel. It built upon the work of Craig Ott, Gene Wilson and (especially) Ben Witherington. What will be original, however, is our application (in subsequent chapters) of this model to discerning and replicating patterns of multicultural teams in Acts.

The argument of this chapter concluded with the examination of a possible supporting line of evidence, what Christopher Little has called the *imitatio Pauli*. Although (contra Little) we could not conclusively prove that Paul expected his readers to imitate his methods, we did conclude that this seems likely. Hence, we included the *imitatio Pauli* as a secondary stream of evidence.

Thus far, we have discovered that the patterns of Acts are meant to be imitated, whenever possible, based upon the genre of Acts and the tapestry of patterns in Luke-Acts. This volume will extend the argument by asserting that the Book of Acts records the development of diverse teams and provides them as a positive pattern that is worthy of emulation. In Chapters Four and Five, we will provide a "cultural map" of various "ministry teams" in the Book of Acts. This will demonstrate that multicultural ministry teams did develop throughout the Book of Acts. First, however, it is important to explore what is meant by the term "culture." Since Chapters Four and Five will explore the potential multicultural composition of the teams found in Acts, it is essential to clarify what is meant when we refer to culture. Consequently, the next chapter will (mostly) depart from the Book of Acts. Here, we will engage the social sciences and the world of antiquity to discover a model of culture that "works" in the Book of Acts.

CHAPTER THREE: Understanding Culture like a Twenty-First Century Human

In Chapter One, we set some benchmark definitions for the terms "race" and "ethnicity." We also briefly engaged the issue of culture, most notably through definitions proposed by Paul Hiebert and Michael Rynkiewich. In this third chapter we will engage with both thinkers on a deeper level as the topic of culture resurfaces. The task of Chapters Four and Five will be to provide a "cultural map" of the "ministry teams" discovered in the Book of Acts. To accomplish this task, we must have a working model of culture. This model must be informed by the latest developments within the social sciences. It must rely upon the best theories of culture, both within the social sciences and missiology.

Finally, the model of culture that emerges from this process must "work" in antiquity. If I propose a model of culture that does not make sense of the ways in which culture was viewed in antiquity, then it cannot be used to aid our study of ancient approaches to urban mission. In the following pages we will, therefore, explore modern, postmodern, and postcolonial theories of culture. This will result in a model of culture that we can test against available data from antiquity. We will devote special attention to the role of Hellenism in crafting a model of culture that corresponds to what we might discover in the Book of Acts.

Modern Theories of Culture

Modernity gave birth to a new way of looking at the world.[139] It was a way that prized empiricism, evidence, and certainty. In that intellectual milieu, the social sciences (anthropology, sociology, linguistics, etc.) developed. In a study of culture, anthropology (oftentimes called cultural anthropology) is the most important of the social sciences. In this chapter we will explore the insights of cultural anthropology to build a model of culture.

At this point, a brief apologetic is in order. Some readers might be understandably skeptical about embracing the insights of the social sciences. After all, Christians are governed by the authority of Scripture, not by any secular theory. Yet this does not mean that Christians cannot appropriate accurate insights from secular disciplines. To do so, however, will require careful discernment. After all, the social sciences developed in the wake of the Enlightenment, and oftentimes were founded on unbiblical presuppositions. Charles Taber declares that "the social sciences have not always been 'objective' and uncommitted. In fact, as we will see, when they emerged from the matrix of the Enlightenment, they had quite utopian and even messianic ambitions."[140] These origins can lead to deep skepticism about the social sciences within the Christian community.

However, missiologists must not let this caution lead them to commit the genetic fallacy and consequently end up rejecting insights which agree with the Bible. Taber insightfully notes, "Missiology, like all endeavors that we undertake in behalf of the kingdom of God, is often

---

[139] See the excellent analysis of the development of modernity's "social imaginary" in Charles Taylor, *A Secular Age* (Cambridge: Belknap Press, 2007). See also René Padilla, "El Reino de dios y la Historia en la Teologia Latinoamericana," *Cuadernos de Teologia* 7, no. 1 (1985): 5, who insightfully notes that "The 'modern man' does not believe in transcendent realities."

[140] Charles Taber, *To Understand the World, to Save the World: The Interface Between Missiology and the Social Sciences* (Harrisburg, PA: Trinity Press, 2000), 5.

forced to move beyond its secure knowledge in order to accomplish anything. It often skates on very thin ice."[141]

Taber understands that the discipline of missiology (like the discipline of systematic theology) must integrate truth from a variety of sources, beginning and ending with the authoritative truth of Scripture. He argues that missiology "cannot afford, therefore, to overlook any potentially useful instruments to improve its understanding and performance. The social sciences, used responsibly and critically, are clearly such instruments."[142] Taber is correct to observe that the social sciences can (and should) be used responsibly by missiologists. Some of the analytical tools of the social sciences can sharpen our insight into the human condition in a fallen world. When placed under the authority of the "norming norm"[143] of Scripture, these tools and insights can be useful and enlightening.

When thinking about culture, Christians must first start with Scripture.[144] A missiology of culture should be shaped by the biblical story[145] and should involve significant theological reflection.[146] Although Christians should start with special revelation in thinking about culture, they can then look to the world of natural revelation. As Rah notes, "A healthy approach to culture has a biblical and theological foundation. It is impor-tant, however, that we also have a broader definition of culture that not only reflects sound theology but also draws on an existing common

---

[141] Taber, *To Understand the World, To Save the World*, 138.

[142] Ibid.

[143] This phrase was utilized by Bruce Ashford in a January 2016 lecture at Southeastern Baptist Theological Seminary.

[144] All modern theological reflection upon culture is done in the shadow of H. Richard Niebuhr, *Christ and Culture* (New York: Harper & Row), 1951. For an updated analysis of Niebuhr's seminal work, see D. A. Carson, *Christ & Culture Revisited* (Grand Rapids: Eerdmans, 2008).

[145] For an example of how the biblical story shapes our theology of culture, see Bruce Ashford, "The Gospel and Culture," in *Theology and Practice of Mission: God, the Church, and the Nations*, ed. Bruce Ashford (Nashville: B&H, 2011), 109–127.

[146] For an example of significant theological reflection on culture, see Henry R. Van Til, *The Calvinistic Concept of Culture* (Grand Rapids: Baker, 2001), 25–35.

under-standing in our society about culture."[147] Consequently, we must first outline the development of various modern theories of culture, and then examine their appropriation in the work of missiologist Paul Hiebert.

Anthropology

Anthropology is the social-scientific discipline that describes what it means to be human at any given moment in time. As Guest observes, "Anthropology is the study of the full scope of human diversity and the application of that knowledge to help people of different backgrounds better understand one another."[148] Anthropologists study people. Classically, they spend time in a community (such as a tribal village) conducting fieldwork. The data that they gather from their observations and interactions then becomes an anthropological report. Many anthropologists focus upon gathering data about individual cultures. This culture might be as large as a country or as tiny as a village.[149]

Anthropologists study people within culture. Consequently, they develop theories of culture. Guest opines, "Culture is a system of knowledge, beliefs, patterns of behavior, artifacts, and institutions that are created, learned, and shared by a group of people."[150] In this definition, the emphasis is upon a system (made up of various features). This system can be formally articulated or informally practiced. This distinction is important. A group of university professors might be viewed as a (more or less) formal culture. The members of that group might even describe their culture in a systematic way. Yet another culture of Caribbean nannies in Brooklyn might simply perform their culture without ever systematically

---

[147] Soong-Chan Rah, *Many Colors: Cultural Intelligence for a Changing Church* (Chicago: Moody Press, 2010), 23.

[148] Kenneth J. Guest, *Cultural Anthropology: A Toolkit for a Global Age* (New York: W. W. Norton & Company, 2014), 7.

[149] Of course, a culture could be even larger than a country and even smaller than a village. For fieldwork to be manageable, anthropologists frequently focus upon smaller, more discrete cultures.

[150] Guest, *Cultural Anthropology*, 35.

classifying it.[151] As Roembke notes, "Culture is the way life is organized to give meaning to a particular group of people in their environment. Culture is used to form the person and the group."[152]

In a previous era,[153] anthropologists embraced the theory of "unilineal cultural evolution." This approach, pioneered in the aftermath of Darwin, posited that cultures all around the world were evolving towards the same enlightened destination. Remarkably (and ethnocentrically), advocates of this approach usually believed that the destination resembled something like Western civilization. Franz Boas took a different approach and pioneered a framework that came to be called "historical particularism." Boas maintained that cultures developed independently based upon unique local factors.[154]

"Structural functionalism" is a third approach that was adopted by some anthropologists. In this framework, anthropologists like Bronislaw Malinowski filtered out historical factors, and merely focused upon the culture as it currently existed.[155] In contemporary times, anthropologists like Clifford Geertz pioneered an "interpretive" approach. In this frame-work, culture was a symbolic system.[156] Each element of a culture was thought to possess a deep meaning, one that ought to be discerned by the anthropologist.[157]

In contrast to an older way of thinking (typically called essentialism), anthropologists no longer believe that humans are born as possess-

---

[151] Tamara Mose, *Raising Brooklyn: Nannies, Childcare, and Caribbeans Creating Community* (New York: NYU Press, 2011).

[152] Lianne Roembke, *Building Credible Multicultural Teams* (Pasadena: William Carey 2000), 13.

[153] This summary is indebted to the historical overview provided by Guest, *Cultural Anthropology,* 46–49.

[154] Guest, *Cultural Anthropology,* 46–47.

[155] Ibid.

[156] Ibid.

[157] Theologian Kevin Vanhoozer has adapted this approach to his own field, providing thick theological descriptions of cultural texts. Kevin Vanhoozer, Charles Anderson, and Michael Sleasman, eds., *Everyday Theology: How to Read Cultural Texts and Interpret Trends* (Grand Rapids: Baker, 2007).

ors of a particular culture.[158] As Guest notes, "Humans do not genetically inherit culture."[159] Instead, a host of environmental factors shape a person's cultural identity throughout the entirety of her life. These factors could include (but are certainly not limited to), geographical location, parental influence, language, economic opportunity, and gender. This idea runs directly counter to the concept of essentialism, which argued that a people's culture was an essence that they possessed, usually due to biological factors.

However, as the Protestant missiologist Henning Wrogemann reminds his readers, this approach led to a nightmare scenario with the rise of fascism in Germany. He notes, "This was a line of thought on which the National Socialists picked up and that they developed into a comprehensive ideology of race – with terrible consequences."[160] As a contemporary missiologist, Wrogemann is understandably sensitive to the way that essentialist ideas were appropriated by The Third Reich as a justification for the enactment of an evil agenda.

As anthropology continued to develop in the wake of the Holocaust and the Second World War, it did so with a focus upon cultural relativism. This approach posited that researchers should suspend judgment about all cultures.[161] Instead, anthropologists should merely observe and classify, without making any value determinations. Christians should be concern-ed about this approach, which can tend towards moral relativism.[162]

---

[158] See the helpful discussion of the historical development of anthropological understandings of culture in Brian Howell and Jenell Paris, *Introducing Cultural Anthropology: A Christian Perspective* (Grand Rapids: Baker Academic, 2019), 29–33.

[159] Guest, *Cultural Anthropology*, 36.

[160] Henning Wrogemann, *Intercultural Theology, Volume One: Intercultural Hermeneutics* (Downers Grove, IL: IVP, 2016), 125.

[161] Guest, *Cultural Anthropology,* 44–45.

[162] For a nuanced (and generally favorable) Christian perspective on cultural relativism, see Howell and Paris, *Introducing Cultural Anthropology,* 33–36.

One hallmark of anthropology during the modern era was its view of cultures as static. Regardless of their interpretive framework, many anthropologists approached a culture as if it were a "closed" society. For instance, many anthropologists would take this approach to the study of a remote village in the Amazon. They viewed the inhabitants of the village (cut off as they were from the outside world) as possessors of a fixed cultural identity, one that had clear boundaries.[163] The resulting "culture" was fixed and bounded.[164] Little room was made for the potential of biculturalism or hybrid identities. These understandings would develop later, with the rise of postmodern and postcolonial anthropological theories. Before examining those developments, we will now explore the work of one of the preeminent missionary anthropologists of the modern era: Paul Hiebert. With a careful reading of Hiebert, we will be able to see how missiologists appropriated the insights of anthropology in building their models of culture.

Missiological Anthropology: Paul Hiebert

Paul Hiebert was one of the premier missiologists of the twentieth century. He served as a missionary to India, before eventually settling into professorships, first at Fuller Theological Seminary and then at Trinity Evangelical Divinity School. From his perches there, he authored numerous treatises on the link between missions and anthropology.[165] As a

---

[163] For a classic example of this approach, see Margaret Mead, *Coming of Age in Samoa: A Psychological Study of Primitive Youth for Western Civilization* (New York: HarperCollins, 2001).

[164] Lee and Park note that many missiologists also adopted this approach to culture, and therefore "envision people groups as discrete, separate, and self-contained cultural entities .... " They also opine that many believe in "distinct groups with fixed, clear, impermeable, and non-overlapping boundaries." Peter Lee and James Sung-Hwan Park, "Beyond People Group Thinking: A Critical Reevaluation of Unreached People Groups," *Missiology* 46. no. 3 (July 2018): 215–216.

[165] For a small, but representative sampling of Hiebert's work, see Paul Hiebert, *Cultural Anthropology* (Grand Rapids: Baker, 1983); Paul Hiebert and Eloise Hiebert Meneses, *Incarnational Ministry: Planting Churches in Band, Tribal, Peasant, and Urban Societies* (Grand Rapids: Baker, 1995); Paul Hiebert, *The Missiological Implications of Epistemological Shifts: Affirming Truth in a Modern/Postmodern World* (Harrisburg, PA:

prolific author, Hiebert perhaps did more than anyone else to bring anthropo-logical thinking into the mainstream of missiological theory and praxis.

Throughout his distinguished career, Hiebert demonstrated a commitment to helping missiologists and missionaries adapt the best insights of cultural anthropology. He believed that missiologists and missionaries should utilize the social sciences. For example, in his preface to the second edition of his cultural anthropology textbook, he asserts, "Christians need an understanding of human life that anthropology offers through the study of diverse sociocultural contexts. Anthropologists, I believe, need the understanding that Christianity provides concerning the transcendent nature of humans and the cosmic history within which they live."[166]

Indeed, Hiebert was so convinced that missionaries could benefit from anthropology, that he wrote an entire book about it.[167] He lists five basic ways in which anthropology can aid the cause of missions.[168] First, anthropology helps missionaries to better understand cross-cultural dynamics. Second, anthropology can aid us in accomplishing specific projects, such as Bible translation. Third, anthropology can enable missionaries to truly understand conversion. Fourth, anthropology can assist missionaries as they seek to demonstrate that the gospel is relevant to members of a particular culture. Finally, anthropology can be used to facilitate cross-cultural understanding. These ideas animated Hiebert's writings, from beginning to end. In fact, one can see a certain level of consistency between his early and later writings. He was gripped with the conviction that missiologists needed anthropology.

Trinity Press, 1999); and Paul Hiebert, *Transforming Worldviews: An Anthropological Understanding of How People Change* (Grand Rapids: Baker, 2008).

[166] Hiebert, *Cultural Anthropology*, xvi.

[167] Paul Hiebert, *Anthropological Insights for Missionaries* (Grand Rapids: Baker, 1985).

[168] Hiebert, *Anthropological Insights*, 15–16.

Paul Hiebert's anthropological emphasis led him into a serious and sustained engagement with the concept of culture. In one of his earlier works he declares, "We will define culture as 'the more or less integrated systems of ideas, feelings, and values and their associated patterns of behavior and products shared by a group of people who organize and regulate what they think, feel, and do.'"[169] According to Hiebert, this definition of culture posits ideas, feelings, and values as "the three basic dimensions of culture."[170] Hiebert notes that the gospel relates to each of these elements, and that holistic conversion is necessary for thorough discipleship.[171] For Hiebert, these ideas, feelings, and values are associated with behaviors and products, shared in common by a certain group of people.

This definition has achieved influential status within the realm of missiology. Bruce Ashford cited this definition in one of his earlier works when he was attempting to produce a theology of culture. In fact, he notes, "This definition is perhaps the most oft-quoted and used conception of culture in evangelical missiology, and is as good as any to give us a handle on the concept, from the stance of the social sciences."[172] Indeed, Ashford returns to this definition in one of his most recent works, co-authored with Heath Thomas.[173]

In his final book (a collection of essays that was published posthumously), Hiebert once again discussed the concept of culture. His definition is remarkable, because it is extremely like his earlier proposal, and yet also deviates in certain ways. He asserts, "Here we will define [culture] as the more or less integrated system of beliefs, feelings, and values creat-

---

[169] Hiebert, *Anthropological Insights*, 30.

[170] Ibid.

[171] Hiebert, *Anthropological Insights*, 34. See also, Figure 11.1 in Paul Hiebert, *Transforming Worldviews*, 316.

[172] Bruce Ashford, "The Gospel and Culture," in *Theology and Practice of Mission: God, the Church, and the Nations* (Nashville: B&H, 2011), 111.

[173] Bruce Ashford and Heath Thomas, *The Gospel of Our King: Bible, Worldview, and the Mission of Every Christian* (Grand Rapids: Baker, 2019), 156–157.

ed and shared by a group of people that enable them to live together socially and that are communicated by means of their systems of symbols and rituals, patterns of behavior, and the material products they make."[174] Hiebert's early and later definitions both posit three dimensions of culture: values, feelings, and ideas (called beliefs in the later definition). They both emphasize the symbols and rituals of culture. The primary difference between the two definitions is that Hiebert's more mature definition of culture places an emphasis upon the social nature of culture: it is created and shared.

This emphasis lends itself towards the concept of fluidity in culture (cultural fluidity would eventually become a defining feature of postmodern and postcolonial theories of culture). Perhaps considering the ongoing developments in the social sciences (see the subsequent section), Hiebert seemed to adopt a more open stance towards culture. He notes, "Initially, social anthropology focused its attention on small societies and examined them as closed systems. Social anthropologists saw societies as harmonious organic wholes. The concept of people groups fits best with such a view of small scale societies."[175]

According to Hiebert, this might have been a helpful analytical perspective in the past. However, the times have changed, and societies have shifted. He asserts that "peasant and urban societies cannot be cut up into distinct, bounded people groups without seriously distorting the picture. In large-scale societies individuals participate in many different groups and cultural frames and do not fully identify with any one of them."[176]

Hiebert argues that it is no longer appropriate to view cultures as fixed and bounded entities. He seems to have moved towards a view of

---

[174] Paul Hiebert, *Constants in Context: Anthropological Explorations for Contemporary Missions* (Grand Rapids: Baker, 2009), 150.

[175] Hiebert, *Constants in Context*, 92.

[176] Ibid.

culture as something that was fluid and permeable. At the end of his life's work, Hiebert still viewed culture as a system of ideas, feelings, and values that resulted in certain shared symbols, rituals and behaviors. However, he also maintained that culture could be created, and that it was not as rigid as anthropologists and missiologists once thought.

Having briefly surveyed the theories of early secular anthropology, and the developing ideas of Paul Hiebert, we are now in a better position to classify modern understandings of culture. In the modern era, anthropologists (and the missiologists who relied upon them) viewed culture as a system that incorporated a variety of symbols and artifacts, and it operated on a deep level, touching every realm of the person. These anthropologists (and the missiologists who relied upon them) tended to view culture as static. It was something fixed and bounded, rather than fluid and porous. In Hiebert's case, he seems to have grown in his understanding of culture as the social sciences continued to develop. It is to this development of the social sciences (and their eventual impact upon missiology) to which we now turn. As we do, our investigation will move from the realm of the modern world and into the world of postmodern and postcolonial theory.

Postmodern and Postcolonial Theories of Culture

Postmodernity[177] followed in the wake of modernity,[178] and it brought a new way of thinking about all of life. In this section we will focus on one element of postmodern thought. Postmodernity generated fresh insights into the meaning of culture. These insights (especially when

---

[177] For a balanced (but substantially critical) analysis of the postmodern worldview, see James Sire, *The Universe Next Door* (Downers Grove, IL: IVP, 2009), 214–223. See also Bob Goudzwaard and Craig Bartholomew, *Beyond the Modern Age: An Archaeology of Contemporary Culture* (Downers Grove, IL: IVP, 2017), 72–79.

[178] Some have argued that postmodernism is really connected to late modernity. Sire notes that " ... postmodernism is not 'post' anything; it is the last move of the modern, the result of the modern takings its own commitments seriously and seeing that they fail to stand the test of analysis." Sire, *The Universe Next Door,* 215.

tethered to the emerging field of postcolonial studies) revolutionized the way that anthropologists talked about culture. In what follows, I will provide a brief sketch of the development within the social sciences, before pivoting to the example of a missiologist who attempted to forge "a postmodern anthropology for mission in a postcolonial world."[179]

Development in the Social Sciences

The social sciences did not remain static. Instead, they evolved under the influence of postmodernism and postcolonialism. As postmodernity developed, it influenced nearly all (if not each) academic discipline. In the social sciences, postmodernity's presence was felt on anthropological theories of culture. In a previous era, culture was viewed as something that was fixed and bounded. Now, the boundaries are viewed as blurry. Guest observes, "Although culture is shared by members of groups, it is also constantly contested, negotiated, and changing. Culture is never static."[180] On the one hand, some might wonder if this is a byproduct of the overall postmodern lack of certainty about anything. A lack of certainty, coupled with an unwillingness to label something, might lead one to see boundaries that are blurry, and cultures that are fluid. On the other hand, some might argue that this is simply the way that cultures are, especially in the globalized world of the twenty-first century.

Postcolonialism is not identical with postmodernism, but the two streams of thought often work in tandem. Postcolonial theory is rooted in the historical conquest, colonization, and eventual independence of much of the Majority World. Robert Young declares that "postcolonialism involves first of all the argument that the nations of the three non-western continents (Africa, Asia, Latin America) are largely in a situation of subordination to Europe and North America, and in a position of economic

---

[179] Michael Rynkiewich, *Soul, Self, and Society: A Postmodern Anthropology for Mission in a Postcolonial World* (Eugene, OR: Cascade Books, 2011).

[180] Guest, *Cultural Anthropology*, 37.

inequality."[181] According to Young, postcolonialism is an activist philosophy.[182]

As it relates to culture, postcolonial thought emphasizes hybridity, which Young notes, "involves processes of interaction that create new social spaces to which new meanings are given."[183] For postcolonial theorists, culture is something that can be contested and negotiated, and the end result is often a third cultural location. It is not either/or, it is both/and. It is hybrid.[184] As Eric Baretto notes, "The notion of hybridity opens a valuable, complex, in-between space that can better comprehend the gradation evident in colonial contexts between resistance and accommodation, between the rejection of one's former identity or an identity imposed by the colonizer."[185]

The postcolonial influence can be seen in standard anthropology textbooks, like the one authored by Guest. He asserts that cultures are not "completely isolated or bounded groups of people located in a particular place."[186] Guest's comment is insightful, especially in the context of a city. Indeed, hybridity can be a helpful prism through which to view major urban centers. After all, in cities like Brooklyn, residents are culturally complex. For instance, a West African immigrant might identify as West African, as Senegalese, as Fulani, as a New Yorker, or as an American (to name merely a few options).[187] The particular cultural identity that this

---

[181] Robert Young, *Postcolonialism: A Very Short Introduction* (Oxford: Oxford University Press, 2003), 4.

[182] Ibid.

[183] Young, *Postcolonialism,* 79.

[184] See Eric Barreto, *Ethnic Negotiations: The Function of Race and Ethnicity in Acts 16* (Tübingen: Mohr Siebeck, 2010), 45–53, for a helpful discussion of the concept of hybridity.

[185] Barreto, *Ethnic Negotiations,* 53. To some, it might appear unusual for a New Testament scholar to employ the language of postcolonialism. However, some postcolonial theorists would maintain that the New Testament, birthed amid the Roman Empire, emerged in a colonial context, and so it gives evidence of the power struggle between the "subaltern" and the "Empire."

[186] Guest, *Cultural Anthropology,* 66.

[187] Interestingly, anecdotal evidence suggests that West Africans do not primarily identify themselves as Black.

West African immigrant lays claim to will vary from day to day, based upon the needs of the moment. Today, she might call herself Fulani. Tomorrow she might be a New Yorker.

Are postmodernism and postcolonial theories of culture accurate?[188] Based upon the way that the world is changing in the twenty-first century, postmodern and postcolonial theories of culture have something helpful to offer to missiologists. Three global phenomena lend credence to the idea that culture can be fluid and might be characterized by hybridity. Mass migration, globalization, and urbanization are three potent forces that have remade the world. Each of these phenomena have impacted entire societies, reshaping the culture of individuals, villages, and countries.

Mass migration (and the contemporary refugee crisis) has resulted in large numbers of immigrants moving rapidly from one country to another. Consequently, many immigrants are now able to function in a foreign land. For instance, in Brooklyn, one can overhear conversations in nearly two hundred languages. Jewish, Russian, Spanish, Italian, and Chinese immigrants are some of the many peoples who now call Brooklyn home. The fact that many of them speak their native language is evidence of culture. However, the longer they remain in Brooklyn, the more they (usually) assimilate.[189] The result is that the immigrant is no longer exclusively Chinese or Russian, but someone who is culturally complex.

---

[188] It should be noted, once again, I am not suggesting that postmodernism and postcolonialism should be completely embraced. Instead, I am merely assessing the usefulness of certain elements of postmodern and postcolonial conceptions of culture.

[189] Wan and Casey note, "Assimilation is not an one way endeavor .... As assimilation occurs, an individual's ethnic origin becomes less relevant as individuals on both sides begin to see themselves as more alike than different. This definition of assimilation not only allows for the influence of the mainstream culture on immigrant groups; but also allows for movement by the mainstream toward cultural values of the immigrant group." Enoch Wan and Anthony Casey, *Church Planting among Immigrants in US Urban Centers: The "Where", "Why", and "How" of Diaspora Missiology in Action* (Portland: Institute of Diaspora Studies, 2014), 4.

They have added American (or perhaps Brooklyn) layers to their cultural identity.

Globalization is a process that has remade and is continuing to remake the world. As Susan Baker notes, "Globalization is a word describing a plethora of phenomena that tend to make the world seem smaller as interconnections form a web around it."[190] For example, one can step into an Eastern city and see the same global brands that one would identify from the West. Coca-Cola, Disney, the NBA, and McDonald's are all global forces. The fact that people in Brooklyn and Nairobi enjoy the same drinks and wear the same brand of jeans means that culture is becoming more blurred. Culture is certainly still distinct, but the lines, in many cases, are becoming less clear.

Urbanization might be the key that links these phenomena together. The world is becoming increasingly urban.[191] As it does, the cities of the world seem to become slightly more alike. This is no doubt the result of mass migration to cities and the homogenizing force of globalization, which is most felt in cities. Indeed, migration and globalization seem to be observed more in the major cities of the world, especially "international cities" like Hong Kong, London, Sau Paulo, Dubai and New York.

As we have observed, the social sciences have developed in how they articulate theories of culture. Postmodern and postcolonial anthropologists now argue that culture is fluid, and not fixed. They argue that the boundaries "around" a culture can be porous, and that people (especially immigrants who live in major cities) can be characterized by cultural hybridity. This developing model of culture has slowly been embraced by

---

[190] Susan Baker, "Introduction: Globalization, Urbanization and Mission," in *Globalization and Its Effects on Urban Ministry in the 21st Century*, ed. Susan Baker (Pasadena: William Carey, 2009), 19.

[191] Harvard economist Glaeser observes, "Five million more people every month live in the cities of the developing world, and in 2011, more than half the world's population is urban." Edward Glaesar, *Triumph of the City: How Our Greatest Invention Makes Us Richer, Smarter, Greener, Healthier, and Happier* (New York: Penguin, 2011), 1.

some missiologists. To further clarify these developments, we will now briefly examine a recent book as an example of an emerging missiological model of culture.

The New Social Sciences and Missiology: Michael Rynkiewich

In 2010 Michael Rynkiewich[192] retired from his role as a professor at Asbury Theological Seminary. Prior to his career educating missionaries, he was trained as an anthropologist, earning a PhD for his fieldwork on Pacific Islanders. He authored or edited several books, some from the per-spective of anthropology and some from the vantage point of missiology.[193]

In the book that represents what Rynkiewich calls the "culmination of my life's work,"[194] he argues that missiology needs to evolve along with the social sciences. He argues that "missiology, as it is taught in colleges and seminaries now, tends to be based on an outdated anthropology that is recommended to potential missionaries for a world that no longer exists. In the missiological imaginary, a Western missionary sits across the table from a local person who embodies one identity, one culture, one language."[195] Rynkiewich believes that the social sciences have continued to develop, and that this development can be clearly seen in newer understandings of hybridity in culture.

---

[192] This biographical material is gathered from the author's preface to the book that is now being examined. See Rynkiewich, *Soul, Self, and Society*, xiii–xv.

[193] For a sampling of Rynkiewich's work, see James Spradley and Michael Rynkiewich, *The Nacirema: Readings on American Culture* (New York: Little Brown & Company, 1975); Michael Rynkiewich and James Spradley, *Ethics and Anthropology: Dilemmas in Fieldwork* (Indianapolis: Wiley, 1976); and Michael Rynkiewich, *Cultures and Languages of Papua New Guinea: The Story of the Origins, Migrations and Settlements of Melanesian Peoples, Languages and Cultures* (Goroka, Papua New Guinea: Melanesian Institute, 2004).

[194] Rynkiewich, *Soul, Self and Society*, xv.

[195] Rynkiewich, *Soul, Self and Society*, xii. Rynkiewich was certainly not the first missiologist to make this claim. Intriguingly, Taber was perhaps ahead of his time when, in 2000, he critiqued the "outdated, functionalist view of societies and cultures as permanently closed, self-contained realities." Taber, *To Understand the World, To Save the World*, 99.

After his introductory chapter, Rynkiewich turned immediately to the topic of culture. He opines (with echoes of Hiebert), "Culture is a more or less integrated system of knowledge, values and feelings that people use to define their reality (worldview), interpret their experiences, and generate appropriate strategies for living..."[196] He believes that culture is "a system that people learn from other people around them and share with other people in a social setting; a system that people use to adapt to their spiritual, social, and physical environments; and a system that people use to innovate in order to change themselves as their environments change."[197]

This approach is noteworthy for multiple reasons. First, it demonstrates conceptual connections with Hiebert's definition, which was cited earlier in this chapter. Like Hiebert, Rynkiewich believes that culture is a mostly integrated system that includes values and feelings. Second, this definition is noteworthy because it incorporates the environmental factor. According to Rynkiewich, culture is not something that one is born with; instead, it is learned from others.

Third, this approach is noteworthy because it allows for the possibility of cultural change. Rynkiewich declares that culture can be used by an individual to change and adapt as society changes. These last two notes of emphasis point towards Rynkiewich's dependence upon both postmodern and postcolonial theories of culture. For Rynkiewich, culture is not static. Not only is it fluid, but the system is such that people can exist in a liminal (in-between) cultural state.

Rynkiewich notes that early anthropologists believed that culture was an essence that existed separately from people. However, he argues that is a fundamental misperception of culture. Rynkiewich believes, "If culture is powerful, and it is when it directs what people see as possible,

---

[196] Rynkiewich, *Soul, Self, and Society*, 19.
[197] Ibid.

it is also contingent on the materials at hand, constructed on a daily basis, and contested by others in the same society."[198] For Rynkiewich, culture is shaped by one's environment (contingent), is fluid (constructed), and is communal (contested). These ideas arise from postmodern and postcolonial conceptions of culture. These theories posit that culture is not essentialized but is instead a dynamic system that is negotiated by individuals and societies.

Michael Rynkiewich is a pioneer, seeking to push missiology into a greater appropriation of the newer insights of anthropology. Yet he is not alone in this determination. In a similar vein, Christian anthropologists Howell and Paris argue, "Culture is the total way of life of a group of people that is learned, dynamic, shared, power laden, and integrated."[199] The similarities to Rynkiewich are apparent. In this definition, Howell and Paris maintain that culture is a system (total way of life), is environment-al, not essential (learned and dynamic), and communal (shared). Howell and Paris also note the important power dynamics at work in cultural systems. This last point of emphasis dovetails nicely with postcolonial readings of culture.

In their provocative article about unreached people groups, Lee and Park make some of the same observations. They note, "This porous and fluid nature of social boundaries becomes amplified amidst the changes brought by globalization, modernization, and urbanization. In today's world, virtually all 'people groups' must navigate the liminal space of intercultural contacts."[200] While the precise arguments made by Lee and Park have been (and will be) vigorously debated,[201] they are no doubt

---

[198] Rynkiewich, *Soul, Self, and Society,* 39.

[199] Brian Howell and Jenell Paris, *Introducing Cultural Anthropology: A Christian Perspective* (Grand Rapids: Baker, 2019), 40.

[200] Peter Lee and James Sung-Hwan Park, "Beyond People Group Thinking," *Missiology,* 216.

[201] See for example, Brad Gill, "Beyond Groupism: Refining Our Analysis of Ethnicity and Groups," *IJFM* 35. no. 4 (October-December 2018): 179–184.

correct in at least one crucial part of their argument. The authors are correct to acknowledge that, in the globalized, urbanized planet of the twenty-first century, most cultures are dynamic and changing. Furthermore, they are correct to observe that many immigrants exist in an in-between plane of existence, oftentimes called a liminal space.

In this brief survey of anthropological theories of culture, we have observed an intriguing development. Early anthropologists (including missiological anthropologists) emphasized culture as an essentialized concept. They typically viewed it as fixed and unchanging, and they maintained that the boundaries around an individual culture were often rigid and clear. Later anthropologists, under the influence of postmodern and postcolonial theories, embraced a developing theory of culture. This model held that culture was fluid, rather than fixed and that the borders around a culture could be porous. The new emphasis resulted in models that emphasized hybridity and a liminal space between cultures.

Our overview has demonstrated that Paul Hiebert was a prominent missiological representative of the first approach. He ably adapted the best of anthropology and employed it in the service of missiology. Yet, in his last book, Hiebert articulated an updated understanding of culture that might seem at home in both modernity and postmodernity. Then we examined Michael Rynkiewich as an example of a missiological anthropologist who was influenced by postmodernity and postcolonialism. We discovered that he emphasized the fluid nature of culture and pointed to the frequent reality of hybrid cultures in our world today.

Which of these approaches is best? Since missiology relies so heavily on the social sciences (especially anthropology), missiologists need to ensure that their models appropriate the best insights of social scientists.[202] In the next section we will attempt to craft a model of culture

---

[202] The best insights will only qualify as such if they agree with Scripture and correspond to the real world.

that is rooted in Scripture and appropriates the best insights of both modern and post-modern/postcolonial theories of culture. Once this model is built, we can then test it against the cultural data available from the world of antiquity.

Forging a Theoretical Model of Culture

Models are, by their very nature, tentative. They are theoretical constructs crafted to make sense of the available data.[203] As new data becom-es available, models are reworked and sometimes discarded. This has been the case with anthropological models of culture. As the world changed, and as the social sciences pressed into further insights, models of culture were significantly reworked. In this section we will forge a theoretical model of culture, one that relies on the wisdom of earlier anthropologists and incorporates insights from current anthropologists. The first step in our endeavor is to engage with the construct of biculturalism, as espoused by Kathy Ehrensperger.

Bilingualism and Biculturalism

Kathy Ehrensperger is a New Testament scholar at the University of Wales. In Paul at the Crossroads of Cultures: Theologizing in the Space Between, Ehrensperger explored the helpful concept of biculturalism. Because Ehrensperger doubts "the heuristic value of the concept of hybridity for the analysis of cultural translation processes"[204] she proposes biculturalism as a model for reading certain New Testament texts. It is not that Ehrensperger dismisses hybridity, for she does acknowledges that culture is hybrid. She notes that "culture is always hybrid, involving ongoing negotiations in the process of the emergence of symbolic and

---

[203] See Mike Stallard, *A Proposal for Theological Method: Systematic Theology as Model Building* (http://our-hope.org/blog/wp-content/uploads/2009/09/Method2.pdf).

[204] Kathy Ehrensperger, *Paul at the Crossroads of Cultures: Theologizing in the Space Between* (London: Bloomsbury, 2015), 11.

social worlds. In that sense, all cultures are hybrid, rather than monolithic, influenced by and influencing each other at crossroads and in webs of networks, in ongoing negotiations."[205]

However, since she believes that culture is always hybrid, she believes that the label can become "rather meaningless."[206] Instead of adopt-ing models of fusion, blending, and hybridity, Ehrensperger seeks models that preserve a culture's uniqueness but also allow for dynamics of fluidity and change.[207] In biculturalism, she believes that she has found such a model and it can facilitate an insightful reading of certain New Testament texts. Ehrensperger observes that "there is a consensus among sociolinguists that language, culture and identity are closely intertwined."[208]

It is this consensus that drives her to first examine bilingualism and then its link to biculturalism. According to Ehrensperger, "Bi- or multilinguals are thus people who use more than one language in their daily lives, either simultaneously or consecutively …. What is significant is the insight that bilinguals are not two monolinguals in one person but have 'a distinct compound state of mind—multicompetence.'"[209] Ehrensperger belie-ves that this model can be applied to the world of the New Testament, in particular to the Apostle Paul.

We will return to this possibility when we explore the phenomenon of Hellenization, and its impact upon the cultural makeup of

---

[205] Ehrensperger, *Paul at the Crossroads of Cultures*, 35.
[206] Ibid.
[207] Ehrensperger is driven to this approach by her assessment of the data regarding Hellenism. She believes that there is evidence from antiquity that Hellenization did not produce fused, hybrid cultures, but instead forged new cultures in which multiple cultures existed within one person or group. Ehrensperger, *Paul at the Crossroads of Cultures*, 17–29. A subsequent section of this chapter will examine information from antiquity to ascertain whether the model that is being forged makes sense of the relevant data from that era.
[208] Ehrensperger, *Paul at the Crossroads of Cultures*, 51.
[209] Ehrensperger, *Paul at the Crossroads of Cultures*, 52.

teams in the Book of Acts. For now, it is enough to acknowledge that many people (in both the ancient and modern worlds) speak two or more languages. Since culture is linked to language, this reality is significant. Ehrensperger notes, "Bilingualism and biculturalism are in many cases closely intertwined ... But the combination of the terms indicates that not all bilinguals are perceived to be bicultural nor that all biculturals are bilingual."[210]

In contemporary urban settings (like Brooklyn), this can be seen most clearly in the examples of immigrants. I live in the neighborhood of Crown Heights, where West Indian peoples constitute the dominant cultural group, followed closely by Chasidic Jews. Both Jamaican (as a representative West Indian people) and Jewish residents of Crown Heights self-identify in culturally complex ways. Jamaican Brooklynites might not speak Patois,[211] hence they may not be truly bilingual. However, an ethnographic researcher would quickly note that they are bicultural. They are Jamaican, but they have also become Brooklynites.[212] Jewish residents of Crown Heights are remarkably culturally insulated. However, even though they speak Hebrew and observe the traditions of their ancestors, they have also become Brooklynites in certain ways. They usually speak at least some English, participate in local culture (although certainly not to the extent of their West Indian neighbors), and contribute to the community.[213] Later in this section, we will return to the example of immigrants in Brooklyn.

---

[210] Ehrensperger, *Paul at the Crossroads of Cultures*, 57.

[211] Patois is a creolized language that is primarily English but incorporates words from West African languages. It is spoken in Jamaica, and oftentimes, in Brooklyn.

[212] This phenomenon of biculturalism is also related to an immigrant's position on a spectrum of assimilation. For instance, second and third generation Jamaican Americans in Crown Heights do not display the same degree of biculturalism as do their parents.

[213] For a sociological analysis of this community, see Henry Goldschmidt, *Race and Religion Among the Chosen Peoples of Crown Heights* (New Brunswick: Rutgers University Press, 2006).

Ehrensperger believes that biculturalism is analogous to (and related to) bilingualism. She notes, "Like bilinguals, biculturals have varied degrees of competence in different cultural meaning systems and different levels of integrating these in their identity. Thus, rather than switching between languages biculturals are seen as switching between their different cultural meaning systems depending on the situation."[214] For Ehrensperger, biculturalism provides a means of positing multiple cultural identities within a single person or group. Crucially, this model does not blur the lines between the various identities, thereby flattening (and potentially eliminating) the cultural distinctives.

The model of biculturalism shares important features with the model of hybridity. First, biculturalism shares with hybridity the idea that culture can be fluid. Second, biculturalism shares with hybridity the idea that one can be culturally mixed. Both insights are valid, especially in contemporary urban societies. However, biculturalism could be a step forward in our understanding of cultural identity. While hybridity tends to fuse a person's cultures together into a new hybrid identity, biculturalism creates a compound cultural identity that still preserves the original cultures. Having engaged the concept of biculturalism, we can now set forth our own model of culture. To do so, we will build upon Hiebert's theory of culture, Rynkiewich's theory of culture, and Ehrensperger's articulation of biculturalism. We will then explore the resulting model against the backdrop of contemporary Brooklyn.

A Theoretical Model of Culture

Henning Wrogemann poignantly asks, "What is culture?"[215] This question continues to perplex theologians and anthropologists. As we previously argued, a model of culture ought to be rooted in the narrative of

---

[214] Ehrensperger, *Paul at the Crossroads of Cultures,* 58.
[215] Wrogemann, *Intercultural Hermeneutics,* 112.

Scripture.[216] It must also appropriate the best insights from both early and later anthropologists. From early anthropologists (and from missiologists such as Hiebert who relied upon them), we can learn that culture is an integrated system of artifacts and symbols. From later anthropologists (and from missiologists such as Rynkiewich who relied upon them), we can learn that culture is dynamic and that its borders can sometimes be porous.

With Hiebert, I believe that culture is a more or less integrated system that encompasses feelings, values and beliefs. With Rynkiewich, I also accept that culture is communal and contested and that a person can inhabit multiple cultural identities. I believe that biculturalism could perhaps provide a better model than hybridity. If this is correct, then biculturalism should feature as an element of our proposed model of culture.

In this book, I want to propose the following way to understand culture (this model should be viewed as more of a description than a definition). Culture is the systemic way of life that a group share. This culture has defining traits like beliefs, values, customs, and languages. People can enter and exit each culture, sometimes by choice and sometimes by the force of circumstances. People can exist in a liminal space, exhibiting characteristics of two or more cultures. Some members of a culture will seem to be completely monocultural. Others will give evidence of biculturalism or even multiculturalism. In these instances, people are not operating with a hybrid identity, but instead preserve important distinctives from multiple cultures.

The most salient feature of this descriptive model is that it allows for both monoculturalism and biculturalism (or even multiculturalism). It recognizes that some members of a society can be clearly identified as one

---

[216] See a previous section of this chapter for resources that articulate a biblical theology of culture.

who is rooted in a single culture. It also recognizes that some members of a society are not so easily categorized, and that they exhibit traits of multiple cultures. Previously, I mentioned that I reside in a Brooklyn neighborhood called Crown Heights. It is a diverse neighborhood that has been historically Afro-Caribbean and Jewish. In theory, it should be easy to spot the difference between those who are Jewish and those who are West Indian.

However, the curious case of Matisyahu[217] demonstrates the complexity of culture. Matisyahu is a Jewish Reggae artist. He looks Jewish, with a traditional beard, and sometimes performs in Jewish attire, including a kepah and tassels. However, once he starts singing, a listener is instantly confused. Matisyahu raps and performs reggae as if he hailed from Jamaica. The Afro-Caribbean and Chasidic Jewish elements of Crown Heights have converged in the person of Matisyahu.[218] Is Matisyahu Jewish? Clearly, his attire gives some evidence that he is. Furthermore, his songs speak of a deep spiritual longing for Moshiach (the Messiah). Yet Matisyahu has become skilled at deploying traditional Afro-Caribbean art forms. With ease, he moves in and out of the traditional Chasidic Jewish world of Crown Heights. Apparently, this is because his upbringing in a West Indian community reshaped him, allowing him to exist in a liminal space.[219]

Matisyahu demonstrates the validity of our model's emphasis upon biculturalism and fluidity. However, it should be noted that Matisyahu is an anomaly in Crown Heights. Most people would not be comfortable in Matisyahu's liminal space. They would prefer to move within a more monocultural slice of society. Many of them prefer to identify as either Jamaican or Jewish (or Hipster). This demonstrates the validity of

---

[217] https://www.matisyahuworld.com/.

[218] In fact, in his hit song, "King Without a Crown," he references Crown Heights: https://www.youtube.com/watch?v=ChV5BZ8SmS0.

[219] Once again, we observe how our environment can shape our culture.

our model's inclusion of traditional understandings of culture (as emphasized by early anthropologists and in the earlier writings of Paul Hiebert).

At this point, we need to step back and assess what ground we have traversed and to preview where we are headed. Our exploration has highlighted early and later anthropological models of cultures. It has surveyed the writings of Paul Hiebert and Michael Rynkiewich, discovering in the process that culture is a shared way of life that can be continually negotiated. The discovery process included learning from Kathy Ehrensperger that biculturalism could be a more useful approach than hybridity when examining instances of multiple cultural identities. Finally, we proposed an understanding of culture that could explain the complexities of Crown Heights, Brooklyn. It is a model that allows for individuals to be monocultural (even fiercely so) for the duration of their lives. It is also a model that allows people to slip in and out of a culture, demonstrating biculturalism and/or multiculturalism.

This approach makes sense of certain settings, such as Crown Heights. However, for this model to be of legitimate use in our study, it must also make sense of the Book of Acts. After all, the next two chapters will seek to culturally map some of the ministry teams found in Acts. In some cases, people will be identified who are clearly monocultural (for instance, Jewish or Syrian). In other instances, people will be discovered who defy easy labels, and just might qualify as bicultural individuals.

Before producing this cultural map, we might ask if it is even appropriate to apply this approach to the Book of Acts. Just because the model has explanatory power for Crown Heights does not mean that it is a legitimate tool in the service of New Testament exegesis. After all, some might contend that it is anachronistic to read contemporary understandings of culture back onto the biblical books. Indeed, this is a legitimate concern. Therefore, to establish the appropriateness of this method, we will examine select data from antiquity. If our model (which affirms both monocultural and bicultural individuals) makes sense of the data of antiquity, then it would likely make sense of the Book of Acts. It is to this exploration of cultural identity in antiquity to which we now turn.

Testing the Model: Culture in Antiquity

How did the inhabitants of the ancient world view their own cultural identity? Did they view it as something that was fixed and unchanging? Or did they perceive cultural identity as something that could be fluid? Did they view identity in monocultural terms, or did they embrace the possibility of biculturalism? Obviously, when discussing views of cultural identity in antiquity, it is impossible to be comprehensive. Instead, we will select representative examples. It will quickly become apparent that there was not one overarching view of cultural identity in antiquity. Rather, a diversity of approaches existed.

As we explore culture in antiquity, we will first note examples of a more fixed approach to cultural identity, one that resonates with the insights of early anthropologists. We will then discover examples of a more fluid approach to cultural identity, one that resonates with the insights of later anthropologists. Finally, we will conclude this section (and chapter) by exploring the phenomenon of Hellenism as a potential model of biculturalism in antiquity and in the Book of Acts.

Fixed Approaches to Cultural Identity

The Greek historian Herodotus records how Xerxes once bribed the Athenians to go to war against other Greeks, and that they rebuffed his efforts. Herodotus notes that in their retort, they claimed they could not go to war against other Greek peoples because of "the kinship of all Greeks in blood and speech, and the shrines of gods and the sacrifices that we have in common, and the likeness of our way of life, to all of which it would not befit the Athenians to be false."[220] In this intriguing excerpt, Hero-dotus demonstrates that the Athenians seemed to believe that their eth-nicity and culture were highly fixed.

It is highly unlikely that the Athenians thought in the systematic categories of ethnicity and culture.[221] However, they did express themselves in ways that contemporary researchers can understand using modern cat-egories. Regarding their ethnicity, the Athenians declared that they had a shared blood with the Greek people, and therefore they would not wage war against them. In reference to their culture, they posited that the "like-ness of our way of life" was held in common with other Greeks. In other words, the Athenians asserted that they shared a culture (a systematic way of life) with the Greek people that Xerxes wanted to defeat.

It seems the Athenians whom Herodotus describes believed that their culture was fixed and was shared with those who had a unique con-nection to them (namely the connections of shared blood and place of origin). The Athenian approach to cultural identity (at least as described by Herodotus) stressed fixed cultural boundaries. These boundaries enclosed a specific way of life, one characterized by certain religious and linguistic practices.

This example from ancient Athens resonates closely with the in-sights of early anthropologists, and of the missiologist Paul Hiebert. Hiebert (and many of the anthropologists upon whom he relied) stressed that culture was an integrated way of life that touched several different spheres, including worldview, customs, and artifacts. The Athenians represent an ancient view of culture that is like that espoused by early anthropologists. The Athenians believed that their way of life marked

---

[220] Herodotus, *The Histories,* 8.144: perseus.uchicago.edu/perseus-cgi/citequery3.pl?dbname=GreekFeb2011&query=Hdt.%208.144.2&getid=1.

[221] For an excellent survey of Greek ethnic identity in antiquity, see Jonathan Hall, *Hellenicity: Between Ethnicity and Culture* (Chicago: The University of Chicago Press, 2002).

them off as a distinct people, albeit ones who shared a way of life with other, closely related Greek people. In modern terms, this is cultural identity. The Athenians believed they shared a fixed cultural identity with other Greek people, based upon shared language, customs, and religion.

Like the early anthropologists, the Athenians seem to have viewed their own culture as fixed and bounded. Moreover, little evidence suggests that they viewed themselves in terms of hybridity or biculturalism. You were either part of Greek culture or you were not. This distinction was crucial, and in this example from military history, it was deadly serious. It is not my goal to demonstrate that all people in antiquity emphasized fixity regarding cultural identity. Rather my goal is to demonstrate that some people in antiquity approached cultural identity in this manner. Having established this through Herodotus' description of the Athenians, we can now survey those who approached cultural identity from a different vantage point.

Fluid Approaches to Cultural Identity

Shaye Cohen notes that, in the ancient world, "One could be a Macedonian and a Hellene, a Syrian and a Hellene, a Cappadocian and a Hellene. Similarly, one could be a Macedonian and a Jew, a Syrian and a Jew, a Cappadocian and a Jew."[222] Cohen is here acknowledging the complex nature of ethnic and cultural identity in antiquity. His assertion sheds light on an overall approach to culture.

A person in my north-central Brooklyn neighborhood could be ethnically Haitian but culturally American. Cohen seems to imply that this same mixed dynamic was at play in the way that Jewish identity was conceived of in the ancient world. One could be ethnically Jewish but

---

[222] Shaye Cohen, *The Beginnings of Jewishness: Boundaries, Varieties, Uncertainties,* (Berkley: University of California Press, 1999), 135.

culturally Greek.[223] For some in the ancient world, cultural identity was characterized by fluidity. To illustrate this point, we will briefly examine the examples provided by Philo and Josephus.

In his treatise about the misdeeds of Flaccus, Philo describes the Jews of the diaspora as those who view "the holy city as their metropolis in which is erected the sacred temple of the most high God, but accounting those regions which have been occupied by their fathers, and grandfathers, and great grandfathers, and still more remote ancestors, in which they have been born and brought up, as their country."[224] In this text, Philo describes the Jewish people as those who are in an orbital relationship to the Mother City, Jerusalem. Yet according to Philo, they also legitimately claim to be citizens of other countries. This statement does not explicitly address the issue of cultural identity.

However, it is not hard to see that Philo could be saying that Jews of the Diaspora negotiated a complex world, one which oftentimes required dual identities. These two identities would have potentially shaped Diaspora Jews into bicultural individuals. It is not implausible, for example, to read Philo's description as something that might make sense of an ethnically Jewish, culturally Egyptian individual in the first century.[225] Since Philo does not explicitly frame the issue in this way, it is important that we are not too dogmatic. However, it does appear that Philo's emphasis upon dual identities (from the Mother City and the countries of the Diaspora) can foster an approach similar to biculturalism.

---

[223] This specific construction of identity will be engaged with more deeply when the phenomenon of Hellenism is explored as an example of biculturalism in antiquity.

[224] Philo, *Flaccus 45–46*. www.earlychristianwritings.com/yonge/book36.html

[225] For an insightful discussion about Philo's statement about Diaspora Jews and their relationship to Jerusalem, see Cynthia Baker, "'From Every Nation under Heaven:' Jewish Ethnicities in the Greco-Roman World," in *Prejudice and Christian Beginnings: Investigating Race, Gender, and Ethnicity in Early Christian Studies,* ed. Laura Nasrallah and Elisabeth Schüssler Fiorenza (Minneapolis: Fortress Press, 2010), 86–91. See also, Jutta Leonhardt-Balzer, "Diaspora Jewish Attitudes to *Metropoleis:* Philo and Paul on Balanced Personalities, Split Loyalties, Jerusalem, and Rome," in *The Urban World and the First Christians,* ed. Steve Walton, Paul Treblico and David Gill (Grand Rapids: Eerdmans, 2017), 89–92.

Indeed, Philo's world of dual identities would cohere with the writings of later anthropologists (and missiologists such as Michael Rynkiewich). They emphasized that culture could be characterized by various forms of hybridity. This might be what Philo is describing, although the evidence is inconclusive.

At the very least, Philo reminds contemporary readers that, just like today, cultural identity was complicated in the world of antiquity. Jewish identity was not simply derived from one's ethnic heritage and embrace of the religious traditions of Jerusalem. Instead, this identity was negotiated amid the various cities of the Diaspora. It produced people who were good Jews and good citizens of their adopted homeland. This was, perhaps, an early indicator of the complex nature of cultural identity; it lent itself towards hybrid or bicultural modes of being.

In Josephus' book *Antiquities of the Jews*, he records a fascinating anecdote that illustrates the complexity of identity in the ancient world. In Chapter 2 of Book XX, he recounts how Queen Helena and her son, King Izates, became Jewish.[226] Under the influence of Jewish acquaintances, both Helena and Izates adopted the Jewish religion. However, converting to Judaism involved more than simply embracing certain religious rites and rituals. Judaism was tied to the ethnic and cultural identity of the Jewish people.

Consequently, when Helena and Izates converted, they sought to become more culturally Jewish. Josephus notes that Helena and Izates "changed their course of life, and embraced the Jewish customs" even to the point of (in Izates' case) circumcision.[227] Josephus provides an intriguing example of an ancient cultural identity that was marked by at least some measure of fluidity.

---

[226] Josephus, *Antiquities of the Jews: Book XX*, Chapter 2: www.sacred-texts.com/jud/josephus/ant-20.htm.
[227] Ibid.

To become a proselyte of Judaism (as Helena and Izates did) involved changing one's culture. For some converts, this could mean altering their diet. For others, it could mean altering their bodies (circumcision). During the process of conversion, a person's culture shifted, sometimes in significant ways, and other times in more subtle ways. This description of the fluid nature of culture coheres with the findings of later anthropologists (and more recent missiologists like Michael Rynkiewich).

In our brief exploration of antiquity, we discovered that some writers viewed culture as something that was fixed and bounded. Herodotus is a prime example of this approach. He cited an example of a specific people whom he believed shared a specific culture. Our investigation also discovered that some writers (Philo and Josephus) held less tightly to the idea of a fixed culture. Instead, they seemed to make room for shifting cultural identities and for biculturalism. The approach of early anthropologists fits nicely with the writings of Herodotus. The approach of later anthropologists fits more closely with the writings of Philo and Josephus. In the next section we will explore how the phenomenon of Hellenism sometimes produced bicultural individuals in antiquity.

Hellenism, Hybridity, Biculturalism, and Multiculturalism

The ancient phenomenon of Hellenization provides us with a unique opportunity to explore two models we previously discussed: hybridity and biculturalism. Hellenization occurred throughout the ancient world as Greek language and culture spread, primarily through Alexander's conquests. Conquered peoples had to discover a new way of life under an imperial power. This inevitably meant a certain amount of acculturation and a certain amount of resistance. We will primarily examine how the so-called Hellenistic Jews navigated this tension. This issue is important to our study since some of these Hellenistic Jews will feature as key members of ministry teams in the "culture map" produced in Chapters Four and Five.

As I previously noted, hybridity is a model that has gained popularity with the rise of postmodern and postcolonial studies. It is attractive because it seems to make sense of a lot of contemporary situations. Humans in the twenty-first century live in an era characterized by fusion. Contemporary people fuse worship styles together. They fuse different foods together (I love Korean tacos and sushi burritos). Fusion is a way of life, especially in global cities like New York, London, and Hong Kong. Hybridity is a theoretical model that could be described as cultural fusion.

According to postcolonial theory, hybridity results from the interactions between those in power and the "subaltern."[228] The conquered people(s) must determine how much cultural ground they will give up. In this case, will the Hellenistic Jews accommodate to the hegemony of Hellenic culture? Will they resist it? Or will they stake out a middle ground? Baretto argues, "The notion of hybridity helps provide critical conceptual grounds for analyzing how individuals and communities navigate the complex interstitial realities of various competing and complementary ethnic claims."[229]

I am sympathetic to the hybridity model. However, it seems that scholars might be in danger of reading the colonialism of modernity into every ancient text, including the Bible. Interpreters should be wary of seeing "Empire" as the all-consuming theme of everything. Apart from this concern, however, it is apparent that that those who advocate hybridity are at least partially correct, on linguistic and anthropological grounds. Anyone who has lived in another culture or has been forced by circumstances to learn another language, can explain how the experience changed them. As we learned in our earlier exploration of the social sci-

---

[228] Baretto, *Ethnic Negotiation*, 52.
[229] Baretto, *Ethnic Negotiation*, 44.

ences, most cultures are not closed systems. When someone interacts with a member of another culture, or a regulation from another culture, or learns the language of another culture, they are inevitably altered.

This can be illustrated by the example of a child of missionaries. If an African-American child from the State of Alabama grows up with her missionary parents on their "mission field" in Japan, she will be forever changed. Does she identify as American, or as African-American? Certainly, she will not identify as Japanese! When she returns home to attend college at the University of Alabama, she will discover that she no longer "fits in" as easily with "her people." She has probably developed an affinity for elements of Japanese culture and might be uncomfortable with many elements of her native culture. She is not exactly African-American, and she is not Japanese, so what is she? She has become a "third culture kid."[230] This is what happened to many Hellenistic Jews.

For Jews who were confronted with the phenomenon of Hellenization, it would have been impossible to resist all change. For many, Collins notes, "The plaintive question of the psalmist by the waters of Babylon"[231] would have been their daily struggle: "How shall we sing the song of the Lord in a foreign land" (Psalm 137:4)? Indeed, living under the auspices of Roman rule and Greek culture must have seemed like the antithesis of Zion. Profiling the Jews in Egypt, Collins observes that many Jews resisted, and that the Jewish people were characterized by a high degree of cultural resistance. As he notes, "They were more cohesive and more resistant to assimilation" than some other ethnic groups.[232] Yet, he con-

---

[230] K. R., "Growing Up a Third Culture Kid: A Sociological Self-Exploration," *Human Architecture: Journal of the Sociology of Self-Knowledge* volume 9, no. 1, Winter (2011): 29–42.

[231] John Collins, *Between Athens and Jerusalem: Jewish Identity in the Hellenistic Diaspora*, (Grand Rapids: Eerdmans, 2000), 1. Although Collins focuses upon the struggle of diasporic Jews, this struggle for cultural identity would have characterized all participants of Second Temple Judaism, regardless of their geographical location.

[232] Collins, *Between Athens and Jerusalem*, 12.

cludes, "Even the most conservative strands of Diaspora Judaism still attempt to strike a balance with Hellenistic culture."[233]

It is this insight that hybridity theorists instinctively understand. Most exchanges between people of different cultures will likely result in both people being changed in some fashion. Those who live in global cities understand this is true. One cannot live among immigrants, hear various languages, learn new postures and customs, celebrate new holidays, and eat new foods without being altered on some level. Baretto contends it is for this reason that hybridity is such a potent model. He notes, "An alternative type of ethnic reasoning between bare accommodation and wholesale resistance, hybridity is a valuable and strategic position for a movement hoping to carve a cultural niche for themselves among the many peoples of antiquity."[234]

However, even though it seems evident that cultures can shift and mix, I prefer the previously discussed model of biculturalism as articulated by Kathy Ehrensperger, who is "not convinced that paradigms of syncretism, fusion and blending are the appropriate lenses for the analysis of cultural translation processes."[235] Instead, as we noted, she proposes bilingualism and biculturalism. She opines, "Given the ethnic, cultural and linguistic diversity in the Roman Empire of the first century CE, it is no surprise then to find significant evidence for the existence of bilingualism and biculturalism."[236] Ehrensperger is certainly not disputing that cultures act upon one another and alter one another. She

---

[233] Collins, *Between Athens and Jerusalem,* 274. See also Russell Moy, who declared that "in response to this Hellenistic culture, the Pharisees, Sadducees, and the Qumran community in their own ways creatively redefined their understanding of the Mosaic tradition and so transformed Judaism." Russell Moy, "Biculturalism, Race, and the Bible," *Religious Education,* Volume 88 No. 3 Summer (1993): 429.

[234] Baretto, *Ethnic Negotiation,* 53.

[235] Kathy Ehrensperger, *Paul at the Crossroads of Cultures: Theologizing in the Space Between,* (London: Bloomsbury T&T Clark, 2013), 1.

[236] Ehrensperger, *Paul at the Crossroads of Cultures,* 2.

is merely dissatisfied with hybridity as a heuristic model. Hence, her proposal of biculturalism.

Is hybridity a model with insufficient explanatory power? It would seem so. Although hybridity is a step in the right direction, the model ultimately does have some weaknesses. First, hybridity, when taken to its logical conclusion, could lead to deep cultural confusion. If every person who interacts with another person is culturally altered (especially when there are power dynamics involved), then ethnicity and culture ultimately dissolve, and we all become hybrid humans. It is true that members of various cultures interact and produce change, but that does not always alter a person's ethnicity or culture. If it did, at some point it would become meaningless to refer to ethnicity or culture. However, ethnicity and culture continue to rear their heads, even long after some theorists predicted we would all melt together into one big pot.

Second, hybridity does not seem to fully account for the biblical data concerning culture. Culture is an intrinsically valuable element of the imago dei. The doctrine of creation demonstrates that this is something worthy of honor. The doctrine of the Incarnation also reminds us of the cultural particularity of Jesus the Messiah of Israel. The fact that he was a Jew forces us to acknowledge that our culture (and even our skin color) means something. Finally, our eschatology also points to the worth of who we are as embodied beings. Humans will carry culture and language with them onto the New Earth (Revelation 21–22).

Hybridity can result in a jumbled ethnic mashup, one in which people lack a basic cultural identity. It is not a bad model; it is merely insufficient. It is better to search for a model that elevates and preserves a person's culture. In the case of someone with multiple cultures (as in the case with biculturalism), this will result in a thick description of who they are as a multifaceted human being with distinct cultures, rather than simply seeing them as the fusion of various inputs. This thicker description honors a person's full cultural identity as one who bears the image of God.

Third, when applied to the New Testament, hybridity insufficiently explains the ethnic and cultural data. People are identified throughout the New Testament as representatives of an ethnic or cultural group. Barnabas was a Cypriot. Paul was a Hebrew of the Hebrews. Aquilla was a Jew. Silas was a Jew. Titus was a Gentile, probably an Antiochene. These designations make little sense if hybridity so blurs the lines as to make cultural identity meaningless. However, when one reads the New Testament (especially the Book of Acts), one can note that people often did possess (or perhaps perform) more than one culture. For instance, Stephen and Philip were Hellenistic Jews who were clearly distinct from the Hebraic Jews of the Church in Jerusalem. Were they Jewish, or were they Greek? If biculturalism is the appropriate model, the answer is "Yes!"

This may be what Aaron Kuecker was advocating when he utilized social identity theory (SIT) to map intergroup reconciliation in the Book of Acts. He argued for the existence of nested identities, which he notes, "can create a complex nexus of identity."[237] He believes that these nested (or dual) identities are the "possession of multiple social identities based upon participation in multiple social groups. These identities become salient based upon contextual factors, such as the social identity of the person with whom one is interacting."[238] Kuecker is right to note that the Holy Spirit, even when bringing about transethnic reconciliation, does not erase ethnicity or culture.

If Kuecker is correct, then this idea lends itself towards Ehrensperger's embrace of the bicultural model. Both Ehrensperger and Kuecker want to make us aware of the fact that ancient people did not lose their ethnic or cultural identities when they became Christians. Nor did their culture dissolve or fuse with another when they interacted in a multi-

---

[237] Aaron Kuecker, *The Spirit and the 'Other': Social Identity, Ethnicity and Intergroup Reconciliation in Luke-Acts* (London: Bloomsbury T&T Clark, 2011), 29.

[238] Kuecker, *The Spirit and the 'Other',* 49.

cultural setting. Instead, something far more sophisticated occurred. People developed along bicultural lines, possessing multiple (what Kuecker would call "nested") identities. These identities were richly textured and defied easy categorization.

Immigrants and ethnic minorities (including Jews) struggled to discover their place in the Greco-Roman world. Many social science theorists would plot them at some point along the acculturation continuum. About this phenomenon, Harland notes, "Acculturation can involve the selection, adoption, and adaptation of a variety of cultural elements including language, values, and other cultural conventions that compose the lifestyle and worldview of a particular culture group. This process is selective and transformative."[239] Some, such as the Essenes, sought to resist assimilation as much as possible. Others embraced a bicultural lifestyle, in which an individual, according to Harland, could be "highly encultureated into the minority group culture and highly acculturated to the majority culture."[240]

Harland describes the inscription on the family sarcophagus of P. Elius Glykon and Aurelia Amia (ca. 200 CE) as an intriguing example of acculturation in Antiquity.[241] Although this epitaph dates from the second century, it is still reasonable to infer that this type of biculturalism would have been present a few generations earlier during the time of the Book of Acts. According to Harland, the epitaph provides no direct statement regarding the culture of the deceased. Yet it does leave tantalizing clues that point in multiple directions.

Harland asserts that the epigraphic evidence demonstrates that Glykon was a Roman citizen who observed both Jewish and Roman religious festivals. It is possible that Glykon was a Gentile. However, since

---

[239] Philip Harland, *Dynamics of Identity in the World of the Early Christians* (New York: T&T Clark, 2009), 102.

[240] Harland, *Dynamics of Identity,* 102.

[241] Harland, *Dynamics of Identity,* 128–142.

Glykon left behind money for the continued observance of Jewish festivals even after his death, it seems more plausible to conclude that Glykon was ethnically Jewish. However, his seamless dance between Jewish and Roman cultures (and religions) would lend credence towards the idea that he (and perhaps his family) was bicultural. Clearly, Le Donne was correct when he asserts, "Hellenism seeped into the pores of Jewish life in innumerable ways and to varying degrees."[242]

The potential for this type of biculturalism was investigated by Barclay as he surveyed the Jewish diaspora. He constructed an assimilation continuum, ranging from high assimilation to low assimilation (and included unknown assimilation).[243] Barclay acknowledged varying degrees of integration with Hellenism. He notes that, "it mattered a thousand times more if a Jewish man was Hellenized in respect of his genitals than if he was Hellenized in respect of his speech."[244]

This statement (although meant to indicate the weight given to circumcision), indicates the possibility of both higher and lower levels of assimilation to Hellenistic culture. In other words, when Jews were shaped by Hellenization, some of them emerged as bicultural individuals. Indeed, Barclay's insights cohere well with Ehrensperger's bicultural approach. According to Barclay, the Jews may have, in some cases, developed bicultural sensitivities, but they never stopped being Jewish. They did not develop an identity characterized by fusion, but instead one characterized by dual cultures and nested identities. Erich Gruen rightly notes, "The interaction of Jew and Greek in antiquity still weaves a spell, fascinating

---

[242] Anthony Le Donne, "Complicating the Category of Ethnos toward Poliscentrism: A Possible Way Forward within Second Temple Ethnography," in *The Urban World and the First Christians,* ed. Steve Walton, Paul Trebilco, and David Gill (Grand Rapids: Eerdmans, 2017), 13.

[243] John M. G. Barclay, *Jews in the Mediterranean Diaspora: From Alexander to Trajan (323 BCE–117 CE)* (Berkley: University of California Press, 1996), 103–124, 320–335.

[244] Barclay, *Jews in the Mediterranean Diaspora,* 91.

inquirers and stimulating researchers."²⁴⁵ At this point, I believe bicultural-ism is a preferred model for understanding the way in which multiple cult-ures converged in the person of Hellenistic Jews.

Conclusion

In this chapter we have surveyed the development of anthropological and missiological theories of culture. We have incorporated insights from both early and later anthropologists and missiologists into a theoretical model. This model allows for the existence of monocultural and bicultural/multicultural individuals within the same societies. When we examined select data from antiquity, we discovered from Herodotus that some viewed culture as more fixed. We also discovered from Josephus that some viewed culture as more fluid.

When we assessed the phenomenon of Hellenization, we observed that this process sometimes resulted in the creation of individuals whose cultural identity could best be described using the framework of biculturalism. To summarize, I conclude that culture can be both mono and multi, both fluid and fixed. The next two chapters will rely upon this discovery to produce a "cultural map" of some of the ministry teams described in the Book of Acts.

---

[245] Erich Gruen, *Heritage and Hellenism: The Reinvention of the Jewish Tradition* (Berkley: University of California Press, 1998), xiii.

CHAPTER FOUR: Mapping Culture from Jerusalem to Antioch

In the last two chapters we have grappled with how to read the Book of Acts and how to read culture. For reading Acts, I proposed a representative patterns approach, in which we look for repeated patterns throughout the text of Acts (in this book we are looking for patterns of diverse teams). For reading culture, I proposed a theory of culture that incorporates both monocultural and bicultural elements. With these introductory matters out of the way, we can now engage the central issue of this volume. Our quest started with a *big idea*: diverse teams were a crucial element of the ancient approach to urban mission pioneered in the Book of Acts. If we want to replicate this method in contemporary cities (an approach I will argue for in the final chapter), then we first must prove that this was, in fact, an ancient approach to urban mission.

Over the next two chapters I will seek to do just that. In this chapter, I will examine the ministry teams in Jerusalem (early Acts) and Antioch (middle Acts). We will look closely for traces of cultural diversity. In the next chapter I will explore various Pauline teams (later Acts); again, hunting for cultural diversity.

Cultural Makeup of the Jerusalem Church

Jerusalem is the natural place to begin when mapping culture in the early Church.[246] It was the birthplace of the Christian movement, the site of Christ's death and resurrection. It was here that the Apostles waited for the Spirit, and it was here that they eventually received power

---

[246] For a helpful methodological discussion centered upon the use of the modern term "culture" and its relation to the Book of Acts, see C. Kavin Rowe, *World Upside Down: Reading Acts in the Graeco-Roman Age* (Oxford: Oxford University Press, 2009), 13–14. Rowe rightly acknowledges that, despite its limitations, the term "culture" can still be usefully applied to our readings of the Book of Acts.

for mission on the Day of Pentecost. Before we can examine the composition of the ministry team that emerged in Jerusalem, it is first necessary to explore the cultural makeup of the Church at Jerusalem. The first step in this process is to examine the cultural context of this first-century city.

According to Eckhard Schnabel, "Jerusalem had become a world city, not least on account of the reign and the building activities of Herod I. The capital of the Jewish commonwealth could compete with the leading cities of the Roman Empire in terms of its magnificence and prestige (not with regards to its size)."[247] Jerusalem was an important city even beyond its spiritual significance to the Jewish people. In this city, one could expect to encounter people drawn from various corners of the Roman Empire (indeed, this would have been the expectation in many major cities of the Greco-Roman world).[248]

Schnabel points to Jerusalem as a spiritual center when he reminds us that its population would have swelled during annual festivals. He notes, "According to Josephus, about 2.5 million pilgrims congregated in Jerusalem for the large festivals."[249] Since these pilgrims descended upon Jerusalem from "all parts of the Roman Empire," Schnabel notes that "Jerusalem was an international city."[250] It is possible that these pilgrims feature prominently in the early pages of the Book of Acts.

Luke describes the emergence of the Church with his narrative of Pentecost (Acts 2). In a key comment, he notes, "Now there were Jews staying in Jerusalem, devout people from every nation under heaven" (Acts 2:5). It is possible these are the pilgrims to which Schnabel and

---

[247] Schnabel, *Early Christian Mission,* 1: 204–205.

[248] Fiensy declares that "The predominantly Jewish city of Jerusalem was bicultural." David A. Fiensy, "The Composition of the Jerusalem Church," in *The Book of Acts in Its Palestinian Setting,* ed. Richard Bauckham (Grand Rapids: Eerdmans, 1995), 230.

[249] Schnabel, *Early Christian Mission* 1:205. Josephus has a checkered record as a reliable narrator of history. However, even if a reader were to dramatically reduce this number (from 2.5 million), she would still be left with a significant influx of pilgrims who were not residents of Jerusalem.

[250] Schnabel, *Early Christian Mission,* 1:205.

Josephus refer, and they constituted many of the listeners of Peter's Pentecostal sermon. However, Keener argues the listeners of verse five are Diaspora Jews who have resettled in Jerusalem. He believes the evidence is vague, but it points in the direction of a diaspora resettlement of Jerusalem.

Keener makes this argument primarily on linguistic grounds, noting that the word used to describe their "stay" in Jerusalem seems to be used in Acts to depict a long-term residence.[251] Indeed, the standard Greek lexicon cites Acts 2:5 as an example of those who settle down somewhere.[252] If Keener is correct, and this word is employed in this way throughout the Book of Acts, then it seems best to conclude that the "devout people from every nation under heaven" were those who had returned to Jerusalem and settled there.[253] The careful reader might lean towards Keener's view without being able to firmly resolve the issue. Regardless of the residency status of these individuals, they come from "every nation under heaven."

Luke's statement is probably meant in a hyperbolic manner, although he provides an impressive list of nations as proof that devout people from every nation under heaven are in the city. He identifies Parthians, Medes, Elamites, Mesopotamians, Judeans, Cappadocians, Phrygians, Egyptians, Libyans, Cretans, and Arabs, along with those from Pontus, Asia, Pamphylia, and Rome (Acts 2:8–11). The reader might be left to wonder: are these individuals Jews or Gentiles? Some might question the assumption made by Keener (and others) that these people

---

[251] Keener, *Acts: An Exegetical Commentary*, 1:833–834.

[252] Frederick William Danker, κατοιχεω, *BDAG* 534. The first gloss for κατοιχεω is "to live in a locality for any length of time, live, dwell, reside, settle (down)." Danker includes the individuals of Acts 2:5 as examples of those who are carrying out this activity.

[253] Conversely, F. F. Bruce argues that the people mentioned in Acts 2:5 are indeed temporary pilgrims. He notes, "From the far-flung lands where the Jews of the dispersion lived, great numbers had come to Jerusalem to celebrate the Feast of Weeks, for only at the Jerusalem temple could they attend the special sacrificial services prescribed for that 'holy convocation' (Num. 28:26ff.)." F. F. Bruce, *Acts,* NICNT (Grand Rapids: Eerdmans, 1976), 59.

from various nations were ethnically Jewish. However, it appears that the linguistic support for this view is solid. Bruce notes that "the Greek word translated 'devout men' in v. 5 appears in [the] NT to be reserved as an epithet for Jews."[254]

Danker's citation, although perhaps not as definitive, also strongly points in this direction. He identifies three instances in Acts of "devout people." One is the passage in question, the second one is a clear reference to a Jewish man (Ananias; Acts 22:12), and the third one is a potentially ethnically ambiguous reference to those who buried Stephen (Acts 8:2). However, the final reference in Danker's lexicon is from Luke's first volume, the Gospel of Luke. Here, the term "devout man" obviously refers to a Jewish man (Simeon; Luke 2:25). [255] On lexical grounds then, it seems probable that these individuals were mostly ethnic Jews.

When the reader stands back to expand the scope of her inquiry, additional evidence indicates the likelihood that these "devout people" were Jews. First, Luke refers to "visitors from Rome (both Jews and proselytes)" (Acts 2:10). In referring to proselytes, he acknowledges the category of people that Schnabel describes as "non-Jews (pagans, polytheists) [who] turned to the Jewish faith and were circumcised, thus becoming 'proselytes.'"[256] Since only the Romans are described as Jews and proselytes, it is possible that Luke meant for his readers to assume that the rest of the peoples in the nations list were predominantly Jewish.

Second, the narrative of Acts is structured around the fulfillment of Christ's promise in Acts 1:8 that the disciples would eventually take the gospel to the ends of the earth. This signifies not merely a geographic focus, but a peoples focus, as the disciples took the gospel from the Jewish center in Jerusalem to the edges of the multicultural Roman Empire. Luke does not attempt to highlight significant numbers of Gentile conversions

---

[254] Bruce, *Acts*, 61.
[255] Danker, ευλαβης, *BDAG* 407.
[256] Schnabel, *Early Christian Mission*, 1:124.

at this early stage of the Church's history. Instead, he is crafting a story that starts Jewish in Jerusalem and ends multicultural in Rome.

Third, Peter's sermon is addressed primarily to Jews and Israelites, although it does seem to acknowledge that non-Jewish residents might be listening (Acts 2:14, 22). Although these three arguments are inconclusive, they do point in the direction of an ethnic Jewish identity for most of these "devout people from every nation under heaven." Thus far, the reader of Luke's Pentecostal narrative can be expected to conclude that many ethnically Jewish people (and some proselytes) were in Jerusalem and heard Peter's seminal message. It was these listeners who observed the miraculous speaking in tongues (Acts 2:4–13). Indeed, 3,000 of their number accepted Peter's message, were baptized, and joined the church.[257]

At this point, the reader should ask herself, what are the implications of this event for our present study? In the previous chapter, we explored the model of biculturalism. Specifically, we examined the phenomenon of Hellenization, noting that it was a construct that lent itself to the bicultural model. Many (if not all) Hellenistic Jews would have been characterized by a certain degree of biculturalism. The Jews of the Diaspora would have oftentimes existed in a liminal space, exhibiting both "Jewish" and "Gentile" traits.[258] As Michael Bird notes, "There were various degrees of acculturation and assimilation in the Greek polis. Hellenism was not necessarily inimical to Jewish customs but often brought Jewish culture to new expressions."[259] The "new expressions" of which Bird speaks no doubt could be found in the cultural customs of the

---

[257] The phrase "joining the church" should not be taken in a modern sense in which a person responds to an invitation and commits to a church. However, it is clear that the 3,000 were "added" to the group of disciples that Jesus had left behind. This seems to indicate some sort of primitive membership.

[258] For a fourth century example of someone who lived in this type of liminal cultural space, see Justo Gonzalez, *The Mestizo Augustine: A Theologian Between Two Cultures* (Downers Grove, IL: IVP, 2016).

[259] Michael Bird, *An Anomalous Jew: Paul among Jews, Greeks, and Romans* (Grand Rapids: Eerdmans, 2016), 75–76.

Diasporic Jews of Acts Chapter Two. These individuals hailed from places as distant as Africa, Asia, and Europe.[260]

This means the birth of the Church occurred at a multicultural gathering on the Day of Pentecost. It also means that Jews who were exclusively culturally Hebraic were likely in the distinct minority. The new Christians at Pentecost quickly constituted the largest group within the church, easily dwarfing the more Hebraic group of Apostles and disciples whom Jesus had left behind. We should not argue that the Church on the Day of Pentecost was multiethnic. It was overwhelmingly (perhaps exclusively) ethnically Jewish. Yet there is a strong possibility that this same body of believers was a multicultural community.

If the Hellenistic Jews of the Diaspora (from places like Crete and Cyrene) were bicultural individuals, then it is reasonable to infer that the early church in Jerusalem was multicultural, at least on some level. As Bruce notes, "The church of Jerusalem comprised both 'Hebrews' (Aramaic-speaking Jews, most of them natives of Palestine) and Hellenists or 'Grecian Jews' (Jews whose habitual language was Greek, many of whom were natives of the Greco-Roman lands of the dispersion or at least had affinities with those lands)."[261]

So far in this chapter we have uncovered the multicultural composition of the Church at Jerusalem in the early pages of the Book of Acts. What remains to be seen is whether this multiculturalism was reflected in the group of leaders that emerged to guide the church on its mission. In

---

[260] This type of situation is what prompted Cadbury to declare, "Homogeneity was not characteristic of population in the Roman Empire, even locally. Mixing occurred—in the army, through trade and migration, by the process of slavery, and in other ways." Henry Cadbury, *The Book of Acts in History* (New York: Harper & Brothers Publishers, 1955), 12.

[261] Bruce, *Acts,* 127–128. See also David Fiensy, who argues that "Jerusalem in the 1st century AD was a moderate-sized urban centre with a socially and culturally pluralistic population .... Although the sources, especially the Book of Acts, give only hints about the make-up of the Jerusalem church, the indications are that nearly all levels of society were represented. The church seems to have been a microcosm of the city." David A. Fiensy, "The Composition of the Jerusalem Church," in *The Book of Acts in Its Palestinian Setting,* ed. Richard Bauckham (Grand Rapids: Eerdmans, 1995), 213.

the next section we will seek to answer this question: were the leadership/ministry teams in the Jerusalem Church monocultural or multicultural?

Cultural Makeup of the Jerusalem Team

The leadership team in the Jerusalem Church can best be examined in two stages. Both stages in question are found in the early part of the Book of Acts. First, the Apostles led the Church between the Ascension and Pentecost and continued to lead thereafter. Second, the Seven (sometimes referred to as the first deacons) emerged and served alongside the Apostles in Jerusalem (and in some cases, beyond). The Apostles and the Seven had different roles and different functions. However, the unique role both groups play in Luke's narrative indicates that both are considered significant actors in the Church at Jerusalem.[262] We will examine each group in turn.

The Hebraic Apostles

The first chapter of Acts lists the Apostles whom Jesus left behind when he returned to heaven: Peter, John, James, Andrew, Philip, Thomas, Bartholomew, Matthew, James the son of Alphaeus, Simon the Zealot, and Judas the son of James (Acts 1:13). These Apostles (Acts 1:2) gathered with various women and with the family of Jesus in the Upper Room (Acts 1:13–14). In the first volume of his masterpiece on the history of early mission, Eckhard Schnabel provides a brief overview of each of the Twelve.[263] Interestingly, he makes almost no comments regarding the culture of the Apostles. One of the rare exceptions is when he speculates

---

[262] Richard Thompson notes that both groups are described using ideal images. Richard Thompson, *Keeping the Church in Its Place: The Church as Narrative Character in Acts* (New York: T&T Clark, 2006), 30–37, 96–103.

[263] The terms Apostles and The Twelve are used interchangeably throughout this section.

that the family of Peter and Andrew might have been "open to Hellenistic culture."[264]

Overall, Schnabel seems to accept the fact that the Twelve are all ethnically and culturally Jewish. In fact, his comments on the symbolism of the number twelve highlight this belief. He notes that "the Twelve are to be seen as a symbol of Israel: they represent the hope for Israel's eschatological restoration."[265] Schnabel continues, "The number 'twelve' indicates that Jesus pursued a program of gathering the entire people of Israel, taking up the hope of the prophets who had prophesied the return of Israel's dispersion in the messianic last days."[266] For Schnabel, the Twelve, as representatives of Israel, must surely be Jewish.

This conclusion is solidly within the mainstream of New Testament scholarship. In fact, the text of Acts bears witness to this fact when it records the words the angels spoke to the Eleven:[267] "Men of Galilee, why do you stand looking up into heaven?" (Acts 1:11). The Apostles were Israel-ites (from Galilee) who symbolized what God was doing and would do through Israel in the last days. They were not Diasporic Jews; they were from Israel. Little evidence exists in the pages of Scripture that these individuals were anything other than ethnic Jews. In fact, when expanding the search to include culture, there is little evidence to suggest that the Twelve were anything other than culturally Jewish (Schnabel's speculative comment about Peter and Andrew notwithstanding). The Apostles were Hebraic Jews. Hence, in the initial chapters of the Book of Acts, there is no reason to conclude that the leadership team of the Jerusalem Church

---

[264] Schnabel, *Early Christian Mission*, 1:266.

[265] Schnabel, *Early Christian Mission*, 1:270.

[266] Schnabel, *Early Christian Mission*, 1:271. In a similar vein, Goheen argues that the number of Apostles is theologically significant. Michael Goheen, *A Light to the Nations: The Missional Church and the Biblical Story* (Grand Rapids: Baker, 2011), 84. Obviously, this issue engages the doctrine of eschatology, which is outside the scope of this book. Suffice it to say that Jesus intentionally selected Twelve Apostles to signify what he was doing in these "last days."

[267] At this point in the narrative, Matthias had not yet replaced Judas Iscariot.

was multicultural. Instead, it was characterized by a high degree of cultural homogeneity.

The Hellenistic Six

The Church at Jerusalem eventually added further servant-leaders to its number. In Acts Chapter Six a cultural conflict emerged within the nascent church. Luke tells us, "In those days, as the disciples were increasing in number, there arose a complaint by the Hellenistic Jews against the Hebraic Jews that their widows were being overlooked in the daily distribution" (Acts 6:1). Some speculate that this conflict had little to do with cultural factors but was instead merely about logistics.

However, Bruce notes that tensions existed between Hellenistic Jews and Hebraic Jews in that era, and it seems likely that this tension continued among those who entered the church.[268] He seems to believe the tension is over a "trifling matter."[269] However, when one considers the necessity of food for survival, the matter takes on a more serious light. Since widows were usually unable to care for themselves, the daily distribution could be a matter of life and death. The complaint was that the widows of the culturally dominant group[270] seem to get preferential treatment in this all-important daily distribution of food. That is why Chrysostom could call this "no small evil."[271]

It is unlikely that this issue stemmed from intent. As Chrysostom notes, "This did not arise from malice, but perhaps from the carelessness

---

[268] Bruce, *Acts*, 128.
[269] Bruce, *Acts*, 128.
[270] This statement is not meant to imply that the culturally dominant group (Hebraic Jews) constituted the largest group within the congregation. Precise data on the cultural composition of the Jerusalem Church eludes the researcher. It is impossible to state with certainty which group was in the majority. However, this study has referred to the Hebraic Jews as the culturally dominant group because the leaders of the Church (the Apostles) were Hebraic Jews. Typically (but perhaps not always), the leaders of a church will be a part of the culturally dominant group. Even if they are in the minority, a group of leaders, because of their status and power, can end up being in the culturally dominant group.
[271] Chrysostom, *The Homilies on the Acts of the Apostles*, 213.

of the multitude."²⁷² Chrysostom seems to believe that the neglect was real, and not just perceived. Indeed, this appears to be the likeliest explanation. Culturally dominant groups may operate with unconscious bias and pre-judice that blinds them to the needs of those in the cultural minority.²⁷³ Skinner notes, "What may be only a logistical problem for a growing sub-culture of Jews from different regions cannot be treated as 'simply' logistical because the wrinkles or offenses fall along ethnic or cultural lines. Clearly some perceive prejudice: the Hellenist widows suffer be-cause they are Hellenists."²⁷⁴ Skinner astutely observes, "It takes little imagination to understand how this might have developed or how it might have extremely negative consequences for the church's ability to thrive and bear witness to Jesus as a unified, just community. Truly the problem needs resolution, lest the church devolve into a collection of sniping fact-ions."²⁷⁵ The Hellenistic Jews believed that their widows were being neg-lected, and this perceived (and probably real) neglect threatened the unity of the church.²⁷⁶

The apostolic solution to the problem was to appoint "seven men of good reputation, full of the Spirit and wisdom" (Acts 6:3). They asked the congregation to select these seven individuals, and to entrust them with the task of overseeing the daily distribution. The seven men who were selected were Stephen, Philip, Prochorus, Nicanor, Timon, Parm-enas, and Nicolaus (Acts 6:5). We will examine the first six as a group, and then consider Nicolaus in a subsequent section.

Before we investigate the first six Hellenistic leaders, an import-ant detour is in order. We must clarify whether the Hellenists of Acts 6 are primarily a cultural group or an ideological group (or perhaps both).

---

²⁷² Chrysostom, *The Homilies on the Acts of the Apostles*, 213.

²⁷³ Ken Wytsma, *The Myth of Equality* (Downers Grove, IL: IVP, 2017), 137–151.

²⁷⁴ Matthew Skinner, *Intrusive God, Disruptive Gospel: Encountering the Divine in the Book of Acts* (Grand Rapids: Brazos Press, 2015), 39.

²⁷⁵ Skinner, *Intrusive God, Disruptive Gospel*, 39.

²⁷⁶ Bock, *Acts,* 258, notes, "The linguistic and social differences produced cultural differences that created a division in the church."

It has been common in the field of New Testament scholarship to view the early church as split into two "tribes": the Hebrews and the Hellenists. According to this theory (which was made popular by Ferdinand Baur[277]), the early church suffered from a schism between two ideological factions. These two factions would have both been Jewish, with one being Hebraic Jews and the other Hellenistic Jews. This theory attempts to account for the genuine evidence of conflict within the first-century Church.[278]

Typically, this theory has been articulated as follows: Hebraic Jews were from Palestine, and hence were more provincial and Torah-focused. They tended toward legalism and ethnic exclusivity. Hellenistic Jews, on the other hand, were from the Diaspora, and hence were more open-minded. They were universalistic in outlook, did not care as much about the temple and were quick to move beyond the Old Testament and embrace the mission to the Gentiles. If this theory is true, it would certainly help to explain certain factors, from the controversy over the care of widows, to the founding of the Antiochene church, to the Jerusalem Council, and to the Incident at Antioch. However, this theory is not as tenable as scholars once believed.

Recent studies in Second Temple Judaism have demonstrated that such a clear-cut distinction did not always exist between Palestinian Judaism and Diaspora Judaism. Instead, a rich tapestry of diverse ideas flourished within this ancient movement. Consequently, insufficient evidence exists to prove that there were two ideological factions in the early church. As I. Howard Marshall notes, "If no hard and fast distinction can be made between Palestinian and Hellenistic Judaism, it is unlikely

---

[277] Ferdinand Christian Baur, *Paul the Apostle of Jesus Christ: His Life and Works, His Epistles and Teachings* (Grand Rapids: Baker, 2011).

[278] The history of the Jerusalem Council and the Antioch Incident demonstrate that there was some conflict in the early Church. Indeed, the complaint about the daily distribution in Acts 6 is evidence of some level of conflict and tension.

that one can press the distinction between Palestinian and Hellenistic Jewish Christianity."[279]

Furthermore, the idea that two formal ideological factions were operating within the Church was always an attempt to "read between the lines" of the New Testament.[280] It led to both overreading and underreading, with scholars constructing, reconstructing and finally deconstructing the historical scenarios that lie behind the text of Acts.[281] It seems best to conclude that, although the reader can spot evidence of some tension within the early church,[282] it is not possible to definitively trace the contours of distinct ideological factions.

Instead, it is preferable to focus upon the Hellenists as a cultural group,[283] rather than as an ideological group. As has been previously noted, they were bicultural Jewish men and women who embraced Jesus the Messiah. This does not mean that the cultural group known as Hellenists did not employ a certain ideology. Some scholars, such as Schnabel, be-lieve that they did. He notes, "The missionary work of the early Christians was significantly advanced by the theological position of Hellenistic, Greek-speaking Jewish Christians in Jerusalem during the first years of the existence of the Jerusalem church."[284]

However, it is not easy to draw definitive lines between the theology of the Hellenists and the Hebrews. Indisputably, the Hellenists were essential to the burgeoning mission of the early church. However,

---

[279] Cited by Craig Hill, *Hellenists and Hebrews: Reappraising Division within the Earliest Church* (Minneapolis: Fortress Press, 1992), 16.

[280] Hill, *Hellenists and Hebrews,* 48, notes, "Scholars interested in Hellenists must commit themselves to reading between the lines the moment they step past the limits of Acts 6:1."

[281] Todd Penner provides an enlightening survey of the literature on these themes. Todd Penner, *In Praise of Christian Origins: Stephen and the Hellenists in Lukan Apologetic Historiography* (London: T&T Clark, 2004), 1–59.

[282] How can one not acknowledge this tension, given Paul's description of his confrontation with Peter? See Bird's helpful analysis of the Antioch Incident in Bird, *An Anomalous Jew*, 170–204.

[283] Given the diversity of this era, it even makes sense to imagine that the Hellenists could have represented multiple cultural groups.

[284] Schnabel, *Early Christian Mission,* 1:653.

our goal is not to concern ourselves with the theology of the Hellenists, but instead is to focus more upon their cultural identity. This study is centered upon the question of culture, and the Hellenists of Acts 6 (and later chapters) are fertile ground for exploring questions of culture.

Having briefly engaged (and set aside)[285] the question of the ideology of the Hellenists, we can now return to mapping the culture of the leaders who emerged in Acts 6. As a result of the cultural conflict surrounding the daily distribution, the Hebraic Apostles devised a plan to select seven men (Acts 6:3). These Seven would ensure that the daily distribution was conducted without any taint of cultural bias or discrimination. In this instance, those with power chose to give it away. As Keener notes, "This time, instead of twelve Hebrews, the food distribution program is assigned to seven Hellenists. Because they belong to the offended minority, they have special sensitivity to both the minority's needs and perceptions, and they are less vulnerable to criticism than Hebrews would have been."[286] In making this statement, Keener aligns himself with a prominent view that the Seven were Hellenists.[287]

However, Penner has disputed this idea. He remarks, "Delimiting the meaning of Ἑλληνιστης is difficult because it is not even clear that Stephen and the seven belong to this group. Although they are often assumed to be part of the Ἑλληνιστης designation—based largely on the fact that they all have good Greek-sounding names! - it is not entirely evident in the narrative whether they belong to the 'Hebrews,' or 'Hellenists,' or a combination of both."[288] Penner is correct that the reader should tread carefully where the text is not clear.

---

[285] Another issue that must be set aside due to the limited nature of this research is the relation of Acts 6 to the office of Deacon. Some see this text as the origin of that office, viewing the Hellenistic Seven as proto deacons. This issue, although important, will not be engaged in this research. This allows us to keep the focus on the salient issue of the cultural identity of The Seven.
[286] Keener, *Acts,* 2:1279.
[287] Apart from Nicolaus, who was a Gentile from Syrian Antioch (Acts 6:5).
[288] Penner, *In Praise of Christian Origins,* 69.

Still, it seems extremely likely that the Seven men (all with Greek names) were chosen from among the discriminated group, so that they could empower that very group. Bock asserts that "most of the names in question here are not commonly used in Judaism."[289] This would point in the direction of Hellenistic origins for the Seven. As Bock astutely notes, "The fact that so many Hellenist leaders exist point to the early church's multiethnic[290] and multicultural makeup."[291]

It is plausible to infer that The Seven were bicultural Hellenistic Jews, based upon their names and the function they serve in Luke's narrative.[292] However, when assessing the cultural identity of specific Hellenistic leaders, not much information is to be found. Of the seven men, only three (Stephen, Philip, and Nicolaus) yield substantial fruit of investigation.

The first Hellenist leader that is mentioned, of course, is Stephen, who would go on to become the first recorded martyr of the Church. However, it would be insufficient to view Stephen as merely an ethnically Jewish leader who spoke Greek. This is the misstep that many might make since they do not understand the relationship between language and culture. For instance, John Pilch argues, "Since the Hellenists and Hebrews in Jerusalem referred to were Israelites, the distinction between them is linguistic rather than ethnic."[293] This is true, yet incomplete (as Pilch himself would probably acknowledge). The Hellenists and Hebrews

---

[289] Bock, *Acts,* 261.

[290] Based upon the criterion we have employed I would differ slightly with Bock's conclusions. The church in Jerusalem was, indeed, multicultural, but probably not multiethnic (at least not in any significant way).

[291] Bock, *Acts,* 261.

[292] The Lukan narrative is fixated upon demonstrating the gospel's flow from Jerusalem, to Judea, to Samaria, and to the ends of the earth in fulfillment of Acts 1:8. Along with this geographical focus, Luke is concerned to illustrate that the gospel is also flowing across ethnic and cultural boundaries. The Hellenists play a key role in advancing the gospel across both geographic and cultural boundaries, and so their introduction in Acts 6 is significant.

[293] John Pilch, *Stephen: Paul and the Hellenist Israelites* (Collegeville, MN: Liturgical Press, 2008), 2.

might have been ethnically identical, yet culturally dissimilar.[294] Language is a potent agent that can sometimes change culture. Those Jews who spoke Greek (and preferred Greek) were not simply adopting another language. They were allowing themselves (even subconsciously) to be altered on a cultural level.[295]

Consequently, it is plausible to infer that Stephen emerged as one of the first bicultural leaders of the Christian movement. He was comfortable in the "religious" world of Jerusalem,[296] as well as the linguistic and cultural worlds of Athens and Rome. Yet his bold preaching on behalf of the gospel stirred up trouble from among his own people. Luke tells us, "Opposition arose, however, from some members of the Freedmen's Synagogue, composed of both Cyrenians and Alexandrians, and some from Cilicia and Asia, and they began to argue with Stephen" (Acts 6:9). According to Thompson, "It was their cultural identity that put them at odds with Stephen and his message, though Stephen may have shared this same cultural identity. Maybe that is why he continued to engage them—even to the end."[297] Stephen is depicted in the Book of Acts as a fearless bicultural prophet. He was someone who helped broker the gospel across cultural lines.

Philip was also one of the Seven (Acts 6:3–5). He served in Jerusalem, preached in Samaria, and evangelized the Ethiopian Eunuch (Acts 6, 8). Many have observed that Philip helped to push the boundaries of mission by engaging the Samaritans and the Ethiopians with the gospel. Leopoldo Sanchez declares, "Philip is a deacon and then an evangelist

---

[294] It is better to follow Skinner, who believes that "Both groups are Jews who follow Jesus as Messiah, the problems that arise relate to their cultural and linguistic differences." Skinner, *Intrusive God, Disruptive Gospel,* 39.

[295] Contra Richard Thompson, who asserts that "the reader may realistically conclude that the distinction refers to language and not to race or theology." Thompson, *Keeping the Church in Its Place,* 97.

[296] Although, as the events of Acts 7 indicate, he might not have been completely comfortable with the religious milieu of Jerusalem.

[297] Robin Thompson, "Diaspora Jewish Freedmen: Stephen's Deadly Opponents," *Bibliotheca Sacra* 173 (April-June 2016): 175.

among marginal characters, amidst people excluded at some level from the community because of their cultural-linguistic or ethnic-religious identity."[298] However, not as many note the likely reasons for Philip's mission-al success. In addition to being Spirit-filled, Philip was a bicultural (Hellenistic) Jew. As Hertig notes, Philip was "a trailblazing missionary who traveled to new lands, [and] radically enacted Stephen's theology. As Hellenists, both [Stephen and Philip] were capable of bridging Jewish and Gentile worlds. Bicultural people are equipped to cross cultural borders."[299]

Philip naturally occupied the liminal space between Jerusalem and Athens (the Ethiopians and Samaritans also occupied a liminal space).[300] He was someone who could move between cultures; someone who understood what it meant to not fit entirely into any group. For this reason, Philip was perfectly poised to serve as a cultural broker—a bridge for the advance of the gospel across new frontiers.[301] Indeed, Spencer notes that Philip's "evangelistic exploits, recounted in Acts 8, represent for Luke genuinely trailblazing and barrier-breaking steps, not merely transitional bridge-building efforts, in forwarding the global dissemination of the Christian message."[302]

Of the first six members of the Seven, the only substantial data that can be gathered concerns Stephen and Philip. However, even the

---

[298] Leopoldo A. Sanchez, "Can Anything Good Come Out of ____? Come and See! Faithful Witness in Marginality and Hospitality," *Concordia Journal* volume 41, no. 2, Spring (2015): 119.

[299] Paul Hertig, "The Magical Mystery Tour: Philip Encounters Magic and Materialism in Samaria," in *Mission in Acts: Ancient Narratives in Contemporary Context*, ed. Gary Gallagher and Paul Hertig (Maryknoll, NY: Orbis Books, 2004), 103.

[300] Andrew Walls notes that "The whole way the story [of the Ethiopian Eunuch] is framed is a reminder that Africa, the lands beyond the Nile, will have a Christian history too—one that is not yet charted, and one that is distinct from the story of Asia and Europe, which is the concern of the Acts of the Apostles." Andrew Walls, *The Cross-Cultural Process in Christian History* (Edinburgh: T&T Clark, 2002), 86.

[301] Keener, *Acts* 2:1489, notes, "Both in Eretz Israel and in the Diaspora, Samaritans spoke Greek and were substantially Hellenized." In the Spirit's perfect plan, a Hellenized missionary would take the gospel to a Hellenized people.

[302] F. Scott Spencer, *The Portrait of Philip in Acts: A Study of Roles and Relations* (Sheffield, England: Sheffield Academic Press, 1992), 272.

sparse data available on the other individuals does point to a Diasporic Jewish identity. For instance, Keener notes, "The name 'Prochorus' was rare everywhere and means something like 'leader of the dance'; it would be more likely to arise in the Diaspora."[303] It is this Diasporic and Hellenistic identity that leads me to conclude that the first six men listed in Acts 6 were bicultural Jews. They were ethnically Jewish but existed in a liminal space between their Jewish and diasporic cultures. In God's providence, they were well-suited to serve as "bridges" who could take the gospel across cultural barriers. As Jennings poetically notes, "The seven are of the diaspora, their bodies already bearing both difference and sameness, both foreign and home."[304]

Nicolaus the Proselyte

Only the first six "men of good reputation" (Acts 6:3) were bicultural Jews. The seventh, Nicolaus of Antioch, was a Gentile. He features at the end of Luke's list as Νικολαον προσηλυτον 'Αντιοχεα. Danker identifies the term proselyte as a reference to "one who has come over from polytheism to Judean religion and practice." Crucially, he elaborates that it is "a designation for a Gentile won for the Israelite community through missionary efforts."[305] In a similar vein, Gonzalez matter-of-factly notes that Nicolaus "was not even a Jew by birth, but by conversion."[306]

Keener's comments about Nicolaus are worth consideration. He notes that Nicolaus "is a proselyte, a former Gentile now in leadership in the church....This foretaste of diversity points the way forward to the later

---

[303] Keener, *Acts*, 2:1283.
[304] Willie Jennings, *Acts,* BTCB (Louisville: Westminster John Knox Press, 2017), 66.
[305] Danker, προσηλυτος, *BDAG* 880. See also Keener's helpful excursus on proselytes in Keener, *Acts*, 1284–1287.
[306] Justo Gonzalez, *Acts: The Gospel of the Spirit* (Maryknoll: Orbis, 2001), 90. Similarly, Levinskaya asserts that in the Book of Acts, "The term is used technically and denotes gentile converts." Irina Levinskaya, *The Book of Acts in Its Diaspora Setting* (Grand Rapids: Eerdmans, 1996), 46.

diverse leadership team in Nicolas's home city of Antioch (13:1)."[307] Keener is right to note that Nicolaus' origin in Antioch is probably intentionally noted by Luke. It is a literary foreshadowing that will eventually lead to the multicultural leadership team in the Antiochene Church.

In the meantime, we need to assess the state of our research in this chapter. Thus far, we have determined that the leadership team in the church at Jerusalem originally consisted of the twelve Hebraic Apostles. Later, it was supplemented by six bicultural Hellenistic men, and one Gentile convert. When we summarize the cultural map produced thus far, the results begin to crystallize. The apostles constituted the dominant group, and they were all Hebraic Jews. They were both ethnically and culturally Jewish. The Hellenists of Acts 6 were either bicultural Jews (in the case of the first six men) or Gentiles (in the case of Nicolaus of Antioch). Over one-third of the leaders in the church at Jerusalem were bicultural or culturally "other."

However, it should be clearly noted that two tiers of leaders existed in this church. In the top tier (the apostles), no cultural diversity is evident. The multiculturalism exists solely when the lower tier of leaders is factored into the equation. Furthermore, this diversity did not initially exist at all. In the next section, we will push forward with an examination of the church in Nicolaus' hometown: Antioch. Here we will discover that the cultural make-up of the church's leadership teams continued to multiply in almost exponential ways.

Cultural Makeup of the Antiochene Church

Syrian Antioch in the first century was a diverse[308] cosmopolitan city in the Roman Empire. It witnessed the intersection of ethnicity, class,

---

[307] Keener, *Acts*, 2:1284.
[308] Bruce Metzger notes, "Archaeological remains corroborate literary evidence that here met and mingled the Greek and Roman traditions on the one hand, and the

124

and religion. As historian Glanville Downey observes, "Antioch, as a meeting point of the Greek and Oriental civilizations, [was] filled with Orientalized Greeks and Hellenized Orientals, of all classes and all degrees of education."[309]

Indeed, Thomas Robinson describes Antioch as a "crossroads for ethnic and cultural interchange: a Macedonian/Greek city in origin, established in the midst of a Syrian countryside, under Roman rule, and with various immigrant populations including Jews and Samaritans."[310] Robinson opines that, as a city of at least 100,000 situated on important trading routes, it was "probably almost as diverse as most large cities in the twenty-first century and certainly as diverse as any city in the Roman Empire."[311]

Antioch was more densely populated than the contemporary island of Manhattan[312] and, according to Stark, was probably a "city filled with hatred and fear rooted in intense ethnic antagonisms and exacerbated by a constant stream of strangers .... A city where crime flourished and the streets were dangerous at night."[313] Apparently, the first-century city of Antioch was dense, diverse, and dangerous, not unlike many cities of the modern world. It is for these reasons, perhaps, that it was a unique, multicultural church that flourished in what Zetterholm describes as an "urban melting pot."[314]

---

traditions of Semitic Arabia, Palestine, and Mesopotamia on the other. There was in addition the varying influence of Persia." See Bruce Metzger, "Antioch-on-the-Orontes," *The Biblical Archeologist,* volume 11 no. 4 (1948): 87.

[309] Glanville Downey, *A History of Antioch in Syria: From Seleucus to the Arab Conquest* (Princeton: Princeton University Press, 1961), 272.

[310] Thomas Robinson, *Ignatius of Antioch and the Parting of the Ways: Early Jewish-Christian Relations* (Peabody, MA: Hendrickson, 2009).

[311] Robinson, *Ignatius of Antioch and the Parting of the Ways,* 15.

[312] Rodney Stark, *The Rise of Christianity* (New York: Harper Collins, 1996), 149–150.

[313] Stark, *The Rise of Christianity,* 160–161.

[314] Magnus Zetterholm, *The Formation of Christianity in Antioch: A Social-Scientific Approach to the Separation Between Judaism and Christianity* (New York: Routledge, 2003), 41.

Luke describes the founding of the Church in this diverse city in Acts Chapter Eleven. He records, "Now those who had been scattered as a result of the persecution that started because of Stephen made their way as far as Phoenicia, Cyprus, and Antioch, speaking the word to no one except Jews. But there were some of them, men from Cyprus and Cyrene, who came to Antioch and began speaking to the Greeks also, proclaiming the good news about the Lord Jesus. The Lord's hand was with them, and a large number who believed turned to the Lord" (Acts 11:19–21).

As the Jerusalem Church scattered due to persecution, the Christians were forced to migrate. Refugees from Jerusalem shared the gospel with Jews of the diaspora.[315] A notable shift occurred, however, when some of these refugees arrived in Antioch and began proclaiming the good news to the Gentiles (Acts 11:20). According to Luke, these refugees came from Jerusalem but traced their roots back to Cyrene and Cyprus. As a result, Gentiles were saved, and the first recorded significantly multiethnic church emerged.[316]

Who were these Cyrenian and Cypriot refugees who arrived in Antioch by way of Jerusalem? The anonymous refugees were apparently Hellenistic Jews of the Diaspora, with roots in the Mediterranean island of Cyprus and the North African city of Cyrene. As we previously noted, Hellenistic Jews had a foot in at least two cultural worlds. They would have been fluent in the practices of Judaism and intimately acquainted with Jewish culture as represented in Jerusalem. They would have also been conversant with the customs and traditions of their unique context (Cyrene[317] and Cyprus). As Crowe notes, "It was impossible to live in that

---

[315] The fleeing Christians of Acts Chapter Eleven fit the description of refugees provided by the United Nations: https://www.cdc.gov/immigrantrefugeehealth/about-refugees.html.

[316] With both Jews and Gentiles present in the church, it would have been, to a certain extent, multiethnic.

[317] Thomas Oden believed that the Cyrenian refugees were uniquely positioned to share the gospel cross-culturally. He notes, "Jewish believers in Christ from Cyrene who already had a cosmopolitan, mercantile trading background were among the first to grasp and implement the relevance of the ministry of Jesus of Nazareth not to Jews alone but

world, to speak the Greek language, to engage in commercial, civic, and social relations, without undergoing significant change."[318] This demonstrates an intriguing fact: at the intersection of every culture is a process of cultural transmission that, at the very least, slightly changes both cultures in question.

It would seem, therefore, that God used these Hellenists to be "bicultural bridges"[319] to facilitate the spread of the gospel to the Gentiles. Indeed, the narrative of Acts demonstrates that Luke was deeply concerned with enabling Theophilus to understand the ethnic expansion of Christianity in its earliest era.[320] Polhill believed that Acts 6–12 demonstrates the ways in which the Hellenists were used to advance the mission. He asserts, "It is much more the story of the growing universalism of the Christian gospel, a gospel which begins in the heart of pious Judaism, breaks the racial, national, and religious barriers in which it was born, and moves to the very heart of the Gentile world."[321] It was the Hellenists who were connected with both Jews and Gentiles, thus enabling them to serve as the bicultural bridge that would facilitate the gospel's leap from one ethnic group to another.[322]

The refugees who shared the gospel with the Gentiles were bicultural. They were ethnically Jewish, but culturally mixed, in large part due to the forces of Hellenization at work in the Diaspora. These men from Cyrene and Cyprus would have no doubt possessed what Bond terms

---

also to Gentiles who spoke Greek." See Thomas Oden, "A Libyan History Awaiting Discovery," *Bibliotheca Sacra* 167 (January-March 2010): 10.

[318] Jerome Crowe, *From Jerusalem to Antioch: The Gospel Across Cultures* (Collegeville, MN: Liturgical Press, 1997), 88.

[319] See Harold Dollar's discussion of the Hellenists as "Bridging People," in Harold Dollar, *St. Luke's Methodology: A Cross-Cultural Challenge* (Pasadena: William Carey, 1996), 61–78.

[320] Aaron Kuecker, *The Spirit and the 'Other': Social Identity, Ethnicity and Intergroup Reconciliation in Luke-Acts* (New York: Bloomsbury, 2011).

[321] John B. Polhill, "The Hellenist Breakthrough: Acts 6–12," *Review and Expositor* 71 no. 4 Fall (1974): 475.

[322] The idea of the Hellenists as bicultural bridges is an inspiration drawn originally from Donald McGavran, *The Bridges of God: A Study in the Strategy of Missions* (Eugene, OR: Wipf & Stock, 2005), 24. See also Harold Dollar's work, cited above.

"Creolian [mixed] consciousness."[323] These words of Bond help me to make sense of my own neighborhood: Crown Heights, Brooklyn. Crown Heights is a prominent diasporic Caribbean community, and this is reflected in the church which I am privileged to pastor. Indeed, some of the leaders of this church speak Creole and give evidence of in-betweenness, what Bond terms "Creolian consciousness."

Borrowing Bond's language, the Antiochene church was founded in a diverse city by Creolian (bicultural) refugees, producing a church that was initially both multicultural (as evidenced by Cyrenian-Jews and Cypriot-Jews) and multiethnic (as evidenced by the presence of both Jews and Gentiles). Indeed, it is possible that the term "Christian" was coined by Antiochenes who were astounded to see this diverse group worshipping together.[324]

Cultural Makeup of the Antiochene Team

In the previous section I pointed out that the city of Antioch was multicultural, and that its first church emerged as a multiethnic community, founded by bicultural Jewish refugees. What remains to be discovered, however, is how the Antiochene leadership team was constituted. At first glance, no biblical data about any Antiochene leadership team is evident. It appears that the church emerged organically as the result of the missionary witness of the refugees from Cyprus and Cyrene.

It is possible that, at the beginning, no leaders surfaced. This supposition seems credible since the first mention of leadership in Antioch is a reference to Barnabas, who was sent there by the church in Jerusalem

---

[323] Bond notes, "Creolian consciousness is one of the enduring characteristics of diasporas wherein identities are mixed and the power to control cultural boundaries and police purity are highly threatened." Gilbert Bond, *Paul and the Religious Experience of Reconciliation: Diasporic Community & Creole Consciousness* (Louisville: Westminster John Knox Press, 2005), vii.

[324] Stephen Strauss, "The Significance of Acts 11:26 for the Church at Antioch and Today," *Bibliotheca Sacra* 168 (July-September 2011): 283–300.

(Acts 11:22).[325] Barnabas eventually recruited Saul of Tarsus to join him as a leader of the Antiochene church (Acts 11:2–26). The next time one reads of leaders in the Antiochene church, five men are listed. Luke records, "Now in the church at Antioch there were prophets and teachers: Barnabas, Simeon who was called Niger, Lucius of Cyrene, Manaen, a close friend of Herod the tetrarch, and Saul" (Acts 13:1). The leadership team of prophets and teachers illustrated Nissen's maxim that "Multiplicity and not uniformity is what characterizes Christianity."[326] We will explore the cultural identities of these five individuals. The resulting data will allow us to fill in our emerging cultural map of the leadership teams in the Book of Acts.

Barnabas

Barnabas is the first leader of the Antiochene church who is mentioned in Luke's list (Acts 13:1). He is described as "Joseph, a Levite from Cyprus by birth, the one the apostles called Barnabas" (Acts 4:36). Since Barnabas was from the tribe of Levi,[327] he was ethnically Jewish. However, Luke's description of the "Son of Encouragement" adds a cultural layer to his identity when he notes that he is "from Cyprus."

Barnabas exemplifies the Hellenistic model of biculturalism that we previously articulated. Ethnically Jewish, yet "from Cyprus," this man of means[328] navigated two worlds. The nature of Hellenization in the first-

---

[325] It should be noted that Barnabas only arrived in Antioch after the church was initially founded.

[326] Johannes Nissen, *New Testament and Mission: Historical and Hermeneutical Perspectives*, 4th ed. (New York: Peter Lang, 2007), 164. John B. Polhill, *Acts*, NAC (Nashville: B&H, 1992), 289, concludes that these five men constituted the "congregational leadership" of the church at Antioch.

[327] An ancient tradition also maintains that Barnabas was the uncle of John Mark. If this is true, this bicultural Jewish family was one of the most influential families in the early Christian movement. Thomas C. Oden, *The African Memory of Mark* (Downers Grove, IL: IVP, 2011), 48.

[328] Fiensy notes the proceeds from the sale of Barnabas' land (Acts 4:37), and suggests that Barnabas "owned a medium-sized" estate. David A. Fiensy, "The Composition of the Jerusalem Church," in *The Book of Acts in Its Palestinian Setting*, ed. Richard Bauckham (Grand Rapids: Eerdmans, 1995), 227.

century world meant that he had to move between his Jewish heritage in Jerusalem and his cultural experience on Cyprus. This would have no doubt produced a certain level of tension as Barnabas existed in a liminal space.

It is possible this is one of the reasons he was sent to Antioch as the representative of the church in Jerusalem. Indeed, Keener speculates that Barnabas "probably knew many of the Cypriot believers scattered from Jerusalem."[329] In addition to being "a good man, full of the Holy Spirit and of faith" (Acts 11:24), Barnabas brought certain cultural assets to his Antiochene mission. First, he was someone who was probably comfortable with liminality. Second, he was familiar with the cultural background of some of those who had originally founded the church in Antioch (Acts 11:20). The bicultural Barnabas was uniquely suited for this mission.[330]

Simeon, Called Niger

"Simeon called Niger" is an enigmatic figure of whom little is known. His Latin surname means "black" and some writers believe that he might have been black skinned.[331] Since his given name is Simeon, and since he is "called Niger," this seems to indicate that Niger is a nickname. If Niger is a nickname, it probably is a reference to Simeon's skin color. Consequently, Hays argues, "The brief mention of Simeon called Niger ... establishes with high probability that Black Africans were part of the Christian Church and part of the Church leadership by the mid-first

---

[329] Keener, *Acts,* 2:1840–1841.

[330] It is important to remember, as Moy notes, that "...biculturalism is not a linear process; rather, it is a dialectical continuum that swings back and forth during a person's life." This would have been true of Barnabas the Levite from Cyprus. Russell Moy, "Biculturalism, Race, and the Bible," *Religious Education* 88 no. 3 (Summer 1993): 425.

[331] See, for example, Darrell Bock, *Acts,* 439. Witherington also seems to be an example of this perspective when he declares, "In view of Luke's obvious interest in ethnography throughout this book, the word probably does suggest that this Simeon was from northern Africa." See Witherington, *The Acts of the Apostles,* 392.

century AD."[332] In fact, Hays boldly declares that Acts 13:1 demonstrates that "the multiethnic aspect of the early Church extended to leadership and not just membership."[333]

However, I would nuance this differently. If Simeon was black (and this is highly likely), this does not definitively establish his ethnicity. One cannot declare that the leadership team in the Antiochene church was multiethnic simply because one of its number was dark-skinned.[334] After all, Simeon could have been a dark-skinned Hellenistic Jew. Instead, a more modest conclusion is called for: Simeon was probably ethnically Jewish and culturally African. It is likely, based upon the Latinized name "Niger," that the Antiochene leadership team was comprised of individuals of varying shades of skin color. One of them, named Simeon, was undoubtedly Jewish (the name Simeon is Semitic).

Still, as Keener cautions, the nickname Niger "leaves open the question ... of his original ancestry."[335] Gonzalez notes that some identify "Simeon called Niger" with "Simon of Cyrene," who carried the cross of Christ.[336] While this speculative idea is plausible, it does not seem to be verifiable.[337] It would not be surprising for Simeon to have originated in north Africa, since there was a strong link between Cyrene and Jerusalem.[338] However, dark skin does not constitute proof of one's place of origin.

It is true, however, that Simeon's skin color does relate to our quest for traces of diversity on the ministry teams described in Acts. Simeon is called black, and this has become a part of his identity. Indeed, his

---

[332] J. Daniel Hays, *From Every People and Nation: A Biblical Theology of Race* (Downers Grove, IL: IVP, 2003), 178.
[333] Hays, *From Every People and Nation,* 178.
[334] See Keener's balanced and nuanced discussion of Simeon. Keener, *Acts* 2:1984–1987.
[335] Keener, *Acts* 2:1986.
[336] Gonzalez, *Acts: The Gospel of the Spirit,* 152.
[337] However, eminent scholars such as Bruce have given much credence to this possibility. See Bruce, *Acts,* 260.
[338] Thomas C. Oden, *Early Libyan Christianity: Uncovering a North African Tradition* (Downers Grove, IL: IVP, 2011), 63–85.

status as a dark-skinned Jewish man points to the intriguing possibility of multiple layers of cultural identity. Simeon is Jewish, yet he is also black. He seems to be different from at least some of the other Antiochene leaders. This leads the reader to infer that Simeon was culturally "other." It is plausible to conclude that Simeon was a dark-skinned Jewish man who was culturally different from at least some of his fellow Antiochene leaders.

Lucius of Cyrene

Lucius of Cyrene was the third leader listed by Luke (Acts 13:1). As Bruce notes, he was probably one of the original men of Cyrene who first brought the gospel to the Gentiles of Antioch (Acts 11:20).[339] Oden has documented the strong first-century connection between Cyrene (a city in the country of Libya in northern Africa) and Jerusalem. He notes that a significant number of Jews resided in Libya. Oden asserts, "Through a combination of forced expulsions and voluntary immigrations and through sustained trade relations and family relations between Palestinian and Cyrenaic Jews, the Jews of Libya became well adapted to Libya while yet remaining devout Jews."[340] Apparently, it was some of these Libyan Jews who relocated to Jerusalem, were converted to Christianity, and then were scattered by Saul's persecution of the church. Some of these men ended up in Syrian Antioch where they proclaimed the gospel to the Gentiles. Lucius of Cyrene was likely one of these refugees who participated in the emergence of the Antiochene church.

One early tradition identifies Lucius of Cyrene with Luke the Physician (and the author of Acts).[341] Both Bruce and Keener doubt the

---

[339] Bruce, *Acts,* 260.
[340] Oden, *Early Libyan Christianity,* 54.
[341] This idea apparently first emerged in the writings of Ephrem the Syrian. See "Lucius of Cyrene" in the *DACB* (Boston: Boston University, n.d.): https://dacb.org/stories/libya/lucius/.

validity of this tradition.³⁴² Although certain textual variants might indicate a very early identification of Lucius and Luke,³⁴³ the primary challenge relates to the ethnic backgrounds of both Lucius and Luke. Lucius is clearly identified as culturally African, and the reader can reasonably infer that he was ethnically Jewish (probably a bicultural Hellenist). However, Luke is described by the Apostle Paul as a Gentile (Col. 4:11).³⁴⁴ It would seem, then, that Lucius of Cyrene and Luke the author of Luke-Acts were two different individuals, hailing from different cultural backgrounds. As far as we can tell, Lucius of Cyrene was a bicultural Jewish man of African origin who served as a prominent leader in the church at Antioch.

Manaen

Manaen is listed by Luke as the fourth member of the Antiochene leadership team (Acts 13:1). He is described as "a close friend of Herod the tetrarch" (Acts 13:1). Brought up with Herod the Tetrarch, Manaen was a συντροφος, one who had aristocratic connections in Herod's court.³⁴⁵ These powerful connections are unsurprising, since Manaen was probably a foster-brother of Herod.³⁴⁶ Ethnically, Manaen was probably Jewish, since, as Bruce notes, his name is "a Greek spelling of the Hebrew name Menahem."³⁴⁷ It is interesting to observe an element of socioeconomic diversity here in the Antiochene leadership team. Although he was ethnically Jewish, Manaen mixed in the social circles of power that would have been foreign to most Jews.

---

³⁴² Bruce, *Acts,* 260 and Keener, *Acts,* 2:1987.

³⁴³ Bruce, *Acts,* 260.

³⁴⁴ Allen disputes this interpretation and argues that Luke was Jewish. His argument will be engaged more fully in the subsequent chapter under the section on Luke the Physician. David Allen, *Lukan Authorship of Hebrews* (Nashville: B&H, 2010), 261–323.

³⁴⁵ Bock, *Acts,* 439.

³⁴⁶ Bruce, *Acts,* 260 –261.

³⁴⁷ F. F. Bruce, *Paul: Apostle of the Heart Set Free* (Grand Rapids: Eerdmans, 1981), 150.

Indeed, his status as a foster-brother to Herod, and his upbringing at the royal court would have opened new cultural vistas for Manaen. As a Jewish man, he would have been exposed to Roman culture through his privileged lifestyle and education. It is plausible to think that he might have been subtly shaped by these experiences. At the very least, one can conclude that Manaen was a powerfully connected, ethnically Jewish leader of the Antiochene church.

Saul of Tarsus

Saul of Tarsus was the final, and most well-known, member of the Antiochene leadership team (Acts 13:1). At first glance, Paul might seem indisputably Jewish. However, Paul is more complex than we might readily recognize. Michael Bird has called him "Paul the Jew…of sorts."[348] He notes that, on the one hand, "Paul was Jewish. It is impossible to deny this basic fact, given Paul's own explicit testimony to his ethnic identity and religious heritage as a Jew, Hebrew, and Israelite."[349] On the other hand, Bird notes that "Paul's self-description and praxis often make him look like he's moving away from the Jewish sphere."[350] Indeed, many authors have grappled with this dilemma of Pauline identity. Studies abound that emphasize one element or another of his identity. Frequently, the research centers upon where to locate Paul on a continuum of Jewishness.[351]

Part of the "problem" results from the fact that Paul was a gifted cross-cultural missionary who excelled at contextualization. He adapted himself well to a variety of environments. He knew how to be "all things to all people" (1 Cor. 9:22). However, he always operated from within a

---

[348] Bird, *An Anomalous Jew,* 1–30.
[349] Bird, *An Anomalous Jew,* 1.
[350] Bird, *An Anomalous Jew,* 3.
[351] See, for example, Caroline Johnson Hodge, *If Sons, Then Heirs: A Study of Kinship and Ethnicity in the Letters of Paul* (Oxford: Oxford University Press, 2007); Love Sechrest, *A Former Jew: Paul and the Dialectics of Race* (London: T&T Clark, 2010); and N. T. Wright, *Paul and the Faithfulness of God* (Minneapolis: Fortress Press, 2013).

distinctly Jewish sense of ethnicity. Paul was, as he himself said "A Hebrew of the Hebrews" (Phil. 3:5).

An analysis of Paul's cultural identity cannot ignore the testimony of Paul's self-description. Clearly, Paul was a Jew. However, Paul was, in some ways, more than a Jew, at least in his outlook and sympathies. As Kathy Ehrensperger notes, he "was a go-between."[352] Gilbert Bond declares, "Paul is a Creole .... Paul's mystical encounter with the Spirit of the risen Christ results in the birth of Creolian consciousness."[353] What both Ehrensperger and Bond are hinting at is that Paul has learned to live in a culturally liminal space. This is not to deny Paul's Jewishness. Clearly, he was an ethnic Jew. However, through the missional process of theologizing across cultures, Paul adapted himself to new cultural modes. Paul the ethnic Jew was a gifted missionary, one capable of reaching bicultural Hellenistic Jews and culturally "other" Gentiles.

Let us now step back and review where we have been. We noted that Antioch was a diverse city, not unlike many contemporary cities. We also observed that the church in Antioch began when bicultural refugees arrived from Cyprus and Cyrene and began to share the gospel with the Gentiles. An exploration of the cultural identities of the leaders on the Antiochene team revealed a mix of various cultures.

Barnabas was a bicultural Jew from the Mediterranean island of Cyprus. Simeon was a black man who can reasonably be viewed as a bicultural individual, possibly from Africa. Lucius was a bicultural Jew from the North African city of Cyrene. Manaen was a Jewish man who had been raised a foster-brother of Herod the Tetrarch. Saul of Tarsus was the most classically Jewish Jew on the Antiochene team. Yet even he learned to adapt to minister to those who existed across cultural divides, and even to those who lived in liminal spaces.

---

[352] Ehrensperger, *Paul at the Crossroads of Cultures*, 1.
[353] Bond, *Paul and the Religious Experience of Reconciliation*, vii.

It is clear from this emerging cultural map that the leadership team of the Antiochene church was culturally diverse. If culture is a shared way of life that is continually negotiated (as I proposed in Chapter Three), then it seems multiple cultures were present on the Antiochene team. At least three (and possibly four) different cultures were present in Luke's list (Acts 13:1). Based on this data, we can classify this leadership team as multicultural.[354]

Conclusion

This chapter has advanced the overall goal of this book by providing the initial building blocks for a cultural map of some of the leadership teams of the Book of Acts. We discovered that the leadership team at the church in Jerusalem (early Acts) was eventually diverse, but only when the "lower tier" of leadership was factored in. In the highest levels of leadership, this team was decidedly monocultural. We then discovered that the leadership team at the church in Antioch (middle Acts) was decisively multicultural. In the subsequent chapter, we will mine the second half of the Book of Acts for further data to complete our cultural map. Here, we will examine the Pauline "missionary teams" and analyze them for traces of cultural identity. The resulting data will then provide us with a clearer picture of the cultural composition of the leadership teams in Acts, from beginning to end.

---

[354] The present study will not classify the Antiochene team as multiethnic, since it appears that all five leaders were ethnically Jewish.

CHAPTER FIVE: Mapping Culture on Paul's Teams

Many different ministry teams flourished in the Book of Acts. In the last chapter we examined two important urban teams. The first, in Jerusalem (early Acts) was not substantially diverse. The second, in Antioch (middle Acts), was incredibly diverse. In this chapter we will push forward on our journey and explore the Pauline teams throughout the second half of the Book of Acts. Once again, these teams were primarily urban, since most of Paul's ministry took place in cities. Because Paul undertook at least three distinct journeys (sometimes called missionary journeys),[355] this chapter will be divided into sections that examine the various teams employed by Paul during these three journeys.

When a reader examines the travels and letters of Paul, she can clearly see that Paul was rarely alone in his missionary endeavors.[356] Sometimes Paul was physically present with others, working alongside them to further the gospel. At other times, he dispatched them on his behalf to accomplish important tasks,[357] such as carrying an important letter (Rom. 16:1–2) or appointing elders in a new church (Titus 1:5). In fact, Eckhard Schnabel notes, "Of the approximately one hundred names that are connected with Paul in the Book of Acts and in the Pauline letters, thirty-eight people are coworkers of the apostle."[358] Paul referred to many of these individuals as his συνεργός, his missionary coworkers (Rom. 16:3,

---

[355] See Schnabel's discussion of the term "missionary journey" in Eckhard Schnabel, *Early Christian Mission* (Downers Grove, IL: IVP, 2004), 2:1455.

[356] See Stanley Porter, "How Do We Define Pauline Social Relations?" in *Paul and His Social Relations*, ed. Stanley Porter and Christopher Land (Boston: Brill, 2013), 7–33, for a helpful discussion of various ways of studying the Pauline Circle.

[357] James Thompson, *The Church According to Paul: Rediscovering the Community Conformed to Christ* (Grand Rapids: Baker, 2014), 229.

[358] Schnabel, *Early Christian Mission*, 2:1425.

Phil. 2:25). Although some have challenged this translation,[359] Danker reminds us that a συνεργός was Paul's "helper, fellow-worker."[360]

Paul surrounded himself with a plurality of missionaries.[361] This does not mean an officially organized Pauline team stayed together throughout Paul's ministry. Rather, the situation was much more fluid. Schnabel was correct to note that the composition of Paul's coworkers "frequently changed."[362] Instead, the Pauline teams served together in a specific season to accomplish a specific mission. These missions were as varied as delivering an offering to Jerusalem (Acts 20:1–5), evangelizing Ephesus (Acts 19) and establishing a church in Philippi (Acts 16). Short-term teams emerged to accomplish each of these tasks under the direction of Paul. As these various teams are culturally mapped, the status of certain individ-uals mentioned in Acts will be ambiguous. For others, their cultural iden-tity will be much clearer. Overall, we will uncover evidence of diversity on most of the Pauline urban mission teams.[363]

---

[359] Kathy Ehrensperger, *Paul and the Dynamics of Power: Communication and Interaction in the Early Christ-Movement,* (New York: T&T Clark International, 2007), 47–48.

[360] Danker, συνεργος, *BDAG* 969. See also E. Earle Ellis, "Paul and His Co-workers," *New Testament Studies* 17, no. 4 (July 1971): 440–441.

[361] George Murray, "Paul's Corporate Evangelism in the Book of Acts," *Bibliotheca Sacra* 155 (April-June 1998): 189–200.

[362] Schnabel, *Early Christian Mission,* 2:1425.

[363] As I noted in the introduction, the focus of this book is cultural diversity, which means that my assertion is more modest in scope than that of William Brooks. He argued, "Paul's coworkers were diverse in ethnicity, in gender, and in socioeconomic background." William Brooks, "A Biblical Understanding of the Diversity of Paul's Missionary Coworkers," in *Reflecting God's Glory Together: Diversity in Evangelical Mission,* ed. Scott Moreau and Beth Snodderly (Pasadena: William Carey, 2011), 209. This is likely true; yet this book is narrowly focused upon questions of culture, leaving the important topics of gender and social standing to others.

The Pauline Team on the First Missionary Journey[364]

According to Luke's record, Barnabas and Saul were sent out by the church at Antioch to engage in the missionary work to which the Holy Spirit had called them (Acts 13:2–3). Since the cultural identities of Barnabas and Saul of Tarsus were already mapped in the previous chapter, the present section will focus on the third member of their missionary team.[365] Luke mentions, "They also had John as their assistant" (Acts 13:5).

John Mark was an important figure in the early Church. He was a relative of Barnabas (Col. 4:10). With a Hebrew name and a Latin nickname, it is likely that John Mark was a bicultural Jew.[366] His missionary work on Cyprus was no doubt enhanced by his biculturalism. John Mark accompanied Paul for a part of his first missionary journey, and then departed, precipitating a later split between Paul and Barnabas (Acts 15:35–41).

John Mark was probably an eyewitness to certain events from the life of Christ. He penned a gospel that was likely based on the sermons and recollections of Peter. He also served as a (controversial) member of an early Pauline missionary team. Not many people could claim that they served alongside both Peter and Paul. John Mark was one of them. Still, there might be more to John Mark's story than meets the eye.

According to Oden, the ancient African traditions concerning John Mark are more credible than Western historians care to admit. He recites the tradition, found in ancient Coptic liturgies: John Mark was a Jew who

---

[364] It is perhaps a misnomer to refer to the team on the first missionary journey as a Pauline team. On this first journey Barnabas appears to begin as the leader, and Saul seems to be described in a secondary role. It is only during the course of this journey that Paul (as he is now known) takes on the leading role.

[365] To review, it was determined that Barnabas was a bicultural Jew from Cyprus and that Saul of Tarsus was a culturally Jewish man.

[366] Oden, *The African Memory of Mark*, 21, maintains that Mark's Hebrew and Latin names provide traces of his "multicultural family background."

was born in Cyrene in North Africa, migrated to Jerusalem, served with Peter and Paul and returned on mission to Africa, where he was eventually martyred for his faith.[367] Much of the source material for these assertions is rooted in tradition and can seem more liturgical and less empirical. However, as Andrew Walls notes, "Anyone who has experienced anything of either Egyptian or Ethiopian Christianity will bear witness to the overwhelming sense of antiquity that they still hold. Talk with a Coptic bishop, and Athanasius does not seem a very remote figure; he could be in the next room."[368]

Not all cultures preserve history in the Western way. To dismiss the sources and traditions of other cultures, simply because they do not measure up to Western standards for history, would be a mistake. As Oden declares, "Treating as myth two thousand years of testimony is bad historical method. It displays moral callousness toward those who suffered torture and death on behalf of their conviction based on the truth they proclaimed."[369] Although the data is extra-biblical (and therefore should not be given as much weight as the text of Scripture), I see no good reason to reject this ancient and venerable recollection (especially since it seems to be so deeply rooted in the rich oral tradition of the Coptics). If the African memory of Mark is accurate, then John Mark would take his place alongside Barnabas as a bicultural Hellenistic Jewish coworker of the Apostle Paul.

On the first Pauline missionary journey, the team consisted of Barnabas, Saul, and John Mark. Based upon the research employed by the last two chapters, it is possible to create a cultural map of the Pauline team on this journey. Barnabas was a bicultural Jew from Cyprus, Saul was culturally Jewish, and John Mark was a bicultural Jew, possibly from

---

[367] Oden, *The African Memory of Mark*, 37–43.

[368] Andrew Walls, *The Cross-Cultural Process in Christian History* (Edinburgh: T&T Clark, 2002), 90.

[369] Oden, *The African Memory of Mark*, 256.

North Africa. In the next section, we will continue by examining the teams on Paul's second missionary journey.

Pauline Teams on the Second Missionary Journey

Paul's second missionary journey had a distinctive urban flavor to it. Over the course of this expedition, he engaged in missionary work in at least five cities: Philippi (Acts 16), Thessalonica (Acts 17:1–9), Berea (Acts 17:10–15), Athens (Acts 17:16–34), and Corinth (Acts 18:1–18). Only in Athens did Paul minister alone. In each of the four other cities he worked with other people to engage in missionary work. It is these urban "missionary teams" that will be explored in subsequent sections. The cultural identities of the various workers on these Pauline teams will be analyzed, furthering the overall research efforts of our study. The resulting data will bring us one step closer to a "cultural map" of some of the ministry teams in the Book of Acts.

The Philippian Team

When the Holy Spirit redirected Paul into Europe (through the famed Macedonian Vision), he and his companions traveled to the important Roman colony of Philippi (Acts 16:6–12). Here, Paul began missionary work that resulted in the eventual formation of a church (Acts 16:12–40). The "team" in Philippi (understood in an informal sense) seems to have consisted of Paul, Silas, Timothy, Luke, and Lydia. Since Paul's cultural background has already been assessed, our research can continue with an analysis of the other four individuals.

Silas

When Paul separated from Barnabas, he took Silas with him on his subsequent missionary journey (Acts 15:40–41). He even eventually co-authored at least one New Testament letter with Silas (1 Thess. 1:1). Silas was a prominent member and leader at the church in Jerusalem

(Acts 15:32). He delivered the decree of the Jerusalem Council and ministered for a short time in Antioch (Acts 15:30–33). No doubt Silas was Jewish, based upon the following lines of evidence.

First, he was a prophet in the Jerusalem Church (Acts 15:32) and described as a leading man "among the brothers" (Acts 15:22). This seems to indicate that he was a Jewish leader in a Jewish church. Second, he was sent as a representative of the Jewish congregation to the Gentile congregation in Antioch (Acts 15:27). It would make little sense to dispatch Silas if he were not Jewish. Third, he had two names, one Jewish and one Latin. Like Paul, Silas was apparently a Roman citizen (Acts 16:37) and, like many Jewish Roman citizens, had multiple names.[370] According to Bauckham, Silas probably was given "his Roman name Silvanus, along with its Semitic sound-equivalent Silas"[371] at birth.

It seems quite reasonable to conclude that Silas would have been (like Paul) culturally a Hebrew. His Roman citizenship might have opened him up to new cultural vistas. However, like Paul, he seems to have been someone whose identity can be characterized as culturally Jewish. Also, like Paul, Silas proved himself adept at cross-cultural missionary work. Perhaps because of Silas' successful season of ministry in the multicultural urban context of Antioch, Paul selected Silas as his companion for the cross-cultural missionary enterprise.[372] Paul would quickly build a diverse team on his second missionary journey, one which would enable him to reach a variety of people groups. The first building block of that team was the Jewish leader Silas, someone who could both minister to Gentiles and assist Paul in taking the gospel "to the Jew first."

---

[370] F. F. Bruce, *The Pauline Circle* (Eugene, OR: Wipf & Stock, 1985), 24, theorizes, "Silas was a Jewish name, corresponding to the Talmudic name *Shila*."

[371] Richard Bauckham, "Paul and Other Jews with Latin Names in the New Testament," in *Paul, Luke and the Graeco-Roman World,* ed. Alf Christophersen et al. (New York: Sheffield Academic Press, 2002), 218.

[372] Bruce, *The Pauline Circle,* 25–26.

Timothy

Timothy was Paul's "son in the faith" (1 Tim. 1:2), his missionary co-worker, a key Pauline representative, and the recipient of two canonical letters. Timothy presents a puzzle of cultural identity. He was born to a Greek father and a Jewish (Christian) mother (Acts 16:1).[373] Contradictory opinions abound concerning Timothy's identity. Bock, leaning upon Witherington's arguments, believes that Timothy was Jewish.[374] Bruce asserts, "Timothy would have ranked as a genuine Jew."[375] Curiously, Schnabel discusses Timothy without delving into his ethnic identity.[376]

Cohen vigorously argues that Timothy would have been considered a Gentile. At issue is the principle of matrilineal descent in rabbinic law, which Cohen maintains is a development of the second century CE.[377] In contemporary Judaism, a person can be deemed Jewish if they can trace their Jewish heritage back on their maternal side.[378] Yet Cohen notes that this is a later development and would not have been the governing paradigm during the era described in the Book of Acts. He asks two separate questions: "Did Luke view Timothy as Jewish?" and "Would contemporaries of Timothy have viewed him as Jewish?" His answer to

---

[373] Paul circumcised Timothy "because of the Jews who were in those places" (Acts 16:3). This circumcision was significant, especially since it follows (in Luke's narrative) the decree from the Jerusalem Council that did not require Gentiles to be circumcised. Although circumcision is a significant theological issue, it is beyond the scope of this study to explore circumcision on theological grounds. Instead, it is enough to note that the text of Acts indicates that Timothy was circumcised "because of the Jews." The salient point for this study is that a careful reading of Acts 16 does not necessarily clarify the issue of Timothy's Jewishness.

[374] Bock, *Acts*, 522–523.

[375] Bruce, *The Pauline Circle*, 31.

[376] Schnabel, *Early Christian Mission*, 2:1428–1429.

[377] Shaye Cohen, "The Origins of the Matrilineal Principle in Rabbinic Law," *AJS Review*, 10, no 1 (Spring 1985): 19–53.

[378] About 25 percent of the residents of this writer's neighborhood (Crown Heights) are Chasidic Jews. This writer personally knows of a Christian visitor to this neighborhood who was aware of some Jewish heritage on her mother's side. She was told by members of the Chasidic community that she did not need to remain Christian, because she was authentically Jewish.

both is clear, as he argues, "Was Timothy Jewish? In all likelihood Luke did not think so. The majority of ancient and medieval exegetes did not think so. There is no evidence that Paul or the Jews of Asia Minor thought so."[379]

Another set of scholars assert that Timothy was neither Jew nor Gentile. Brooks states that Timothy was a unique "exception" to the Jew-Gentile binary.[380] In a similar fashion, Keener emphasizes Timothy's in-be-tween status. Although he believes that Luke viewed Timothy as "essentially Jewish," he also believes that there was more to the story. According to Keener, Timothy had an "ambiguous ethnic status" that dovetailed with the overall story of Acts. He notes, "Just as the culturally hybrid Hellenist Jews carried forward the mission in chapters 6–8 and the culturally hybrid Paul continues it, Timothy's interethnic and intercultural heritage continues to symbolize the direction that the Spirit is moving God's people."[381]

Baretto (who advocates the hybridity model of culture that was discussed in Chapter Three) argues that debates about Timothy's ethnic status are missing the point. He asserts, "Acts 16:1–5 wades directly into contested ethnic ground, reflects these ambiguities, yet ultimately leaves largely unresolved these critical questions."[382] Baretto is correct that Luke does not clarify Timothy's ethnic identity.[383] An unaddressed tension remains in the text, one which the human author seems to ignore. Why does the text of Acts leave us with uncertainty concerning Timothy's identity?

---

[379] Shaye Cohen, "Was Timothy Jewish (Acts 16:1–3)? Patristic Exegesis, Rabbinic Law, and Matrilineal Descent," *JBL* 105, no 2. (1986): 268.

[380] Brooks, "A Biblical Understanding of the Diversity of Paul's Missionary Coworkers," 211.

[381] Keener, *Acts*, 3:2318.

[382] Baretto, *Ethnic Negotiation*, 98.

[383] Some might argue that the record of Timothy's circumcision was Luke's way of clarifying Timothy's ethnicity. However, this might be stretching the text too far. All that Acts 16 tells us is that Timothy was the product of a mixed marriage, that Paul circumcised him because of the Jews, and then that Paul took Timothy on a cross-cultural missionary journey to reach both Jews and Gentiles.

Baretto believes it is because Luke was not interested in resolving this question. Instead, he believes Luke was interested in demonstrating the ethnic flexibility of Christian mission.[384]

What are we to make of these contradictory opinions swirling around the text of Acts 16, and how do these relate to the issue of cultural identity addressed in this book? First, it would be wise to recognize (with Cohen) that we should be cautious about utilizing the matrilineal principle, given its later formal codification in rabbinic law. Second (with Brooks, Keener and Baretto), we should emphasize Timothy's in-between status. He occupied a unique liminal space in the Pauline mission. Baretto cites Wall, who declared that "Timothy is the right person for the work ahead because his ethnic mix envisages the very mixture of Paul's mission....Paul wanted Timothy as a traveling companion not because of his professional resume but because he personifies and presumably has a grasp of the tensions between 'being Greek' and 'being Jewish" that will characterize the Pauline church."[385]

Thus far, most of the scholarly discussion has centered upon Timothy's ethnic status. However, as we noted in previous chapters, cultural identity is not identical to one's ethnic status. When assessing the ethnically ambiguous Timothy, it seems clear his cultural identity has at least two layers. With a Greek father and a Jewish mother, Timothy would have existed from birth in a liminal space. Like the Hellenistic Jews profiled earlier in this study, Timothy would have probably been characterized by biculturalism. One key difference is that Timothy was not a clearly defined Jew. Instead, his ethnicity is ambiguous. This would have led to a compound cultural identity. It is likely that two nested cultures existed within Timothy. Therefore, it is safe to conclude that (whatever his ethn-

---

[384] Baretto, *Ethnic Negotiation*, 114–115.
[385] Baretto, *Ethnic Negotiation*, 16.

icity) Timothy was a culturally mixed individual who was an effective agent for the spread of the gospel.

Luke

Luke was another important member of the Pauline Circle, and someone who was present during Paul's missionary efforts in Philippi (Acts 16:11–17). Luke was a physician (Col 4:14) who, according to ancient Christian tradition, was the author of the two volume Luke–Acts.[386] Based upon the famous "we passages," we can deduce that Luke sometimes traveled and ministered with Paul. Paul also sent greetings from Luke to the Colossian Church, indicating once again that Luke was working alongside Paul (Col. 4:14).

Both Metzger and Bruce refer to the third century tradition that Luke was from Syrian Antioch and a part of the church there.[387] The textual variant in Acts 11:28 could indicate an early "we passage" in Syrian Antioch.[388] At the very least, the variant indicates the existence of a distinguished tradition about the Antiochene residency of Luke. As Ramsay notes, the tradition is based upon the words of Eusebius, whose statement might be open to interpretation.[389] However, it seems best to read Eusebius' words in the traditional manner, as indicating an Antiochene origin for Luke. If he did hail from the multiethnic church in this city (as seems likely), it could explain Luke's interest in ethnicity and culture in Luke–Acts.

Furthermore, this means that a substantial portion of the New Testament was penned by someone who was likely an urbanite. Luke-Acts

---

[386] Rick Strelan, *Luke the Priest: The Authority of the Author of the Third Gospel* (New York: Routledge, 2016), 70, does not believe that Luke was a doctor. Rather, he maintains that Luke was a priest, one who was a healer of souls. This interpretation is intriguing, but not entirely convincing.

[387] Metzger, "Antioch-on-the-Orontes," 70, and Bruce, *The Pauline Circle,* 40.

[388] Bruce Metzger, *A Textual Commentary on the Greek New Testament,* 2nd ed. (New York: UBS, 1994), 344, refers to this variant as "An important Western reading."

[389] William Ramsay, *St. Paul the Traveler and Roman Citizen,* Full-Color Updated & Revised Ed. (Grand Rapids: Kregel, 2001), 302–304.

cised are my coworkers for the kingdom of God" (Col. 4:11). He then lists Epaphras, Luke, and Demas as additional co-workers (Col. 4:12–14). Since Paul referred to the first three as his only Jewish co-workers, some have concluded that Epaphras, Luke, and Demas were Gentiles.

McKnight is one of the interpreters who believes that Luke was likely a Gentile. He notes that "the Greek text has the more evocative and ritual-reminding 'those who were of the circumcision."[395] McKnight concludes, based upon Paul's wording, that Luke was a Gentile. Allen disputes this interpretation, yet his arguments are unconvincing considering the apparent meaning of Colossians 4:10–14. Ladd is probably correct when he declares, "The fact that Luke is excluded from 'men of the circumcision' (v. 10) suggests that he was a Gentile."[396]

Luke was probably the most important Gentile in the New Testament. As Paul's traveling companion and chronicler, he was able to record details of the earliest Christian mission. As far as we know, no other Gentile authored a book of the New Testament. It is to Luke that this honor was entrusted. As one of Paul's close companions, no one was better suited for the task. This means that someone who was an urbanite Gentile (probably a Syrian Gentile) penned Luke-Acts, and even features in Acts as an occasional member of the Pauline Circle, making his first official appearance during Paul's ministry in Philippi.

Lydia

Lydia is a fascinating figure who was influential in the founding of the Church at Philippi. She was converted down by the river and then swiftly opened her home as a center for Pauline outreach in Philippi (Acts 16:13–15). In fact, when Paul and Silas were released from the Philippian

---

[395] Scot McKnight, *The Letter to the Colossians*, NICNT (Grand Rapids: Eerdmans, 2018), 390.

[396] George Eldon Ladd, "Paul's Friends in Colossians 4:7–16," *Review and Expositor* 70, no. 4 (Fall 1973): 512.

comprises over 25% of the New Testament, making Luke the most prolific New Testament author. It is unsurprising that an urbanite from Syrian Antioch would choose to devote so much attention to the urban mission that characterized the early church in the Book of Acts.

Luke was probably also a Gentile. In Colossians 4:10–11, Pau[l] referred to three men as the only Jewish coworkers he had with him a[t] that time. In the subsequent verses he referenced others who were als[o] with him, including Luke. Given the contrast of these verses, it seems pr[o]bable that Luke was a Gentile. Some have challenged this consensu[s] view,[390] including David Allen.[391] Allen posits that Luke wrote not on[ly] Luke-Acts, but also the epistle of Hebrews.[392]

During the course of his detailed argument for Lukan authorsh[ip] of Hebrews (which cannot be engaged here), he argues that Luke was p[ro]bably Jewish. Allen maintains, "On the question of Luke's birthpla[ce] Antioch in Syria has the greatest evidence."[393] However, although [he] accepts the Antiochene connection, Allen rejects the traditional view t[hat] Luke was a Gentile. He instead argues that "Luke was a Hellenistic J[ew] with cosmopolitan training and interests."[394] The central challeng[e to] Allen's thesis lies in one's interpretation of Colossians 4:10–14.

As Paul concluded his letter to the Colossian church, he inclu[ded] greetings from some of his colleagues. He mentions Aristarchus, [John] Mark, and Jesus/Justus (Col. 4:10–11), noting, "These alone of the circ[umcision]

---

[390] Robert Wayne Stacy, "Colossians 4:11 and the Ethnic Identity of Luke," *Eruditio Ardescens: The Journal of Liberty Baptist Theological Seminary* 2 no. 1, arti[cle] (2015).
[391] Allen, *Lukan Authorship of Hebrews*, 261–323.
[392] For a related perspective, see Andrew Pitts and Joshua Walker, "The Authorship of Hebrews: A Further Development in the Luke-Paul Relationship," in *P[aul] and His Social Relations*, ed. Stanley Porter and Christopher Land (Boston: Brill, 201[3]) 143–184, who argue that Luke took notes of some of Paul's sermons during his "Jewi[sh] mission" and used them to develop the book of Hebrews. In their reading, Luke is the author, but it is Paul's voice which comes through.
[393] Allen, *Lukan Authorship of Hebrews*, 264.
[394] Allen, *Lukan Authorship of Hebrews*, 266.

prison they returned to Lydia's house where they "saw the brothers" (Acts 16:40). Apparently, the new convert Lydia was exercising considerable hospitality and hosting this urban church in her home. Ascough asserts, "Lydia was the host and patron of the first community of Jesus followers established in the land mass that would later be known as Europe, and she was the nexus for the network of Jesus believers in and around Philippi."[397]

Lydia was able to serve as the patron of the Church in Philippi due to her financial resources. She was in the somewhat unusual position of being an independent businesswoman in the Greco-Roman world. Lydia was a "dealer in purple cloth" and in charge of her own household (Acts 16:14-15). As McKarty notes, "The various aspects of her life referenced in Scripture—purple-dealing, autonomy, heading a household, showing hospitality, and traveling—each contribute to a picture of some wealth."[398] Lydia provides the striking portrait of a strong, independent businesswoman, plying her trade as a dealer in purple cloth.[399] She acquired financial resources (either through her business or through the receipt of an inheritance) that positioned her to be the host and benefactress of the Pauline urban mission team that planted the Philippian church (Acts 16:15, 40).

Lydia is described as a σεβομένη τὸν Θεόν (a "God-fearer"). Danker notes that this "is a term applied to former polytheists who accepted the ethical monotheism of Israel and attended the synagogue, but who did not

---

[397] Richard Ascough, *Lydia: Paul's Cosmopolitan Hostess* (Collegeville, MN: Liturgical Press, 2009), 1.

[398] V. K. McCarty, "Lydia in Acts 16: 'The Lord opened her heart'," *ICJ* 13, no. 1 (2014): 15.

[399] Alexandra Gruca-Macaulay, *Lydia as a Rhetorical Construct in Acts* (Atlanta: SBL Press, 2016), 10, recounts the history of the interpretation of Lydia, and notes, "In the late fourth century, John Chrysostom's portrayal of Lydia launched a key trajectory of interpretation." According to this interpretive tradition, Lydia was a lowly woman of little means. See Chrysostom, *The Homilies on the Acts of the Apostles,* 498. The evidence of Lydia's wealth and status contradict the interpretive tradition inspired by Chrysostom.

obligate themselves to keep the whole Mosaic law."⁴⁰⁰ This was a standard, technical term for Gentiles who had almost entirely converted to Judaism. Lydia was with the Jewish women at the river because, as a Gentile, she had decided to worship the God of Israel. When Paul arrived, she was more fully introduced to that God and became a key Gentile member of Paul's team in urban Philippi.

What might Luke's readers have thought about Lydia's cultural background when they first encountered her in the text? Clearly, they would have viewed her as someone from the city of Thyatira, since this is the explicit statement of Acts 16:14. Gruca-Macauley makes the interesting observation that Lydian culture frequently carried certain unflattering stereotypes. She notes, "Overall, in a broad spectrum of writings ranging from the classical period to well into antiquity, the ethnography of Lydian woman and 'Lydias' features prostitution, sexual licentiousness, and impropriety."⁴⁰¹ It would appear that this is an example of what Justo Gonzalez terms "The Great Reversal."⁴⁰²

The original reader might have expected for Paul's first European convert to fit the template of the powerful Macedonian man.⁴⁰³ Instead, the reader's sensibilities would have been shattered at the encounter of a woman who stereotypically would have been an unsavory character from Thyatira.⁴⁰⁴ In classic Lukan style, a great reversal ensues, and the Philippian church begins with the "least likely" convert. Overall, we can conclude that Lydia was a wealthy businesswoman. She was a Gentile, from the Lydian city of Thyatira, a place where women where rumored to

---

⁴⁰⁰ Danker, σεβω, *BDAG* 917–918.

⁴⁰¹ Gruca-Macauley, *Lydia as a Rhetorical Construct in Acts,* 127.

⁴⁰² Justo Gonzalez, *Luke,* BTCB (Louisville: Westminster John Knox Press, 2010), 5, notes, "Reversal is a central theme of Luke-Acts, and this too is of particular interest to us today. A grand reversal is part of Luke's geopolitical narrative."

⁴⁰³ See Gruca-Macauley, *Lydia as a Rhetorical Construct in Acts,* 162–179, for her analysis of the Macedonian man.

⁴⁰⁴ This is not to say that Luke thought that Lydia was a prostitute. Rather, he intentionally engaged a literary stereotype in order to highlight God's scheme of Great Reversal.

be loose with their morals. Culturally, then, Lydia was clearly the possessor of a "foreign" culture, at least in comparison to that of Paul, Silas, Timothy, or Luke.

What can we conclude about the cultural identities of the various members of this urban church planting team? First, Paul and Silas were culturally Jewish, although they possessed Roman citizenship. Second, Timothy was culturally mixed. Third, Luke was culturally a Gentile, probably a Syrian urbanite. Fourth, Lydia was culturally a Gentile, from the city of Thyatira. Consequently, it is reasonable to infer that at least four cultures were evident in this five-person band of co-workers in Philippi. This is a clear example of the argument of this book: diversity was a key part of the ancient urban approach to mission.

The Thessalonian and Berean Teams

After leaving Philippi, Paul, Silas, and (possibly) Timothy traveled to the city of Thessalonica. Stallard notes, "It was in this major cosmopolitan city of 200,000 people that Paul and Silas, on Paul's second missionary journey, established a church (1 Thess. 1:9)."[405] Luke apparently remained behind in Philippi, perhaps on business, or perhaps to help the fledgling church (or both). He records only that Paul and Silas traveled to Thessalonica, and then subsequently to Berea (Acts 16:38–17:10). In Berea, the reader once again encounters Timothy (Acts 17:14). Was he present and unmentioned the entire time in Thessalonica? Or did he travel directly from Philippi to Berea? It is impossible to say, since the text of Acts does not clarify this matter. Consequently, very little data is available concerning the missionary teams in Thessalonica and Berea.

In Thessalonica, at least Paul and Silas ministered, possibly alongside Timothy. In Berea, the three of them served together. If

---

[405] Mike Stallard, *First & Second Thessalonians: Looking for Christ's Return* (Chattanooga: AMG, 2009), 4.

Timothy did not minister in Thessalonica, then this raises an intriguing possibility regarding the cultural composition of the leadership team. It is possible that Paul and Silas constituted a monocultural two-person team in Thessalonica. If this happened, it would have been the first (and ultimately, last) instance since the early days of the leadership team of the Jerusalem church. After Thessalonica, it is certain that the culturally Jewish Paul and Silas served alongside the culturally mixed Timothy in Berea.

The Corinthian Team

The last major ministry project of Paul's second missionary journey occurred in Corinth, when he planted a church (Acts 18:1–18). Here, Paul labored alongside Silas, Timothy, Aquila, and Priscilla. Since Paul, Silas, and Timothy have already been culturally mapped, subsequent sections will merely explore the cultural identities of Aquila and Priscilla.

Aquila

Luke notes, "After this [Paul's solo ministry in Athens], he left Athens and went to Corinth, where he found a Jew named Aquila, a native of Pontus, who had recently come from Italy with his wife Priscilla because Claudius had ordered all the Jews to leave Rome" (Acts 18:1–2). Aquila and his wife Priscilla (to be discussed in the subsequent section) were tentmakers who apparently employed Paul while he engaged in bi-vocational ministry (Acts 18:3).[406] They eventually hosted a church in their home (Rom. 16:3–5).

Regarding Aquila's ethnic and cultural identity, Bruce notes, "He was an immigrant Jew from Pontus, on the Black Sea coast of Asia Minor."[407] Bruce's comment is illustrative, because it reminds us of the

---

[406] Wayne Meeks, *The First Urban Christians: The Social World of the Apostle Paul* (New Haven, CT: Yale University Press, 2003), 59, declares, "They are artisans, but independent, and by ancient standards they operate on a fairly large scale."

[407] Bruce, *The Pauline Circle,* 47.

multiple layers of cultural identity that oftentimes operate simultaneously.[408] In this case, his cultural identity has at least four layers.[409] As Bruce notes, Aquila was ethnically Jewish (Acts 18:2), a native of Pontus (Acts 18:2), and an immigrant to Corinth from Italy (Acts 18:2). He might have also noted that Aquila could be viewed as a refugee, since he was expelled from Rome by Claudius (Acts 18:2).

No doubt, Aquila was ethnically Jewish. However, as has been noted, his cultural identity is more complex. He was from Pontus in Asia Minor. As a Hellenistic Jew, he would have been characterized by a certain degree of biculturalism. Culturally, he would have had traits in common with both Jews and his fellow residents from Pontus. His migration to Italy would have also left some cultural imprint upon him, as would his eventual expulsion and journey to Corinth. Aquila was a Jewish man who, due to his upbringing in Pontus and his life experiences in Italy, was well-suited to work with the bridge-building Apostle Paul.

Priscilla

Priscilla (also referred to as Prisca) was the wife of Aquila (Acts 18:2). She had been expelled from Rome, along with her husband, and was living in Corinth, engaged in the business venture of making tents (Acts 18:2-3).[410] Both Bruce[411] and Rolston speculated about the possibility that Priscilla might have been a Gentile. For instance, Rolston mentions that "her name was a familiar name for women among the first families of

---

[408] Here it is important to remember the insights of Rynkiewich that were discussed in Chapter Three. Rynkiewich, *Soul, Self, and Society,* 1–5, tells a story of a man named Lakan to demonstrate that people can simultaneously be characterized by multiple layers of identity.

[409] See Keener, *Acts* 3:2711–2712, for a discussion of the citizenship status of Aquila. Keener asserts that "we should not infer citizenship necessarily from the name."

[410] See V. K. McCarty, "Prisca-Fellow Tent-maker and Fellow Missionary of Paul: Acts 18.2-3, 18, 26; Romans 16.3-4; 1 Corinthians 16.19; 2 Timothy 4.19," in *ICJ* 11, no. 2 (2012) 44–60, for a detailed analysis of Priscilla's ministry, as well as her occupation.

[411] Bruce, *The Pauline Circle,* 45.

Rome and it is possible that she was of Gentile origin."[412] Still, he notes, "The probability is that Priscilla was also Jewish."[413]

Bruce observes that it is likely Priscilla had a high social standing, possibly due to her family connection. He observes that "when he [Luke] speaks of Prisca, he reminds us of an ancient and illustrious Roman family, the gens Prisca. It is conceivable the wife of Aquila belonged in some way to that family; if so, she would have come from a much higher social level than her husband."[414] Both Bruce and Rolston offer up the possibility, based upon Priscilla's name, that she was a part of an influential Roman family, and consequently should be viewed as a Gentile.

However, Keener is more cautious when he notes that "we cannot know about Priscilla."[415] Indeed, Keener is correct that conjecture about Priscilla's name cannot fully clarify her cultural identity. She might have been a Jew, or she might have been a Gentile. The text of Acts simply does not say. Since a Jew-Gentile marriage was not out of the question, it is unwise to rule out either option. However, like her husband Aquila, Priscilla was a resident of Rome, and was eventually expelled before tra=-veling to Corinth. Consequently, Priscilla's cultural identity has some complexities, even though the precise nature of her identity cannot be determined. Regarding Priscilla's cultural identity, we are forced to adopt an agnostic posture.

When stepping back to survey the entirety of the Corinthian team, it becomes apparent that, once again, Paul ministered on a diverse team. Paul and Silas were culturally Jewish. Timothy was culturally mixed (and ambiguous). Aquila was a bicultural Jew from Pontus, by way of Rome. Finally, Priscilla's cultural identity is unknown. Therefore, we can

---

[412] Holmes Rolston and Clovis Chappell, *Personalities Around Paul: Men and Women who Helped or Hindered the Apostle Paul* (Richmond: John Knox Press, 1954), 97.

[413] Rolston and Chappell, *Personalities Around Paul,* 97.

[414] Bruce, *The Pauline Circle,* 45.

[415] Keener, *Acts* 3:2712.

conclude that two men who were culturally Jewish served alongside a bicultural Jewish man, a culturally mixed man, and a woman of unknown cultural origin.

Pauline Teams on the Third Missionary Journey

Paul began his third missionary journey (like all his others) from the city of Antioch in Syria (Acts 18:22–23). This point should not be overlooked. His launching pad for mission was an urban, multicultural church. From there, Paul traveled "through one place after another in the region of Galatia and Phrygia, strengthening all the disciples" (Acts 18:23). From the text of Acts, it is not possible to know with certainty all the destinations on Paul's journey. However, Luke does clearly establish two important aspects of this journey. First, Paul spent significant time ministering in the city of Ephesus (Acts 19:1–10). Second, Paul returned to Jerusalem to be present for Pentecost (Acts 20:16). In this section we will look at two Pauline teams. First, we will map the team in Ephesus. Then, we will map the team that coalesced around Paul during his return to Jerusalem.

The Ephesian Team

The members of the Ephesian team mentioned in the Book of Acts are Paul (Acts 19), Timothy (Acts 19:22), Erastus, (Acts 19:22) Gaius (Acts 19:29), and Aristarchus (Acts 19:29). Paul and Timothy have already been discussed earlier in this book, leaving Erastus, Gaius, and Aristarchus in need of cultural mapping. However, when data from the Pauline epistles is correlated with the text of Acts,[416] it becomes apparent that Paul's band

---

[416] See Thomas Phillips, *Paul, His Letters, and Acts* (Peabody, MA: Hendrickson, 2009), 157–189, for a discussion of the Pauline Circle from two different data sets: the Pauline epistles and the Book of Acts.

included additional individuals:[417] Aquila, Priscilla, Apollos, Stephanas, Fortunatas, and Achaicus.[418] The rest of this section will explore the cultural identities of each member of the Ephesian team.

Erastus

Erastus is an intriguing member of the Pauline Circle. He ministered with Paul in the city of Ephesus before he was sent into Macedonia (Acts 19:22). It is possible that Erastus was from the Corinthian isthmus, since Paul identified him as the city treasurer of Corinth (Rom. 16:23).[419] Goodrich has argued convincingly that Erastus occupied an important office. He notes that Erastus was a "quaestor, a high-ranking municipal position exclusively occupied by the economic elite."[420] While others have questioned this extremely plausible scenario,[421] it still appears likely that Erastus was, as Cranfield notes, a "... highly placed official" in Corinth.[422] As such, he would have hailed from the upper economic echelons of society. When Paul wrote to the Church at Rome, he made sure to mention this

---

[417] See Kenneth Davis, *Designing a Church Planting Internship for Seminarians That Is Mentor Led and Is Local Church Based* (DMin diss., Trinity Evangelical Divinity School, 2013), 270–271, for his helpful chart on "Possible Interns of Paul at Ephesus."

[418] Some potential Ephesian team members have been excluded from this list due to the uncertain point of origin of both Colossians and Philemon. In Colossians, for example, Paul acknowledges that Epaphras is with him (Col 4:12). If Colossians was written from Ephesus, as some suspect, then this would mean that further names could be added to the roster of the Ephesian team. See McKnight, *The Letter to the Colossians,* 34–39, for an insightful discussion of Colossians. McKnight leans towards an Ephesian provenance for Colossians, but admits the situation is complex and uncertain. Due to this uncertainty, individuals such as Philemon and Epaphras will not be included in the list of Ephesian teammates.

[419] This presumes that the Erastus of Acts and the Erastus of Romans are one and the same. Keener, *Acts,* 3:2864–2865, notes the challenges and options of identifying "Luke's Erastus" with "Paul's Erastus."

[420] John K. Goodrich, "Erastus, Quaestor of Corinth: The Administrative Rank of ὁ οἰκονόμος τῆς πόλεως (Rom 16.23) in an Achaean Colony," *NTS* 56 (2009): 90.

[421] Friesen argued that Erastus was likely a slave. Steven J. Friesen, "The Wrong Erastus: Ideology, Archaeology, and Exegesis," *Corinth in Context: Comparative Studies on Religion and Society,* ed. Steven J. Friesen, Daniel N. Schowalter, and James C. Walters (Leiden: Brill, 2010), 231–256. Meeks, *The First Urban Christians,* 59, instead agrees with Kent, who argues that "Erastus was probably a Corinthian freedman who had acquired considerable wealth in commercial activities."

[422] C. E. B. Cranfield, *Romans: A Shorter Commentary* (Grand Rapids: Eerdmans, 1985), 383.

important Roman official who was a part of the Church in Corinth. It is impossible to be certain why this city leader from Corinth was in Ephesus with Paul. However, he did serve for a time with Paul, before being sent back onto the Corinthian isthmus.

If the Erastus of Acts 19:22 and the Erastus of Romans 16:23 are one and the same, the social standing of Erastus seems to be reasonably apparent. This leaves the further question: what data can be gleaned about his cultural identity? Unfortunately, precise data eludes us. Erastus seems to have been an influential resident of the city of Corinth. Whether he was born there, it is impossible to say. Indeed, it is possible that he was ethnically Jewish, but probably more likely that he was a Gentile, given his social standing and governmental rank. However, even though the ethnicity of Erastus cannot be definitively determined, it is apparent that he would have possessed a considerable degree of Corinthian culture. It is inconceivable that someone could rise to a position of power and prominence in this Roman city, without acquiring elements of its culture.

This brief foray into the identity of Erastus has uncovered more information about his social standing than his culture. Furthermore, what has been stated about his cultural identity is open to interpretation. One significant challenge is that the preceding analysis rests upon the identification of "Luke's Erastus" with "Paul's Erastus." If these men are two different individuals, then the inferences made here about the cultural identity of Erastus will be incomplete, and perhaps inadequate. Consequently, our conclusions about Erastus' cultural identity must necessarily be provisional. In the summary at the end of this section, we will be sure to note his uncertain cultural status.

Gaius and Aristarchus

Gaius and Aristarchus are mentioned together in Acts, and so will be discussed together here. They are described by Luke as "traveling companions" of the Apostle Paul (Acts 19:29). They traveled with Paul, and presumably assisted him on his sojourn in Ephesus,[423] and later his journey to Jerusalem. Gaius and Aristarchus are also described as Macedonians (Acts 19:29). However, Luke later mentions the pair in Acts 20:4, where he refers to Gaius as someone who hailed from Derbe and Aristarchus as someone from Thessalonica.

Keener acknowledges that it is difficult to untangle the identity of Gaius.[424] An individual named Gaius is mentioned several times in a Pauline context (in addition to the above-mentioned references in Acts, see also Rom. 16:23 and 1 Cor. 1:14). However, it is not at all clear if these men are identical. It is possible two or more men named Gaius played a role in Paul's ministry.[425] However, even if it is not possible to pinpoint the precise cultural identity of Gaius, it is possible to determine some of the possibilities. The Gaius of Acts 19:29 was Macedonian. The Gaius of Acts 20:4 was from Derbe in Asia Minor.

It is possible that the same individual had spent time in each place, and so was referred to in this way by Luke. In that scenario, Gaius would have probably possessed multiple layers of cultural identity, as someone with fluency in both the cultures of Macedonia and Derbe. If the Gaius of Acts 19:29 was not the same individual mentioned in Acts 20:4, then each "Gaius" would have been characterized by a different cultural identity. The Gaius of Acts 19:29 would have possessed a Macedonian cultural identity, while the Gaius of Acts 20:4 would have exhibited traits in common with the cultures of Derbe, in Asia Minor. Either scenario demonstrates that Gaius was culturally "other" than the Apostle Paul.

---

[423] Keener, *Acts,* 3:2906, notes that Paul used the term translated "traveling companions" to refer to his colleagues (2 Cor 8:19).

[424] Keener, *Acts,* 3:2744–2747, 2906. See also Bruce, *Pauline Circle,* 98, who discusses a relevant textual variant, and Richard Fellows, "Name Giving by Paul and the Destination of Acts," *Tyndale Bulletin* 67, no. 2 (2016): 252–253, who argues that Aristarchus might have been identical with Jason.

[425] See also Gonzalez, *Acts,* 229, who advocates for agnosticism on this issue.

The case of Aristarchus is also complex. A Jewish Aristarchus is mentioned in Colossians 4:10–11. Some might identify him with the Aristarchus of Acts. However, Luke's Aristarchus is described as a "Macedonian" (Acts 19:29) and as someone from Thessalonica (Acts 20:4). It is possible these two individuals are identical, and that Aristarchus was a Diaspora Jew who was from Thessalonica and consequently described as a "Macedonian." It is also possible these two individuals are entirely different. How do these scenarios impact our placement of Aristarchus on a cultural map?

It should be noted at this point that the Aristarchus of Acts 19:29 and Acts 20:4 is the one profiled in our study. He was clearly "from" the Greek city of Thessalonica and was termed a "Macedonian."[426] It is possible that he was ethnically Jewish.[427] However, Luke's descriptions of him indicate clear traces of Greek culture. As a Macedonian from Thessalonica, he would have doubtless given evidence of Greek cultural identity. Together, Gaius and Aristarchus illustrate that Paul surrounded himself with people who were culturally complex and were, therefore, perfectly poised to engage with Paul in the mission to the nations.

Apollos

Apollos[428] was a Jew from the Egyptian city of Alexandria (Acts 18:24). Luke notes that Apollos was effective in his ministry, although he suffered from an incomplete knowledge about the ways of God (Acts 18:24–25). He was mentored by Priscilla and Aquila (Acts 18:26), who enabled him to more fully understand Christian theology. He eventually went to minister in Corinth, in the region of Achaia (Acts 18:27, 19:1).

---

[426] Aristarchus (apparently the same one mentioned in19:29 and 20:4) was also described elsewhere by Luke as a "Macedonian from Thessalonica" (Acts 27:2).

[427] At present, I am unable to solve the riddle of Aristarchus' ethnic identity.

[428] Metzger, *A Textual Commentary on the Greek New Testament,* 2nd ed., 412–413, notes that the Western text of Acts uses the longer name "Apollonius."

In Paul's first Corinthian letter, which was written from Ephesus (1 Cor. 16:8), he notes, "Now about our brother Apollos: I strongly urged him to come to you with the brothers, but he was not at all willing to come now. However, he will come when he has an opportunity" (1 Cor. 16:12). Bruce notes, "That Apollos did visit Ephesus while Paul was there is the natural inference from 1 Cor. 16:12."[429] It seems that, at some point during Paul's lengthy sojourn in Ephesus, Apollos returned there and served, presumably alongside Paul.

If, as seems likely, Apollos was one of Paul's fellow-workers in Ephesus, then it is necessary to culturally map this enigmatic individual. According to Luke, Apollos was ethnically Jewish and was a native of the Egyptian city of Alexandria (Acts 18:24). Two textual clues emerge regarding his potential bicultural status as a Diaspora Jew. First, as Keener notes, the varied spellings of Apollos's name in various manuscripts of Acts reveals a probable Egyptian preference.[430] Indeed, Apollonius (the longer version of Apollos' name) was common in Alexandria, due to the prominence of one its governors, who bore that name.[431]

Second, Luke notes that Apollos was "an eloquent man" (Acts 18:24). In fact, Paul seems to provide an implicit contrast between his own "weak" rhetoric and the more eloquent rhetoric of Apollos (1 Cor. 1:10–31). Given Apollos's upbringing in Alexandria, this rhetorical competence is unsurprising. As Keener notes, "Apollos' city of origin could have provided him not only a Greek education, if his family had sufficient means, but probably also a passionate desire for respectability by Greek standards, including a commitment to defend his faith's intellectual integrity."[432] The

---

[429] Bruce, *The Pauline Circle*, 56.
[430] Keener, *Acts*, 3:2799.
[431] Ibid.
[432] Keener, *Acts*, 3:2803.

intellectual milieu of Alexandria prioritized Greek education and rhetoric. Since Apollos hailed from Alexandria and was rhetorically competent, it seems probable that he was exposed to some type of Greek education during his formative years.

This portrait of Apollos adds further layers of complexity to his cultural identity. He was ethnically Jewish but lived in an Egyptian city and probably received a Greek education. Like many Alexandrian Jews, Apollos would have been characterized by some level of biculturalism (or perhaps even multiculturalism). Barclay (who has extensively studied diaspora Jews in Egypt) notes, "Indeed Philo's example indicates that a Diaspora Jew could be, in certain respects, Jewish to the core and Hellenized to the same core."[433] Barclay's insights about Philo are resonant with our reliance upon the social sciences, and their embrace of liminality (see Chapter Three).

Barclay has, through the accumulation of historical evidence, reached the same conclusions held by contemporary anthropologists: it was (and is) possible to have a compound cultural identity, characterized by either biculturalism or multiculturalism. Indeed, Barclay helpfully constructs a scale for plotting Jews of the Diaspora. It involves three levels: assimilation, acculturation, and accommodation.[434] For the purposes of our study, it would seem likely that Apollos gives some evidence of accultureation to Greek culture, and probably to Egyptian culture as well.[435] Consequently, I believe that Apollos was a bicultural Jew from the Egyptian city of Alexandria.

---

[433] John M. G. Barclay, *Jews in the Mediterranean diaspora: From Alexander to Trajan (323 BCE–117 CE)* (Berkeley: University of California Press, 1996), 91.

[434] Barclay, *Jews in the Mediterranean Diaspora*, 92–102.

[435] See also John M. G. Barclay, *Pauline Churches and Diaspora Jews* (Grand Rapids: Eerdmans, 2011), 167–170, for an insightful discussion of how Egyptian and Hellenistic ideas blended together in the ancient world.

Stephanas, Fortunatas, and Achaicus

Stephanas, Fortunatas, and Achaicus are briefly mentioned together, and therefore we will briefly map them together. Writing from Ephesus (1 Cor. 16:8), Paul declares, "I am delighted to have Stephanas, Fortunatas, and Achaicus present, because these men have made up for your absence. For they have refreshed my spirit and yours" (1 Cor. 16:17–18). Who were these three men? Little is known about them. However, we can deduce that Stephanas was from Greece since Paul describes he and his household as "the firstfruits of Achaia" (1 Cor. 16:15). Apparently, Stephanas and his household were some of the initial converts in that region and were baptized by the Apostle Paul (1 Cor. 1:16). Stephanas eventually rose to a position of leadership (1 Cor. 12:15–16). As Brooks notes, "Achaicus, Fortunatas, and Stephanas are from Corinth."[436]

Little information can be gleaned concerning Fortunatas and Achaicus. However, the available data does provide instructive clues. Achaicus was probably a Gentile. His name suggests his origin in the Greek region of Achaia. As Welborn notes, "A cognomen such as Achaicus, [was] derived from a place name or an εθνος."[437] Welborn also declares, "The mention of Fortunatas and Achaicus along with Stephanas suggests that they were members of Stephanas's household, whether as slaves or freedman clients."[438]

Although little data is available about Stephanas, Fortunatas, and Achaicus, the following conclusions can be reached. Each of these three

---

[436] William Brooks, "A Biblical Understanding of the Diversity of Paul's Missionary Coworkers," in *Reflecting God's Glory Together: Diversity in Evangelical Mission,* ed. Scott Moreau and Beth Snodderly (Pasadena: William Carey, 2011), 210.

[437] L. L. Welborn, "Inequality in Roman Corinth: Evidence from Diverse Sources Evaluated by a Neo-Ricardian Model," in *The First Urban Churches 2: Roman Corinth,* ed. James R. Harrison and L. L. Welborn (Atlanta: SBL Press, 2016), 68.

[438] Welborn, "Inequality in Roman Corinth: Evidence from Diverse Sources Evaluated by a Neo-Ricardian Model," 68. See also Laura Nasrallah, "'You Were Bought With a Price': Freedpersons and Things in 1 Corinthians," in *Corinth in Contrast: Studies in Inequality,* ed. Steven Friesen, Sarah James, and Daniel N. Schowalter (Boston: Brill, 2014), 65, who points out the possibility that Fortunatas and Achaicus were slaves.

individuals would have been culturally "other," at least in comparison to the culturally Jewish Apostle Paul. After all, as residents of Corinth, these men would be characterized by strong Greek cultural traits. Therefore, we can identify these individuals as culturally Greek co-workers of the Apostle Paul.

At this point, it is necessary to review our findings about the Ephesian team members. The team that coalesced[439] in Ephesus consisted of a culturally Jewish leader (Paul), bicultural Jews (Aquila and Apollos), a culturally mixed individual (Timothy), culturally ambiguous (and yet culturally "other") individuals (Priscilla, Erastus, Stephanas, Fortunatas, Gaius, and Aristarchus), and a Gentile (Achaicus). Clearly, this team can be characterized as a multicultural ministry team. In the subsequent section, the team that emerged on Paul's journey to Jerusalem will be culturally mapped.

The "Return to Jerusalem" Team

Following his sojourn in Ephesus, and a brief ministry in Greece (Acts 20:1–3), Paul departed for Jerusalem. Traveling with him were Sopater (Acts 20:4), Aristarchus (Acts 20:4), Secundus (Acts 20:4), Gaius (Acts 20:4), Timothy (Acts 20:4), Tychicus (Acts 20:4), Trophimus (Acts 20:4), and Luke (Acts 20:5–6). Since Paul, Aristarchus, Gaius, Timothy, and Luke have already been profiled earlier in this study, subsequent sections will explore the cultural identities of Sopater, Secundus, Tychicus, and Trophimus.

Before proceeding to an examination of the cultural identities of these individuals, it is necessary to note the unique nature of this Pauline journey. Unlike most of Paul's other journeys, this one was not designed to make disciples and plant churches. Instead, it was a return to

---

[439] Again, it should be noted that this team did not exist as a formal construct. Many of Paul's Ephesian co-workers came and went as the mission necessitated.

Jerusalem, with a gift for the church there, from the churches of Paul's mission (2 Corinthians 8–9). Consequently, Schnabel notes, "Paul's travel companions during his return journey from the mission to Ephesus mentioned in Acts 20:4 are a special case because they accompany him as representatives of the churches that he had established, bringing the collection from the Jewish-and Gentile-Christian churches to Jerusalem."[440]

Because Paul desired to demonstrate solidarity with the church at Jerusalem, he gathered representatives from across the churches that he had planted. As Bruce notes, "Paul was not going to make his journey to Jerusalem unaccompanied. A number of Gentile Christians went with him: these were no doubt representatives of the various churches which were contributing to the gift for the relief of the poverty of the Jerusalem Christians."[441] Consequently, this "team" could perhaps be viewed as less of a ministry team, and more as a traveling band of colleagues on a journey to a sister church. Their mission was to deliver the all-important offering.

Paul apparently desired to showcase the diversity and unity of the church. The churches that he had established were primarily Gentile. The original church in Jerusalem was primarily Jewish. Therefore, Paul's band of compatriots were Gentile representatives of various Pauline churches. They seem to have been tasked with the mission of accompanying Paul, administering the benevolence offering to the Christians in Jerusalem, and demonstrating the unity of the fledgling Christian movement (Rom. 15:25–26). Sleeman notes that "Paul thus arrives back in Jerusalem surrounded by the embodied evidence of his ministries among the diaspora and the nations."[442] Having noted the unique nature of this

---

[440] Schnabel, *Early Christian Mission,* 2:1445. See also Witherington III, *The Acts of the Apostles,* 603, for a similar conclusion.

[441] Bruce, *Acts,* 405.

[442] Matthew Sleeman, "Paul, Pentecost, and the Nomosphere: The Final Return to Jerusalem in the Acts of the Apostles," in *The Urban World and the First Christians,* ed.

traveling band of Pauline companions, we can now examine the particular cultural identities of these men.

Sopater

Luke describes Sopater as the "son of Pyrrhus from Berea" (Acts 20:4). Since Berea was in Macedonia, some might immediately assume that Sopater was ethnically Greek. However, Lightfoot cautions us against this reading, noting that the Sopater of Acts 20:4 could be the same as the ethnically Jewish Sosipater of Romans 16:21. If these two individuals are one and the same, Lightfoot points out that Sopater would have been "one of those Berean Jews who were ευγενεστοροι among their countrymen (Acts 17:11)."[443]

Even if Sopater was a Diaspora Jew from Berea, he likely would have been characterized by Greek culture. As we previously noted in this study, Jews of the Diaspora existed in a liminal space, and were consequently shaped by two or more cultures. As a result, even though Sopater's ethnicity might have been (and likely was) Jewish,[444] it seems reasonable to infer some level of biculturalism on the part of this Pauline compatriot from the Macedonian city of Berea.

Secundus

Luke records that one of Paul's traveling companions was "Secundus from Thessalonica" (Acts 20:4). Information about Secundus is sparse. Keener notes, "'Secundus' appears prominently as a name in Thessalonica; ... it was a common Latin name, including in Jewish inscriptions in various languages."[445] On the basis of the name's attestation in Thessalonian inscriptions, and its connections to Roman citizenship,

---

Steve Walton, Paul R. Trebilco, and David W. J. Gill (Grand Rapids: Eerdmans, 2017), 27–28.

[443] J. B. Lightfoot, *The Acts of the Apostles: A Newly Discovered Commentary*, ed. Ben Witherington III and Todd Still (Downers Gove, IL: IVP, 2014), 259.

[444] Bruce, *Pauline Circle,* 98, seems to embrace a Jewish ethnic identity for Sopater.

[445] Keener, *Acts,* 3:2954–2955.

Keener declares, "Secundus was thus likely a person with some status, insofar as we may venture an educated guess."[446] Bruce assumes that Secundus was "evidently" a Gentile, although he does not provide any justification for that claim.[447]

Even if Secundus' ethnic identity cannot be determined with precision, his cultural identity should be clearer to the reader. He was "from Thessalonica" and represented the Gentile church in that city. Furthermore, his name was a common one in Thessalonica. Even if Secundus was Jewish, he was given a name that enabled him to seamlessly navigate the Roman world of Greek Thessalonica. All at once, his liminality should be apparent. If Secundus was Jewish, he would have been a bicultural Jew. If he was a Gentile, he would have been culturally Greek. In either case, he would have been culturally "other" to the Apostle Paul.

Tychicus

Tychicus is mentioned by Luke in his list of Paul's traveling companions. He also appears in some of the Pauline epistles. Apparently, he was the courier who delivered the Ephesian (Eph. 6:21 and 2 Tim. 4:12) and Colossian (Col. 4:7) letters. It is also possible that on other occasions he functioned as a messenger on behalf of Paul (Titus 3:12). Bruce argues that Acts 20:4 indicates that "Tychicus was himself a native of the province of Asia."[448] Philipps asserts that Tychicus was part of "A group of apparently Gentile emissaries."[449] Indeed, the most natural reading of the text (Ασιανοι δε Τυχικος και Τροφιμος) leads one to conclude that Tychicus was from Asia, along with Trophimus (to be considered in the subsequent section). Keener asserts, "The name [Tychicus] means something like 'Lucky' but is attested as a (likely) Jewish name."[450]

---

[446] Keener, *Acts,* 3:2955.

[447] Bruce, *The Pauline Circle,* 98.

[448] Bruce, *The Pauline Circle,* 87.

[449] Thomas E. Phillips, *Paul, His Letters, and Acts* (Grand Rapids: Baker, 2010), 167.

[450] Keener, *Acts,* 3:2956.

It is possible that the name Tychicus could be employed by a Jewish man. However, it is also possible that this is evidence of a Gentile ethnic background (since the connection to fate was a pagan Greek concept).[451] At the very least, it probably illustrates a Gentile influence. Since Tychicus was from Asia, and used such a name, it seems probable that he was ethnically a Gentile. On the level of culture, he was most assuredly culturally "other" from Paul, given his status as a native of Asia. Culturally, then, Tychicus was Asian.

Trophimus

The ethnic identity of Trophimus is more easily identified than some of his traveling companions. Like Tychicus, he was "from Asia" (Acts 20:4). Later, after the band has reached Jerusalem, Trophimus appears once again in Luke's narrative. Luke's reader is told that the Jews rioted because they believed that Paul brought "Trophimus the Ephesian" into the Temple (Acts 21:27–30). If Trophimus was a Jewish Ephesian, why would his presumed entrance into the Temple spark a riot?

Clearly, the Jewish population of Jerusalem understood that Trophimus was a Gentile, and they feared that Paul was scandalously crossing lines and bringing Trophimus past the so-called "Court of the Gentiles." In fact, Paul's opponents (Jews from Asia) said as much, when they charged that "he [Paul] also brought Greeks into the temple and has defiled this holy place" (Acts 21:28). Ethnically, then, Trophimus was a Gentile. Culturally, he was a Greek man from the city of Ephesus.

Here we ought to review our findings about Paul's traveling companions during his return to Jerusalem in Acts 20–21. The team that carried the offering to Jerusalem probably consisted of a culturally Jewish leader (Paul), a bicultural Jew (Sopater), a culturally mixed individual (Timothy), culturally ambiguous (and yet culturally "other") individuals (Gaius, Secundus and Tychicus), and Gentiles from multiple cultural

---

[451] Ibid.

backgrounds (Trophimus and Luke). Importantly, Sleeman notes that "Paul's report in 21:10 of 'the things that God had done among the Gentiles through his ministry' is both discursive and embodied: it is heard and it is seen."[452] Clearly, this band of travelers can be characterized as a multicultural group.

Summary and Review: Patterns of Diverse Teams in Acts?

This book set out to discover if the ancient urban approach to mission included the use of multicultural ministry teams. After discussing preliminary matters such as the genre of Acts (Chapter Two) and the social sciences (Chapter Three), we engaged the text of Acts in a quest to "culturally map" the various ministry teams that were described by Luke. The last two chapters have sought to establish this cultural map, first by charting urban teams in early Acts (at Jerusalem) and middle Acts (at Antioch), and then by charting the Pauline teams of later Acts. At this point, the data from the last two chapters will be summarized. It will then be assessed for possible patterns of multiculturalism on the teams of Acts.[453]

In the previous chapter, we analyzed the ministry team of the original church in Jerusalem (early Acts). We discovered that, initially, the leadership team was monocultural, comprised of twelve culturally Jewish apostles (men who were described as "Galileans"). Later (perhaps several years later), the apostles, in response to a cultural controversy, decided to appoint "The Seven." The Seven were culturally "other" from the apostles. Six of them were bicultural Jews, while one (Nicolaus of Antioch) was a culturally Syrian Gentile.

---

[452] Sleeman, "Paul, Pentecost and the Nomosphere," 28.
[453] See the Appendix for a concise chart that summarizes the findings of Chapters Four and Five.

However, since this diversity only existed in the "lower tiers" of leadership, this was not necessarily what many contemporary advocates are striving for when they advocate for multicultural teams. Based upon this data, the ministry team of the first church can be described as initially monocultural and eventually mildly multicultural. Therefore, the ministry team in the church at Jerusalem should not be classified as an example of a multicultural team.

Following the discussion of the Church in Jerusalem, the previous chapter moved on to an exploration of the Antiochene leadership team (described primarily in Acts 13:1). Here, the leadership team was multicultural, with its leaders possessing Cypriot, Jewish, and African cultural traits. I remain agnostic about whether this team was multiethnic. It is highly likely that all the individuals studied were ethnically Jewish, even while many of them were culturally "other." Therefore, the cultural map of the previous chapter unveiled one monocultural and one multicultural ministry team.

The present chapter assessed the ministry teams on the three Pauline missionary journeys. The team on the first journey was at least bicultural, and most likely multicultural since Paul's two colleagues were each culturally "other." Multiple urban teams emerged on the second journey. The team in Philippi was decidedly diverse, with two leaders who were culturally Jewish and three who were not. The cultural map of the team in Thessalonica is unclear. It is possible that it was bicultural, or even monocultural (depending upon whether Timothy was present). In Berea, the team was bicultural. The ministry team at Corinth was multicultural, with at least three cultures represented in the group of missionaries.

On the third Pauline journey, two teams were culturally mapped. The team in Ephesus was extremely multicultural, with at least five different cultures represented on Paul's team in Ephesus. As we noted earlier in this chapter, the Pauline team in Ephesus was fluid, with team members coming and going, based upon the needs of the mission. The second team from the third journey was Paul's team of traveling companions who returned to Jerusalem with him. It was a unique team, with no goal to make disciples and plant churches. The goal of this team was to take the offering from the Gentile churches back to the Jewish church in Rome, thereby demonstrating solidarity and unity, even amid the emerging diversity of the Christian movement. At least four cultures were present in this group; therefore, this band of travelers qualifies as multicultural.

How does all this data add up? Of the seven Pauline teams examined in this chapter, five of them were multicultural, one was bicultural, and one was (possibly) monocultural. When added to the two teams assessed in early Acts (Jerusalem) and middle Acts (Antioch), this leaves the reader with the following data. Nine ministry teams are mentioned in the Book of Acts. Six of them were multicultural, two of them were monocultural, and one was bicultural. This takes us back to the crucial question posed in the introduction: does the Book of Acts showcase an approach to urban mission that incorporates the use of diverse teams?

Since six of the nine teams were multicultural, the interpreter can now raise the salient issue, and ask: "Is this a pattern?" This question can be answered in different ways. Some might argue that, since one-third of the teams were not multicultural (up to two were monocultural and one was bicultural), a subdominant pattern of the Spirit's use of these types of teams appears throughout Acts. Some might prefer to focus on the larger group of multicultural teams and argue that this constitutes a clear pattern: the Holy Spirit was at work forming multicultural teams to accomplish his mission to the nations.

In resolving this dilemma, the issue of trajectory must be raised. The reader must ask herself, "What was the cultural trajectory of the ministry teams in the Book of Acts?" In answer to that question, the data comes into sharper focus. The first team was clearly monocultural (Acts 2). From that point on, seven out of eight teams were not monocultural.

One of the seven was bicultural, and the other six were multicultural. The teams described in the Book of Acts are clearly moving along a multicultural trajectory. Indeed, this fits the pattern of the overall church in the Book of Acts. Jesus had predicted that the Church would bear witness to his lordship in Jerusalem, Judea, Samaria, and to the ends of the earth (Acts 1:8). The story of Acts seems to follow that outline and tells its readers how the church grew and took the gospel across cultural boundaries. Therefore, it should not surprise the reader to discover that, just as the Church diversified throughout the course of the story, so too did its ministry teams.

In response, then, to the question posed in this study's introduction, the answer seems evident. A progressive pattern from one monocultural team to multiple multicultural teams emerges in the Book of Acts. However, this still leaves the applicational component of that question unanswered. The contemporary urban practitioner is still wondering if these patterns are applicable to contemporary urban settings. In the final chapter of this study, we will explore issues of application as we engage the fields of urban missiology and multicultural studies.

CHAPTER SIX: Diverse Urban Teams in Acts and in the Modern World

Our earliest chapters built a foundation by providing insight regarding interpretive approaches to Acts, as well as outlining social-science perspectives on the topic of culture. In the heart of this book, we culturally mapped the teams in the Book of Acts. This cultural map indicated a progressive pattern from monocultural teams to multicultural teams in the Book of Acts. This is especially clear when the overall trajectory of Acts is taken into consideration. The Church moved from sameness to diversity within one generation, and its ministry teams reflected that rapid shift!

In this final chapter, my goal is to apply what we have learned to urban contexts. Many Christians live and minister in major cities, where diverse teams are frequently a wise approach, and perhaps sometimes even a missional necessity. As I have mentioned, I live in Brooklyn, where over three-hundred languages are spoken. It is in contexts such as this that our discoveries about the Church's ancient approach to urban mission can begin to pay off. We will discover that this ancient approach can still prove useful for churches, non-profits, and mission organizations.

In the following pages, we will explore three ideas. First, we will discover that many contemporary urban settings are contextually like many of the settings of the Book of Acts. We will find that cities in which multicultural teams flourished were extremely similar in many ways to modern cities. Based upon this high degree of convergence, we will argue that practitioners in urban contexts should consider retrieving this ancient approach to urban mission.

Second, we will devote space to an exploration of Luke's model of diverse teams in the urban context. In this section, we will once again re-examine the issue of a mandate for multicultural teams. Third, in our section of most practical application, we will examine specific challenges and opportunities for diverse teams. Here, we will make preliminary recommendations regarding cultural equity, cultural intelligence, and cultural tension.

All but one of the previous chapters directly engaged the field of New Testament studies. One chapter explored the field of the social sciences. In this chapter, the fields of urban missiology and multicultural studies will also be briefly engaged, for the purposes of developing relevant application. This will bring to fruition one of the goals of this volume, which was to provide an original integrative exploration of this theme that brings three unique conversation partners together: the social sciences, New Testament studies, and urban missiology. In this final chapter, the fields of urban missiology (and the related literature on multicultural studies) will drive the conversation as our quest reaches its conclusion.

Similarities Between the Cities of the Book of Acts and Modern Urban Settings

A pattern of diverse teams emerges upon a close reading of the Book of Acts. However, for that pattern to be applicable in contemporary contexts, the practitioner should consider contextual similarities.[454] She should consider whether the cities of Acts, in which multicultural teams flourished, were like contemporary urban centers. This means assessing factors such as diversity, disease, immigration, violence, cultural influence, and poverty (to name only some of the relevant factors). In this section, we will assess some of these variables.

---

[454] Grant Osborne, *The Hermeneutical Spiral: A Comprehensive Introduction to Biblical Interpretation,* revised and expanded ed. (Downers Grove, IL: IVP, 2006), 452, notes that understanding the historical context of a

We will sift through data about ancient cities and compare this with data pertaining to contemporary cities. As a result of this analysis, we will conclude that a high degree of similarity exists between many of the urban centers of mission in Acts and many contemporary cities. Subsequent sections will compare the cities of Acts and contemporary cities through the lenses of diversity, immigration, violence, poverty, and cultural influence. I will use Brooklyn as a case study to illustrate the similarities between ancient and modern cities.

Diversity in the Cities of Acts and Contemporary Cities

First-century cities were oftentimes characterized by ethnic and cultural diversity. Even though the cities of antiquity were small (by modern standards), they were densely populated,[455] and usually diverse.[456] Syrian Antioch, which features prominently in the Book of Acts, and has been an important factor in this book, is a prime example of diversity. As a crossroads city at the edge of the Roman Empire, Antioch played a crucial role in international diplomacy. Downey notes, "We are told, for example, how Nicolaus of Damascus, when he was at Antioch, saw ambassadors from India on their way to visit the Emperor Augustus."[457] This would be comparable to the present-day city of New York, where diplomats (and their considerable entourages) from around the world converge to represent their respective countries at the United Nations.

However, Syrian Antioch was not simply characterized by transient diversity, as diplomats traveled through the city. Instead, it was

---

[455] See Rodney Stark, *The Rise of Christianity* (New York: HarperOne, 1997), 149–150, who argues, for instance, that Syrian Antioch was more densely populated than present-day Manhattan.

[456] See Rodney Stark, *Cities of God* (New York: HarperOne 2006), 32, who notes that the imperial cities were marked by "enormous ethnic and cultural diversity."

[457] Glanville Downey, *A History of Antioch in Syria: From Seleucus to the Arab Conquest* (Princeton: Princeton University Press, 1961), 164. Elsewhere, Downey, *A History of Antioch in Syria*, 272, notes, "Antioch saw the coming and going of peoples of all sorts."

also marked by more permanent ethnic and cultural diversity. Downey argues that, in Antioch, "traditional barriers of race, nationality, and formal religion could easily be crossed."[458] This was due in part to its location on the map of the ancient world. In fact, Robinson describes Antioch as a "crossroads for ethnic and cultural interchange: a Macedonian/Greek city in origin, established in the midst of a Syrian countryside, under Roman rule, and with various immigrant populations including Jews and Samaritans."[459] Robinson even notes the claim of the fourth-century Antiochene, Libanius, who declares that someone who "sits in our market place…will sample every city."[460]

Although Antioch is a prime example of ancient urban diversity, it is hardly alone. The cities were dominated by commercial interests, and so merchants from a variety of cultures flocked to their streets to trade their goods in the agora. Issues of security were also prominent in the ancient urban landscape. Consequently, companies of soldiers from around the Roman Empire were garrisoned in various cities. Meeks notes that urban society in antiquity was initially characterized by diversity. He asserts, "For a very long time groups of foreigners had gathered in each city: merchants and artisans following the armies or in search of better markets or better access to transportation, persons enslaved and displaced by war or piracy and now set free, political exiles, soldiers of fortune."[461]

Contemporary cities are also characterized by diversity. This is unsurprising, since diversity tends to be a cherished ideal for urban

---

[458] Downey, *A History of Antioch in Syria*, 274.

[459] Thomas Robinson, *Ignatius of Antioch and the Parting of the Ways: Early Jewish-Christian Relations* (Peabody, MA: Hendrickson, 2009), 16–17.

[460] Robinson, *Ignatius of Antioch and the Parting of the Ways*, 15. Caution is necessary in utilizing the testimony of Libanius since he wrote about fourth-century Antioch. However, it is likely that the city was not substantially changed from its first-century environment in the Book of Acts.

[461] Wayne Meeks, *The First Urban Christians: The Social World of the Apostle Paul* (New Haven, CT: Yale University Press, 2003), 13.

planners.[462] It is also unsurprising, given that the twin phenomena of globalization and urbanization are remaking the modern world.[463] From a church–planting perspective, Bergquist and Crane argue that cities should be reached since "the world is coalescing in the cities."[464] They note, "Cities connect diverse cultures, languages, and worldviews."[465] Indeed, anyone who has lived in a major American city knows that in such cities they are more likely to encounter the ethnic or cultural "other." The urban theorist Edward Glaeser declares, "During the millennia since Athens first attracted the finest minds of the Mediterranean world, cities have grown by attracting people from diverse cultures. The most successful cities today—London, Bangalore, Singapore, New York–still connect continents."[466]

Where I live in Brooklyn, the setting is highly diverse. Hundreds of languages can be overheard on the streets of this borough, where over one-third of the population is foreign born.[467] For example, great waves of Caribbean migration have reshaped Brooklyn, forging new Caribbean enclaves.[468] I am privileged to live in the historically Afro-Caribbean neighborhood of Crown Heights in north-central Brooklyn. Kasinitz describes this community as "New York's oldest and most diverse Caribbean neighborhood."[469] However, Crown Heights is also historically

---

[462] See Michael Crane, *Sowing Seeds of Change: Cultivating Transformation in the City* (Portland: Urban Loft, 2015), 94, who briefly traces this ideal in both ancient and contemporary literature.

[463] See Michael Goheen, *Introducing Christian Mission Today: Scripture, History and Issues* (Downers Grove, IL: IVP, 2014), 370–400 and Susan Baker, *Globalization and Its Effects on Urban Ministry in the 21st Century* (Pasadena: William Carey, 2009) for a discussion of these phenomena.

[464] Linda Bergquist and Michael Crane, *City Shaped Churches: Planting Churches in the Global Era* (Portland: Urban Loft, 2018), 53.

[465] Bergquist and Crane, *City Shaped Churches,* 53.

[466] Edward Glaeser, *Triumph of the City* (New York: Penguin, 2011), 251.

[467] *World Population Review: Brooklyn Population 2019.* worldpopulationreview.com/boroughs/brooklyn-population/.

[468] Philip Kasinitz, *Caribbean New York: Black Immigrants and the Politics of Race* (Ithaca, NY: Cornell University Press, 1992), 38–89.

[469] Kasinitz, *Caribbean New York,* 59.

Jewish,[470] and it is home to an influential Jewish unreached people group.[471]

The convergence of these cultures in Crown Heights is highlighted by our neighborhood's annual Labor Day parade (known as Carnival in some parts of the world). A group of researchers note, "As parade participants–many with ties to Haiti, Jamaica, Trinidad and Tobago, Barbados, and Grenada—wend their way through Brooklyn, their celebration passes by the worldwide headquarters of the Lubavitch movement of Hasidic Jews at 770 Eastern Parkway."[472] On this same parkway, only a few weeks after the parade, one can encounter Hasidic Jews who are engaging in ritual animal sacrifice for Yom Kippur. The juxtaposition can be jarring, yet this pattern of diversity is replicated in many of Brooklyn's communities, as east meets west, and north meets south.

Immigration in the Cities of Acts and Contemporary Cities

The important topic of immigration is related to the previously discussed issue of urban diversity.[473] First-century cities were oftentimes diverse because of the presence of immigrants within their walls. In fact, a brief review of some of the texts examined in this book will demonstrate that immigration was a ubiquitous phenomenon in urban antiquity.

On the Day of Pentecost, Jerusalem was marked by the presence of pilgrims. As we noted, these ethnically Jewish immigrants had relocated to Jerusalem from "every nation under heaven" (Acts 2:5). Luke ob-

---

[470] Henry Goldschmidt, *Race and Religion Among the Chosen Peoples of Crown Heights* (New Brunswick, NJ: Rutgers University Press, 2006).

[471] Chris Clayman and Meredith Lee, *ethNYcity: The Nations, Tongues, and Faiths of Metropolitan New York* (New York: MNYBA, 2010), 174–175.

[472] Kenneth Jackson and John Manbeck, *The Neighborhoods of Brooklyn* (New Haven, CT: Yale University Press, 2004), 78.

[473] For an insightful and contextual theological reflection upon immigration, see Andrew Walls, *Crossing Cultural Frontiers: Studies in the History of World Christianity* (Maryknoll, New York: Orbis, 2017), 49–61.

serves that these immigrants were Parthians, Medes, Elamites, Romans, Cretans, and Arabs, and representatives remained from Mesopotamia, Judea, Cappadocia, Pontus, Asia, Phrygia, Pamphylia, Egypt, and Libya (Acts 2:9–11). Based upon Lukan testimony, Jerusalem (at least in the era narrated in the Book of Acts) was a city marked by immigration. Antioch was the second of the two cities that dominate the Lukan narrative of the first half of Acts.

In Antioch, the gospel was at first shared only with the Jewish residents of Antioch (Acts 11:19). Subsequently, refugees from Africa and the Mediterranean (Acts 11:20) proclaimed the gospel to Gentiles (Acts 11:20). Luke seems to take great care to demonstrate how the Syrian city of Antioch gave birth to a Jew-Gentile church that was founded by refugee-immigrants from Africa and the Mediterranean. Based upon the text of Acts, both Jerusalem and Antioch were cities marked by at least some level of immigration.

When Luke pivots his narrative to the life of Paul, he continues to describe cities in a similar manner. A sampling of cities from Paul's second missionary journey makes this clear. In Philippi, Luke's readers are alerted to the presence of an important Lydian immigrant from Thyatira (Acts 16:14). This immigrant, named Lydia, was Paul's first convert in Europe, and she ultimately served as a crucial patroness for his Philippian church plant. In both Thessalonica and Berea, Jews and Gentiles lived as neighbors (Acts 17:17:1–4 and 17:10–12). This testifies to the existence of an immigrant movement, at least at some point in the history of these ancient cities.

In Athens, Luke wrote that Paul ministered in a setting in which "all the Athenians and the foreigners residing there spent their time on nothing else but telling or hearing something new" (Acts 17:21). According to Luke, the Grecian city of Athens was home to foreigners, including some Jews (Acts 17:17). Paul's final urban destination on his second missionary journey was the important city of Corinth. Here, one of his most prominent team members (Aquila) was a Jew from Pontus who had migrated to Corinth from Italy (Acts 18:2). As an immigrant, Aquila would have been at home in Corinth, a city which was home to both Jews and Gentiles (Acts 18:4–8). The Lukan record of Acts leads the reader to conclude that immigration was ubiquitous in antiquity. At the very least, it was a prominent feature of the cities in which the early Christian movement flourished.

Contemporary American cities are likewise characterized by immigration.[474] This can be illustrated in multiple ways. First, we will briefly examine salient essays in a volume edited by Robert Orsi. Second, we will engage the field of diaspora missiology. In his book "Gods of the City," Orsi and his team of writers provide compelling case studies of American urban religion.[475] Three of these essays speak directly to the impact of immigration upon contemporary urban centers. Two of them will be considered here.

In "Diasporic Nationalism and Urban Landscape: Cuban Immigrants at a Catholic Shrine in Miami," Thomas Tweed notes that "Fidel Castro's revolutionary army victoriously entered Havana on January 8, 1959, and thereby transformed the cultural landscape of Miami."[476] How was Miami transformed culturally by a military action in another country? The answer lies in the immigration that resulted as thousands of Cubans fled Castro's revolution and resettled in exile in Miami. According to Tweed, "the displaced community simultaneously reclaims Havana and re-maps Miami."[477]

---

[474] Glaeser, *Triumph of the City,* 251, notes, "Immigrants are often a vital part of their [successful cities] economic model, both at the top and the bottom ends of the pay scale, and the success of global cities depends on national policies toward trade and immigration."

[475] Robert Orsi, *Gods of the City: Religion and the American Urban Landscape* (Indianapolis: Indiana University Press, 1999).

[476] Thomas Tweed, "Diasporic Nationalism and Urban Landscape: Cuban Immigrants at a Catholic Shrine in Miami," in *Gods of the City,* 131.

[477] Thomas Tweed, "Diasporic Nationalism and Urban Landscape: Cuban Immigrants at a Catholic Shrine in Miami," in *Gods of the City,* 148.

Another essay, "The Religious Boundaries of an In–Between People: Street Feste and the Problem of the Dark-Skinned Other in Italian Harlem, 1920–1990," illustrates some of the features of Italian immigration in New York City.[478] Orsi maps the complex nature of ethnic and cultural identity in the historically Italian part of Harlem. He notes that Italian immigrants in Harlem were originally discriminated against, then eventually became accepted as "Americans," and then proceeded to discriminate against those who were ethnically "other."[479] In retelling this story of one of New York's most idealized neighborhoods, Orsi's localized insights resonate with others, who have told a broader history of how America's European immigrants "became white."[480]

Orsi notes that the Italian immigrants in Harlem would have been viewed as "in-between." As we noted in chapter three, this concept of liminality is commonly utilized in the social sciences, and it can be seen operating in history, especially during periods of immigration. Orsi's description of a Catholic street festival in Harlem helps to facilitate a comparison of ancient and modern cities. He notes, "During the July celebrations in Harlem, Haitian and Italian women wash each other's faces with wet cloths; an Italian band plays the Haitian national song; Haitian pilgrims sing Italian hymns ... while Puerto Ricans who live in the Madonna's neighborhood but were kept out of her home ignore her as she passes."[481] In Orsi's retelling of Harlem's story, Italians, Haitians, and Puerto Ricans thrived as they mingled and coexisted (sometimes tenuously).[482]

---

[478] Robert Orsi, "The Religious Boundaries of an In–Between People: Street *Feste* and the Problem of the Dark-Skinned Other in Italian Harlem, 1920–1990," *Gods of the City,* 257–288.

[479] Robert Orsi, "The Religious Boundaries of an In-Between People," 262–273.

[480] David Roediger, *Working Toward Whiteness: How America's Immigrants Became White* (New York: Basic, 2018).

[481] Robert Orsi, "The Religious Boundaries of an In-Between People," 282.

[482] This description of Harlem resonates with the insights of another essayist in Orsi's volume, who described a street corner in the Williamsburg neighborhood of Brooklyn. In one direction, the street is named "Avenue of Puerto Rico," and in the other it

The burgeoning new field of diaspora missiology also demonstrates that American cities are characterized by immigration. In the diaspora missiology paradigm, missionaries pursue people groups that are dispersed around the globe. In this innovative approach, missionaries do not need to travel to a people group's homeland. Instead, they can reach them "on the way." As Kim notes, "The People on the Move, the phenomenon of Diaspora, are a demographic trend of the 21st century, and diaspora missiology is becoming the new 21st century paradigm for Christian mission."[483]

Wan and Casey apply the paradigm of diaspora missiology to urban America, noting that major American cities are home to thousands of foreign-born residents.[484] The diaspora has arrived on American shores, and it primarily concentrates in the major urban centers.[485] This makes possible certain disciple-making and church planting initiatives among foreign-born populations. For instance, Algera chronicles how the Christian Reformed Church in North America (CRC) has participated in a diaspora-driven church multiplication project. He notes, "The ends of the earth have come to New York."[486] Immigration is a key feature of the contemporary urban landscape.[487] This is a feature that contemporary cities share with their ancient counterparts in the Book of Acts.

---

is called "Via Vespucci." See Joseph Sciorra, "'We Go Where the Italians Live': Religious Processions as Ethnic and Territorial Markers in a Multi-ethnic Brooklyn Neighborhood," in *Gods of the City,* ed. Robert Orsi (Indianapolis: Indiana University Press, 1999), 310.

[483] Luther Jeom O. Kim, *Doing Diaspora Missiology Toward "Diaspora Mission Church"* (Eugene, OR: Wipf & Stock, 2016), 1–2.

[484] Enoch Wan and Anthony Casey, *Church Planting Among Immigrants in US Urban Centers: The "Where", "Why", and "How" of Diaspora Missiology in Action* (Portland: Institute of Diaspora Studies, 2014), 19.

[485] See www.peoplegroups.info, a website operated by the International Mission Board, for statistical data about unreached people groups in North America. It is clear from the data that cities are home to significant numbers of UPG's.

[486] John A. Algera, "The Ends of the Earth Have Come to New York: A Church Multiplication Movement in the NY Metro Area," in *Globalization and Its Effects on Urban Ministry in the 21st Century,* ed. Susan Baker (Pasadena: William Carey, 2009), 177.

[487] Harvie Conn and Manuel Ortiz, *Urban Ministry: The Kingdom, the City & the People of God* (Downers Grove, IL: IVP, 2001), 318–319.

Violence in the Cities of Acts and Contemporary Cities

Violence is another feature that links both ancient and modern cities. As Joel Kotkin observes, from the very beginning, cities were designed with safety and security in mind.[488] He notes, "Cities must, first and foremost, be safe."[489] However, even though ancient people banded together behind walls, they did not always experience physical safety. Rodney Stark argues, "Compared with even the most crime-prone modern cities, these [Greco–Roman] cities were overrun with crime."[490] Some of this crime included violence, as a quick survey of select texts from the Book of Acts will confirm.

In Jerusalem, Stephen was executed by a frenzied mob (Acts 7:54–60). The city of Damascus was the site of a foiled assassination plot against the Apostle Paul (Acts 9:19–25). Thessalonica was home to a riot (Acts 17:5–9), as was Ephesus (Acts 19:21–41). The city of Jerusalem also experienced a riot in the environs of the Temple, when the crowd seized Paul because they believed he had brought a Gentile past the court of the Gentiles (Acts 21:26–36). Each of these instances of recorded violence was religiously motivated and was directed at the early Christians. Luke does not mention any more "typical" violence, of a non-religious bent. However, at least two textual factors indicate how these outbursts of violence were also mirrored in society at large.

First, the very fact that Luke could so matter-of-factly record these instances indicates that it would not strain credulity for original Greco-Roman readers, like Theophilus. They would have understood that these types of unfortunate events did occur from time to time throughout the Roman Empire. In fact, this relates to the second textual clue regarding the presence of violence in the Greco-Roman world. In Luke's narrative,

---

[488] Joel Kotkin, *The City: A Global History* (New York: Random House, 2005), 9–12.
[489] Kotkin, *The City*, xxii.
[490] Stark, *Cities of God*, 29.

he notes that the citizens were sometimes concerned that they might be charged with rioting, and face consequences as a result (Acts 19:38–41).

Indeed, the presence of Roman garrisons was designed in large part to ensure peace throughout the Empire, including on the streets of the imperial cities. This can be seen in Acts when Luke tells his readers of the response of the Roman regiment to the riot in the Temple. The military responded to the riot by imposing order and reducing violence (Acts 21:30–37). This indicates that the pacification of all significant urban violence was one of the responsibilities of the Roman garrison.

Contemporary cities can also be known for episodic and systemic violence. For instance, the Four Corners neighborhood of Boston has been known, as McRoberts notes, for being a "high-crime, depressed area."[491] Here, urban churches must confront the sometimes-dangerous reality of "the street." Bedford-Stuveysant (known as Bed-Stuy) is a north-central Brooklyn neighborhood immediately adjacent to Crown Heights, where I reside. Historically, Bed-Stuy has experienced its share of violent activity. About Bed-Stuy, a 1940's era grand jury reported, "Gangs of hoodlums armed with ... knives and weapons commit holdups, stabbing, homicides and serious crimes."[492] The grand jury most likely was racially biased, and therefore proposed inadequate solutions. However, their reporting about the conditions in Bed-Stuy seems to reflect a consensus among a broad swath of community stakeholders.[493]

It is not just cities of the past that have been plagued by violence. The problem persists in contemporary times. In my own Brooklyn neighborhood of Crown Heights violence seems endemic. In the northeastern section of the community, an anti-gun violence non-profit called "Save Our

---

[491] Omar McRoberts, *Streets of Glory: Church and Community in a Black Urban Neighborhood* (Chicago: University of Chicago Press, 2003), 84.

[492] Clarence Taylor, *The Black Churches of Brooklyn* (New York: Columbia University Press, 1994), 111.

[493] Clarence Taylor, *The Black Churches of Brooklyn*, 111–113.

Streets"[494] has attempted to reduce violence by adopting a public health approach to reducing violence.[495] I have personally participated in street-corner vigils in the aftermath of violence.[496] I have befriended a grieving father who just lost his adult son in a knife attack and shaken the hand of a young boy paralyzed by a stray bullet.[497] The violence might look different when comparing ancient and modern cities. However, a measure of similarity exists between the violent urban centers of the Roman Empire and the violent urban centers of the 21st century.

Poverty in the Cities of Acts and Contemporary Cities

Poverty is another common factor that links the ancient and contemporary urban contexts. To assess urban poverty, researchers typically raise issues of class. However, it is difficult to uncover information on socioeconomic class in antiquity. This difficulty arises, at least in part, because of modernity's embrace of the concept of class, which was not highly relevant in antiquity. While recognizing this challenge, Stark still uses a class model and argues that the early church "was not a proletarian movement but was based on the more privileged classes."[498] For his part, Wayne Meeks deems it "vague and misleading" to assert that the early Christians were mostly middle class. He argues, "It is vague because it ignores the multidimensionality of stratification. It is misleading because

---

[494] neighborsinaction.org/sos/.

[495] *The Public Health Approach to Violence Prevention,* https://www.cdc.gov/violenceprevention/publichealthissue/publichealthapproach.html?CDC_AA_refVal=https%3A%2F%2Fwww.cdc.gov%2Fviolenceprevention%2Foverview%2Fpublichealthapproach.html.

[496] For the story of how I learned to address gun violence, see Stephen Stallard, "Voices in the Violence: How Black Churches in Brooklyn Can Help Us Find Our Voice as We Minister in Violent Contexts," *JofUM* 6, no. 1 (2020).

[497] Natalie Duddridge, *'He Asked Me Why He Can't Feel His Legs': 11-Year Old Struck by Stray Bullet May Be Paralyzed from the Waist Down,* https://newyork.cbslocal.com/2019/06/24/jayden-grant-stray-bullet-shooting/. Jayden's shooting took place on the block where this writer resides with his family.

[498] Stark, *The Rise of Christianity* (New York: HarperCollins, 1997), 33.

it tacitly assumes that there was something in the ancient Greek city corresponding to the middle class of modern industrial society."[499]

Still, others continue to assert that economics is the best tool with which to map the first Christians. Steven Friesen advocates the use of his "poverty scale" to measure the financial resources of the Pauline assemblies.[500] Friesen's focus on financial resources is helpful in reminding interpreters of the importance of wealth and poverty in antiquity. Yet his analysis falters precisely because it lacks the multidimensionality of Meeks's social status approach.[501] Wealth is merely one factor in determining social status in the biblical world, yet Friesen seems to make it the primary issue.

Both Friesen and Meeks are helpful because they remind the reader of different facets of ancient identity. Friesen reminds his readers about wealth, or the lack thereof, while Meeks focuses his readers more broadly upon the types of complex social statuses that could exist in antiquity. It is apparent from their research that poverty did exist in some parts of the Roman Empire. This problem of poverty seemed to be exacerbated in the imperial cities. Indeed, as Keener notes, "The poor constituted the majority of cities' residents; at Pompeii they even constituted a sufficiently significant voting bloc that 'the beggars' could 'demand' someone's election. In Rome they often lacked enough food, and they had to pay high rent for wretched lodgings."[502]

Poverty is also ubiquitous in contemporary American cities. At this point, two important disclaimers are in order. First, this does not mean that all the poor live in cities. Poverty is a problem for many rural

---

[499] Meeks, *The First Urban Christians*, 54.

[500] Steven J. Friesen, "Poverty in Pauline Studies: Beyond the So-called New Consensus," *JSNT* 26, no. 3 (2004): 323–361.

[501] See two excellent responses to Friesen: John Barclay, "Poverty in Pauline Studies: A Response to Steven Friesen," *JSNT* 26, no. 3 (2004): 363–366; and Peter Oakes, "Constructing Poverty Scales for Graeco-Roman Society: A Response to Steven Friesen's 'Poverty in Pauline Studies,'" *JSNT* 26, no. 3 (2004): 367–371.

[502] Keener *Acts, 2*:1056.

settings, both nationally and internationally. Second, this does not mean that cities are dominated by the poor. Far from it, the very wealthy also usually live and work in urban centers. A city like New York, for instance, is home to Wall Street, and the wealthy bankers and investment managers who work there. The present analysis is not an attempt to discuss wealth and poverty in tandem. Instead, I am merely attempting to point out that poverty is a common factor that was similar between ancient cities (like those found in the Book of Acts) and modern cities.

Poverty seems to be a constant in many contemporary urban centers. As Glaeser notes, "Cities can be places of great inequality; they attract some of the world's richest and poorest people."[503] Churches have long grappled with how to engage in holistic ministry that transforms impoverished communities.[504] This is exacerbated by the ongoing contemporary phenomenon of gentrification, in which people with more wealth move into urban communities that were historically impoverished. In rapid fashion, this can lead to a complete transformation of the neighborhood, with both positive and negative outcomes.[505] While neighbor-hood transformation is underway (as a result of gentrification) in my own neighborhood of Crown Heights, poverty is still ever present.

Tragically, data from 2008 demonstrates that one-quarter of Community District 8 (which roughly corresponds to northern Crown Heights) is impoverished, and that over one-third of children live below the poverty line.[506] Newer data (especially emerging from the 2020 census) will no

---

[503] Glaeser, *Triumph of the City*, 257.

[504] McRoberts, *Streets of Glory*, 100–121. See also Taylor, *The Black Churches of Brooklyn*, 157–160.

[505] For a discussion of gentrification in Brooklyn, and how it impacts both church planting efforts and the urban poor, see Stephen Stallard, "Placemaking in the City: A Theological Vision for Church Planters in Brooklyn's Gentrifying Neighborhoods," *IJUT* 4 (May 2019): 47–59.

[506] *Community District 8 Brooklyn Neighborhood Report*, https://issuu.com/studybrooklyn/docs/community-district-8-brooklyn-neighborhood-report.

doubt demonstrate that these numbers have shifted somewhat as the neighborhood has experienced a measure of renewal.[507]

However, simple observation leads me to conclude that poverty (and corresponding phenomena, such as homelessness) remains a challenge in Crown Heights. For instance, our daughter attends a public school only two blocks from our apartment. On that block, some of our homeless neighbors built a home, using a street bench and a large tarp. At least two people lived there, and we passed it regularly as went about our lives. The temporary shelter existed during long stretches of the COVID-19 pandemic, reminding us that some of our neighbors were at greater risk of catching the Coronavirus. Clearly, poverty continues to thrive in urban contexts, demonstrating once again the link between ancient and modern cities.

Influence in the Cities of Acts and Contemporary Cities

When one reads the early chapters of Genesis one discovers that cities have always been influential (Gen 4:17 and Gen 11:1–9). This was still true in the world of the Acts of the Apostles. Meeks notes, "The cities of the Mediterranean world were at the leading edge of the great political and social changes that occurred during the six and a half centuries from Alexander to Constantine."[508] The cities were centers of commerce and culture, of education and entertainment, and of passion and politics. The polis (to use the Greek term which was used in the first century) influenced its entire region.[509] This can even be discerned through a close reading of the Book of Acts.

---

[507] It should also be noted that poverty can decrease in urban neighborhoods simply because the poor, through gentrification, are displaced to other communities. Under this scenario, the median income goes up because the poor have moved out.

[508] Meeks, *The First Urban Christians,* 11

[509] Anthony Le Donne, "Complicating the Category of Ethnos toward Poliscentrism: A Possible Way Forward within Second Temple Ethnography," in *The Urban World and the First Christians,* ed. Steve Walton, Paul Trebilco, and David W. J. Gill (Grand Rapids: Eerdmans, 2017), 9–13.

Jerusalem was influential even beyond its borders, as evidenced by the fact that pilgrims came from as far as Africa to learn the spirituality of the Hebrews (Acts 8:27). Philippi was an important Roman colony. As Luke notes, it was "a leading city of the district of Macedonia" (Acts 16:12), one that was home to both commercial (Acts 16:14) and spiritual (Acts 16:16–18) influences. Paul spent two years ministering in the city of Ephesus. As a result, the entire region heard the gospel proclaimed (Acts 19:9–10). It is possible that Paul grasped the influential nature of first century cities, and therefore targeted them with his missionary efforts.[510] Attempts to discern a Pauline strategy have not been entirely successful. However, we can determine that the cities in Acts were influential in society, and that Paul spent much of his time ministering in these urban centers.

Contemporary cities are still sites of influence upon society at large. Bergquist and Crane note, "Decisions are made on a daily basis in offices in Tokyo, New York, and London that impact the lives of villagers in remote parts of Nepal or Nigeria. Due to the higher percentage of the world's most influential decision-makers being in cities, particularly global cities, these cities wield disproportionate influence on the world."[511] Indeed, urban theorist Glaeser argues that cities are the site for the planet's most important innovations.[512] Indeed, one can look at Brooklyn and note its cultural influence, both in the past and in the present.

In the more distant past, Brooklyn impacted American society through the work of notable figures such as the poet Walt Whitman. Whitman, a Brooklyn resident for most of his life, even wrote a poem about

---

[510] Volker Rabens, "Paul's Mission Strategy in the Urban Landscape of the First-Century Roman Empire," in *The Urban World and the First Christians,* ed. Steve Walton, Paul Trebilco, and David W. J. Gill (Grand Rapids: Eerdmans, 2017), 99–122.

[511] Bergquist and Crane, *City Shaped Churches,* 50.

[512] This can be seen in the subtitle to his book, *Triumph of the City: How Our Greatest Invention Makes Us Richer, Smarter, Greener, Healthier, and Happier.* See Glaeser, *Triumph of the City* for his detailed argument.

watching the ferry bringing people "home" from Manhattan. In it, he declares, "Brooklyn of ample hills was mine."[513] "Brownstoners" built upon the legacy of Whitman, and they moved to Brooklyn as "pioneers" who settled in (and eventually transformed) the "urban wilderness."[514] The ripple effects of this cultural moment continue to be felt today.

In another cultural stream, Brooklyn has long been a center for influential black culture, alongside of Harlem and the Bronx. As Zukin notes, "When Biggie and Jay-Z rapped 'Where you from?' on the chorus of 'Brooklyn's Finest' (1996), they offered a shout-out to the neighborhoods spanning central Brooklyn."[515] These neighborhoods included, among others, Bed-Stuy, Crown Heights, and Brownsville, neighborhoods from which my church has drawn some of its members. This Black influence extends to the broader American society through hip-hop, politics, and sports.

These various streams of cultural influence converged recently as NBA superstar Kevin Durant chose to play for the Brooklyn Nets[516] in "The house that Jay-Z built."[517] What happens in Brooklyn (and other major American urban centers) eventually happens in other parts of the country. The worlds of art, fashion, athletics, politics, and more are shaped and reshaped in cities, and then eventually exported to the suburbs and beyond. Like many of the cities of the Book of Acts, modern cities have a tremendous amount of social influence.

---

[513] Walt Whitman, *Crossing Brooklyn Ferry*, https://www.poetryfoundation.org/poems/45470/crossing-brooklyn-ferry.

[514] Suleiman Osman, *The Invention of Brownstone Brooklyn: Gentrification and the Search for Authenticity in Postwar New York* (Oxford: Oxford University Press, 2011), 51.

[515] Sharon Zukin, *Naked City: The Death and Life of Authentic Urban Spaces* (Oxford: Oxford University Press, 2010), 56.

[516] Scott Cacciola and Marc Stein, *Kevin Durant to Join Nets in N.B.A. Free Agency*, https://www.nytimes.com/2019/06/30/sports/kevin-durant-nets.html.

[517] David K. Li, *Garden Wilting at No. 2 as Barclays Center named highest-grossing venue in US*, https://nypost.com/2013/07/24/garden-wilting-at-no-2-as-barclays-center-named-highest-grossing-venue-in-us/.

Several commonalities exist between the cities of antiquity (including those described in the Book of Acts) and contemporary cities. These commonalities include (but are not limited to) diversity, immigration, violence, poverty, and social influence. Given these similarities, it makes sense for practitioners in urban settings to consider the benefits of adopting (and adapting) the ancient urban practice of deploying diverse teams. We will explore the potential usage of such a practice in the next section.

Applying the Model from Acts to Contemporary Urban Centers

Earlier in this book we discovered that a pattern of multicultural teams exists within the Book of Acts. These diverse teams were deployed in primarily urban contexts. Since there is much similarity between the cities of Acts and contemporary cities, I have argued for the retrieval of this ancient urban methodology. In this section, I want to consider two additional issues. First, we must grapple with the nature of the teams in the Book of Acts. Were they identical to contemporary church staffs, or were they more analogous to missionary teams? Second, we must reexamine the issue of a mandate. Specifically, does a pattern of diverse teams in the Book of Acts mean that contemporary urban practitioners must employ this method?

Teams from Berea to Brooklyn

In Chapters Four and Five we examined the nine discernably distinct teams in the Book of Acts. Some of them were church leadership teams (Jerusalem and Antioch are prominent examples). Some of them were roving bands of church planters (most of the Pauline teams).[518] One

---

[518] See C. Gordon Olson, *What in the World Is God Doing?* (Cedar Knolls, NJ: Global Gospel Publishers, 2003), 314, who wonders whether Paul's band of colleagues was the "beginnings of a mission agency."

team was charged with a diplomatic mission of benevolence (the "Return to Jerusalem Team"). Consequently, it is not possible to categorize all these teams as church leadership teams. The broader term "ministry team" seems more appropriate.

In Chapter One we set out to discover if diverse teams were a part of an ancient approach to urban mission. We also set out to discover if this ancient approach was one that should be employed today. We sought to discover a model for leadership teams in urban Christian ministries, both inside and outside the church. This focus was intentionally broad enough to cover urban church staffs, urban mission organizations, and urban nonprofits.

A broader statement has at least two advantages. First, it more closely corresponds to what is seen in the text of Acts. In the Book of Acts, the reader observes that the ministry teams are different. Some operate within the church, as the recognized leaders of a local church (Acts 13:1). Some operate outside the church, as roving apostolic bands of disciple-makers who plant churches (Acts 16) and deliver donations (Acts 20:4). Second, the broader term "ministry team" is more readily applicable to a wider swath of urban ministries. For instance, churches, homeless shelters, seminaries, and church planting networks could all potentially utilize aspects of the multicultural team model from Acts.

Two hypothetical examples demonstrate how this model could potentially benefit two different types of urban ministries. The first example will be a church plant in New York, sponsored by a North American church planting network. The second example will be a mission organization that is reaching unreached people groups (UPG's) in New York. In the first example, a church planter with a desire to start a multicultural church could recruit a diverse team to join him in this venture. He could then serve alongside some of these team members, as they eventually constitute the multicultural staff of this church.

In the second example, an urban mission organization could strategically set out to engage certain UPG's with the gospel, with the eventual goal of starting indigenous churches within these UPG's. They could, when possible, recruit team members from various cultures to facilitate the flow of the gospel across cultural boundaries. As disciples are made within these various UPG's, the original diverse team does not "settle down" as the staff of the nascent church(es). Instead, they would continue to function as coaches and catalysts who work to birth new indigenous churches throughout various UPG's.

In both examples, the ministry teams were diverse. In the first, the culturally diverse church planting team eventually became a culturally diverse church staff. In the second, the culturally diverse missionary band continued to foster new disciple-making movements within a variety of cultures.

In contemporary urban contexts both approaches might at times be useful. In fact, some might find that certain cities lend themselves to a combination of the two approaches. In some ways, this has been my experience. I initially recruited a diverse team to assist in the planting of a multicultural church. A multicultural church emerged from this process and was led by the diverse staff. However, the church plant quickly became a leadership incubator, as leaders were continually developed and deployed to engage in both monocultural and multicultural contexts. Thus far, our church plant has sent out a Taiwanese pastor to Manhattan's Chinatown, a Korean planter[519] with a multicultural vision to Queens, a Haitian leader to the Haitian context of south Brooklyn, and a tri-cultural couple who desire to serve as overseas missionaries. Presently, we are developing a Malaysian leader who has a vision for multicultural ministry.

---

[519] The Korean missionary we deployed is not merely pastoring. He also leads a non-profit that operates a food truck that serves gourmet meals to the homeless of NYC. During the early days of COVID, when NYC was locked in a life-and-death struggle, the church that I pastor partnered with this non-profit to provide food relief to some of our physically and financially vulnerable neighbors.

The diverse team that planted our church has not "settled down" to serve as the church staff. Although some have stayed for a time, the situation has been much more fluid. The church strives to be catalytic and mobilize leaders to engage in various monocultural and multicultural contexts. In this way, perhaps our ministry context is somewhat analogous to Paul's sojourn in Ephesus, where he strategically developed and deployed leaders who served with him and then went out on mission.

When assessing the ministry teams of Acts, a pattern of diversity becomes apparent. Ministry teams (of various types) in contemporary cites could consider embracing the model of multicultural teams that is seen in the Book of Acts. However, the fact that these teams might consider a multicultural model does not mean they must embrace a multicultural model. We will explore this question in the subsequent section.

Are Diverse Teams a Biblical Requirement?

So far, we have established that different kinds of diverse ministry teams existed in the Book of Acts. We have also demonstrated a close similarity between many present-day urban contexts and many of the cities of the Book of Acts. However, this leaves unresolved the issue of a mandate. Are diverse teams a best practice for ministries in contemporary cities? Or are they a required biblical mandate, based upon the narrative of Acts?

To answer this question, we must return in part to the data of Chapter Two. There, we examined various proposals for the genre of Acts, as well as various models for applying Acts. We tentatively concluded that both historiographical and biographical genres lend themselves towards mimesis (imitation). Ancient history writing, we learned, was written with an end in mind. In Luke's case, part of the purpose of Luke-Acts was Christian formation (oftentimes called discipleship).

Luke narrates the story of Jesus (in Luke) and then the Apostles (in Acts) to summon his readers to carry on the movement in the way of

Jesus and the Apostles. Indeed, this reading of Luke-Acts helps to explain the enigmatic ending of the Book of Acts. Instead of telling the reader how Paul's story ended, Luke leaves the narrative open ended. This was a brilliant literary maneuver, one that invites the readers into the story. In essence, Luke is encouraging his readers to carry on in the spirit of Paul, who carried on in the spirit of Jesus.

And yet, what does it mean to carry on in the spirit of Paul? As we noted in Chapter Two, some of the Book of Acts is historically unrepeatable and cannot be replicated. For instance, although the church at Jerusalem practiced communal living and fully shared their possessions, we are not told that any other churches did the same in Acts. This seems to have been an isolated incident that was probably due to the famine in Jerusalem and the impoverishment of the Christians in that city. Since no recurring pattern of communal living emerges, it cannot meet the standard established by the "representative patterns" approach to reading Acts that I advocated in Chapter Two.

The issue of diverse teams is more complex since multiple instances of multicultural ministry teams occur in Acts. I have assessed that six out of nine teams in Acts were multicultural. This constitutes a pattern, especially when considered in conjunction with the direction of the narrative. As the story progresses, diverse teams become more common (and homogenous teams are eventually no longer mentioned).

Based upon the pattern of diversity and the multicultural trajectory of Acts, I lean towards the idea of a mandate. In diverse settings (like contemporary cities), we should strongly consider the wisdom of the early church and deploy diverse teams. In my estimation, this is more than a best practice; this is the pattern established by the Holy Spirit and the Early Church. Some readers (both scholars and practitioners) might disagree. I can live with that disagreement and respect an alternative point of view. I am unwilling to say that my way is the only way. However,

I do believe that contemporary urban ministries should retrieve this element of the Church's ancient approach to urban mission.

Challenges and Opportunities for Diverse Teams

I have argued for the retrieval of an ancient approach to urban mission, one that equips and deploys diverse teams. However, utilizing this approach has significant challenges. In what follows, it will be impossible to catalogue all the obstacles that could keep multicultural teams from thriving. Instead, we will conclude this chapter by examining a handful of the challenges and opportunities faced by diverse teams. In subsequent sections we will explore the dynamics of cultural equity, cultural intelligence, and cultural tension, and we will make preliminary recommendations in each area.

Cultural Equity

Equity could be described as the practice of treating people justly. Implicit in this idea is the notion that equity rules out favoritism and partiality.[520] In an equitable system, all people are treated with the same level of justice. In a culturally diverse team, members of the team (and especially its leaders) will need to assess the level of cultural equity on the team. In other words, those who strive for diverse teams should consider whether all members of the team are being treated with the same measure of justice. This is another way of describing the concept of cultural equity.

A brief survey of some of the literature birthed out of the modern American multicultural church movement will demonstrate that practitioners strongly believe that cultural equity is important on multicultural teams. I agree with this assessment and would propose two criteria for evaluating the level of cultural equity on a multicultural team. First, team leaders should assess how many culturally "other" people serve on the

---

[520] Merriam-Webster, *Merriam-Webster's Dictionary*, https://www.merriam-webster.com/dictionary/equity.

team. Second, team leaders should assess how power is shared among the culturally diverse team members. In this section, we will explore both criteria, along with relevant insights from the nascent field of multicultural church studies.

It should be noted at the outset that not all the literature cited will utilize the same terms to refer to diverse teams. The terms multiracial, multiethnic, multicultural, and intercultural will all be referenced in the pages that follow. Typically, the various authors mean something similar to one another. They are referencing the diverse nature of churches and/or teams.

Sociologist George Yancey studied successful multiracial churches and he catalogued the traits exemplified in these churches.[521] One of these traits was that of diverse leadership.[522] However, Yancey cautions his readers against misapplying this insight. For Yancey, the drive to diversify is not, he notes, "a call for direct proportionality."[523] If the membership roll of a church is split equally between Chinese, Spanish, and Russian congregants, it does not follow that the church must employ a staff member from each group. Instead, Yancey believes that multiracial churches should work towards the goal of diverse teams because it illustrates "to members of racial groups who are not in the numerical majority that they have a voice."[524] Yancey understands that perception is usually reality. If those who are served by an urban ministry (whether it be a church, soup kitchen, or homeless shelter) perceive that the ministry is staffed by people who are culturally diverse, they will likely feel as if the ministry exists to meet their needs. They will likely feel at home in such a ministry.

---

[521] George Yancey, *One Body One Spirit: Principles of Successful Multiracial Churches* (Downers Grove, IL: IVP, 2003).
[522] Yancey, *One Body One Spirit*, 85–97.
[523] Yancey, *One Body One Spirit*, 96.
[524] Yancey, *One Body One Spirit*, 97.

The sociological insights of Yancey are matched by the pastoral experiences of both planters and pastors.[525] A notable voice is that of Rodney Woo, who successfully transitioned a Southern Baptist Church in Houston from a predominantly white congregation into a diverse church with over forty nationalities represented.[526] As part of this daunting journey, he notes, "The church needed to raise spiritually effective leadership from each racial group on our congregation."[527] As Woo narrates his story, it is apparent just how difficult that task can be. In addition to seeking to develop a diverse group of leaders, Woo was also committed to developing leaders who could minister effectively in a multiracial context. This included, he notes, a commitment to "shared diverse leadership,"[528] a model that Woo embraced in part because of his recognition of multicultural teams in the Book of Acts.[529]

Those who have studied multicultural ministries (like Yancey) and led multicultural ministries (like Woo) should be recognized as thought leaders in this field. They are representative of a larger group of researchers and practitioners who assert that a diverse team is an important ingredient in a healthy diverse ministry. Indeed, additional anecdotal evidence supports this claim.

My first experience serving at a multicultural church was as the youth pastor of a multicultural church plant in a bedroom community outside of New York City. When a Haitian teenager visited the church after relocating from Harlem, he stayed (by his own admission), because the preacher who spoke when he visited looked like him. The African

---

[525] Mark DeYmaz, *Building a Healthy Multi-Ethnic Church* (San Francisco: Jossey-Bass, 2007), 70–80; Darryl Williamson, "Word and Witness: Church Leadership for Twenty–First Century Gospel Missions," in *All Are Welcome: Toward a Multi-Everything Church*, ed. Leon Brown (USA: White Blackbird Books, 2018), 209–226.

[526] Rodney Woo, *The Color of Church: A Biblical and Practical Paradigm for Multiracial Churches* (Nashville: B&H, 2009).

[527] Woo, *The Color of Church*, 203.

[528] Woo, *The Color of Church*, 210.

[529] Woo, *The Color of Church*, 211–213.

American preacher who spoke that day was the associate pastor, one who was tasked with overseeing discipleship and preaching monthly in the church. This Haitian teenager from Harlem saw someone in the pulpit who looked like him, and so was willing to attend a youth group led by me (even though I did not look like him). This teenager eventually trusted Christ and was baptized alongside his Guyanese friend. All of this was made possible by the existence of a diverse ministry team.

However, cultural equity should extend beyond the mere inclusion of the diverse "other" on a team. To truly strive for cultural equity, the diverse "other" members of the team must possess real power. Roembke asserts, "One cannot speak of the encounter of cultures without dealing with the issue of power."[530] In recognition of this reality, Hong argues that people should be "equals at the table."[531] Her fellow essayist, Daniel Hill, agrees, arguing for what he terms "just power."[532] Hill believes issues of power dynamics existed in the early church, some of which were described in the Book of Acts. He argues, "Luke intuitively understood what any of us who work with intercultural organizations do: that when different cultural groups unite together, the most critical dynamic revolves around how power is shared."[533] In Hill's reading of Acts 6, the apostles "created a pathway for leaders in the marginalized group [the Hellenists] to emerge (Acts 6:3–7). It was both effective and honoring of everyone in the community." [534]

Both Hong and Hill argue for the same ideal. They do not want diversity on leadership teams simply for the sake of multiculturalism.

---

[530] Lianne Roembke, *Building Credible Multicultural Teams* (Pasadena: William Carey, 2000), 31.

[531] Angie Hong, "Equals at the Table," in *Intercultural Ministry: Hope for a Changing World,* ed. Grace Ji-Sun Kim and Jann Aldredge-Clanton (Valley Forge, PA: Judson Press, 2017), 124–133.

[532] Daniel Hill, "Just Power: Ten Principles for Building Intercultural Leadership Teams," in *Intercultural Ministry: Hope for a Changing World,* ed. Grace Ji-Sun Kim and Jann Aldredge-Clanton (Valley Forge, PA: Judson Press, 2017), 111–123.

[533] Hill, "Just Power," 111.

[534] Hill, "Just Power," 112.

They believe that this will make the minority team members feel like mere tokens of diversity. Instead, they want a robust diversity, one that truly empowers the culturally diverse "others" on the team. I have experienced some of these power dynamics while leading a multicultural ministry team in Brooklyn. Currently, the five-person leadership team of our church includes those from European-American, Haitian, Guyanese, and Malaysian backgrounds. Since I am the senior leader, and since I am from the majority culture, it has been important to ensure that the diverse "others" on the team have a real voice in shaping the direction of the church. This means these leaders lead ministries, preach on Sunday's, design the worship services, and occasionally even overrule me. Admittedly, this is not an easy approach. However, like Hong and Hill, I believe the model is worthwhile.[535]

If ministry teams in urban settings adopt a diverse model, this will necessitate cultural equity. This would lead to the inclusion of the culturally diverse "other" on ministry teams of organizations in the urban context. Ideally, this would also lead to the empowerment of team members who hail from minority cultures. It should be noted that what constitutes "majority culture" and "minority culture" varies from place to place. In the United States, European Americans constitute the majority culture. However, in many local contexts (like Manhattan's Chinatown) this will not be the case. Regardless of which group constitutes the dominant culture, it is desirable to learn to follow the approach of Jesus, who laid aside privilege and power to serve others (Phil. 2:5–11). In the subsequent section, we will briefly engage the field of cultural intelligence, to consider how this might benefit diverse teams in urban contexts.

---

[535] See also Grace Ji-Sun Kim and Graham Hill, *Healing Our Broken Humanity: Practices for Revitalizing the Church and Renewing the World* (Downers Grove, IL: IVP, 2018), 76–90, who urge their readers to "relinquish power." They even point to an online "Power Audit" that can be taken by team members: www.theglobalchurchproject.com/power/.

Cultural Intelligence

The field of cultural intelligence is relatively new and was first developed by professors who taught business in London and Singapore. In their pioneering monograph from the early 2000's, Earley and Ang highlight the intercultural challenges of the globalized world. They note, "The challenge for an international sojourner is that in highly novel cultures, most of the cues and behaviors that are familiar may be lacking, so entirely new interpretations and behaviors are required. A person who is able to generate such new and appropriate responses has a high cultural intelligence."[536] In response to this dilemma, Earley and Ang set forth a "theoretical model" to help explain why certain individuals adapt better across cultures.[537] Their theoretical model was refined and popularized by management expert David Livermore, who has written extensively on cultural intelligence (also called CQ), with application to the realms of both business and religion.[538] Because Livermore's work is so crucial to this burgeoning field, it is important to understand his thinking.

According to Livermore, Cultural Intelligence (CQ) is a combination of four capabilities. The first, he notes, is "CQ Drive (Motivation): Having the Interest, Confidence, and Drive to Adapt Cross-Culturally."[539] Livermore notes that one cannot be apathetic towards cultural adaptation. One must possess a strong internal desire to adapt cross-culturally if one is to succeed in developing a high level of cultural intelligence. Livermore asserts that the second capability is "CQ Knowledge (Cognition): Understanding Intercultural Norms and Differences."[540] This is the aspect of cultural awareness that is usually taught in diversity trai-

---

[536] P. Christopher Earley and Soon Ang, *Cultural Intelligence: Individual Interactions Across Cultures* (Stanford: Stanford University Press, 2003), xii.

[537] Earley and Ang, *Cultural Intelligence*, xii.

[538] David Livermore, *Leading with Cultural Intelligence* (New York: AMACOM, 2015); David Livermore, *Cultural Intelligence: Improving Your CQ to Engage Our Multicultural World* (Grand Rapids: Baker, 2009).

[539] Livermore, *Leading with Cultural Intelligence*, 27.

[540] Livermore, *Leading with Cultural Intelligence*, 28.

ning for corporations and non-profits. Employees are generally taught about various cultures with the hope that they will learn how to successfully navigate them. Yet the advocates of cultural intelligence seek to put this cultural training in proper perspective by linking it with the other three CQ capabilities. Livermore, for instance, believed that CQ knowledge could be detrimental if uncoupled from the rest of the desired traits.[541]

The third capability is what Livermore terms "CQ Strategy (Metacognition): Making Sense of Culturally Diverse Experiences and Planning Accordingly."[542] This is one of the crucial differences between cultural intelligence and mere diversity training. Corporations who emphasize diversity training do not always make the leap from teaching about cultures to equipping their employees to apply what they have learned in a multicultural environment. This element of CQ is "the ability to draw on your cultural understanding to solve culturally complex problems."[543]

The fourth capability charted was that of "CQ Action (Behavioral): Changing Verbal and Nonverbal Actions Appropriately When Interacting Cross-Culturally."[544] Livermore rightly maintained that the ability of individuals to act in a culturally appropriate way in a cross-cultural setting was vital to success. The Cultural Intelligence Scale (CQS) was developed by researchers to measure the four CQ capabilities. The CQS scale was first demonstrated to be empirically valid in 2007, and its credibility has only grown since that time.[545] This measurement system

---

[541] Livermore, *Leading with Cultural Intelligence*, 29.
[542] Ibid..
[543] Livermore, *Leading with Cultural Intelligence*, 29.
[544] Ibid.
[545] S. Ang et al., "Cultural Intelligence: Its Measurement and Effects on Cultural Judgment and Decision Making, Cultural Adaptation, and Task Performance," *MOR* 3 (2007): 335–371.

was used as the foundation for various assessment tools which are available online at www.culturalq.com.[546]

Various management experts have attempted to apply the CQ model to teams. Earley and Ang note that cultural intelligence can facilitate diversity on an individual, team, and organizational level.[547] Flaherty warns, "Multicultural teams can experience difficulties with integration that keep them from reaching their potential."[548] However, she also notes that some multinational teams with higher levels of cultural intelligence have successfully mitigated some of those potential problems.[549] Potential problems can emerge when people from various cultures are brought together and given a shared task. These challenges can be seen on athletic teams, academic teams, business teams, governmental teams, and ministry teams. If urban ministries plan to adopt a diverse approach to teams, they would be wise to train their members in cultural intelligence.

Some might wonder how Christians should appropriate the social-science insights of cultural intelligence. Is there a distinctly Christian approach to cultural intelligence? At this point, Hirpo Kumbi and Soong-Chan Rah are helpful interlocutors,[550] having both written on themes related to cultural intelligence. Kumbi writes from the international context as an Ethiopian church planter in the United Kingdom. He

---

[546] In 2018, this writer purchased and utilized one of these tools: the *CQ Pro Self-Assessment*.

[547] Earley and Ang, *Cultural Intelligence*, 256–257.

[548] Jane Flaherty, "The Effects of Cultural Intelligence on Team Member Acceptance and Integration in Multinational Teams," in *Handbook of Cultural Intelligence: Theory, Measurement, and Applications*, ed. Soon Ang and Linn Van Dyne (New York: Routledge, 2008), 193.

[549] Flaherty, "The Effects of Cultural Intelligence on Team Member Acceptance and Integration in Multinational Teams," 192–205. For a similar approach, see Thomas Rockstuhl and Kok-Yee Ng, "The Effects of Cultural Intelligence on Interpersonal Trust in Multicultural Teams," in *Handbook of Cultural Intelligence: Theory, Measurement, and Applications*, ed. Soon Ang and Linn Van Dyne (New York: Routledge, 2008), 206–220.

[550] Hirpo Kumbi, *The Culturally Intelligent Leader: Developing Multi-ethnic Communities in a Multicultural Age* (Watford, England: Instant Apostle, 2017); Soong-Chan Rah, *Many Colors: Cultural Intelligence for a Changing Church* (Chicago: Moody, 2010).

asserts, "The type of leader needed in a multi-ethnic missional community is one who is able to understand the complex and sometimes contradictory elements of such multicultural groups."[551] Kumbi crucially connects cultural intelligence with worldview. He declares, "A cultural quotient (CQ) .... includes a questioning of ... world view."[552] He demonstrated how cultural intelligence could be used in ministry by noting that culturally intelligent leaders would need to grapple with the dynamics involved in honor-shame cultures.[553] For Kumbi, cultural intelligence is an essential part of the tool-kit of an intercultural minister.

Soong-Chan Rah writes from the urban North American context as a Korean American. He notes, "The church, operating out of the context of communicating God's truth, should also see the need for cultural intelligence in order to more effectively communicate God's truth to a changing world and church."[554] Rah injected the cultural intelligence conversation with two key ingredients: theology and history. Theologically, he sought to frame the discussion with a biblical understanding of culture rooted in the imago dei (Gen. 1:26–28). He memorably declared that God wanted humanity to "Be fruitful and culture-fy."[555]

Rah also points to the role of history in formulating one's method of cultural intelligence. In prophetic fashion, he reminds his readers that our collective American culture has been shaped by the sins of our ancestors. He laments the racial injustices perpetrated in American

---

[551] Kumbi, *The Culturally Intelligent Leader*, 58.

[552] Kumbi, *The Culturally Intelligent Leader*, 59. This connection with anthropology reminds the reader of the excellent work done by Paul Hiebert on the connection between mission, anthropology and worldviews. Although he did not use the terminology of cultural intelligence, what Hiebert proposed was a high degree of cultural literacy that would enable missionaries to exegete culture and conduct deep discipleship that would result in worldview transformation. See Paul Hiebert, *Transforming Worldviews: An Anthropological Understanding of How People Change* (Grand Rapids: Baker Academic, 2008).

[553] Kumbi, *The Culturally Intelligent Leader*, 64.

[554] Rah, *Many Colors*, 12.

[555] Rah, *Many Colors*, 27.

history, from slavery to segregation.[556] Rah took care to help his readers spot their cultural biases and reflect upon their own power and privilege. For Rah, this is indispensable when constructing a method for cultural intelligence.

How can one sort through the underlying scientific theories of business experts like Earley, Ang, and Livermore and then attach them to the theology and methodology of both Kumbi and Rah? What is a helpful way for those who lead multicultural teams to appropriate the insights of the field of cultural intelligence? In seeking to answer this question, I am instantly reminded of the limits of cultural intelligence. Livermore poignantly declares, "Becoming culturally intelligent means we have to do more than simply change the way we talk to our culturally diverse colleagues. We have to actually transform the way we see each other."[557]

This sounds somewhat utopian, and a reader might be forgiven if she is left wondering if that is a realistic possibility. Is it possible for such deep transformation to occur? A reader operating from within a Christian worldview will certainly answer in the affirmative. With Christ (and only with Christ) is this possible. What is necessary is to "baptize" cultural intelligence theories with orthodox doctrines, such as the imago dei and the gospel. Doing so will enable practitioners to have a better foundation for developing the four cultural intelligence capabilities.[558]

Like Kumbi and Rah, urban missionaries and activists can learn from the social sciences and from their own history to develop a greater cultural quotient. Those who lead diverse teams will instantly spot the value of such an approach. Yet this cannot be adopted merely based upon

---

[556] Rah, *Many Colors*, 40–59. See also, Mark Charles and Soong-Chan Rah, *Unsettling Truths: The Ongoing, Dehumanizing Legacy of the Doctrine of Discovery* (Downers Grove, IL: IVP, 2019).

[557] Livermore, *Leading with Cultural Intelligence*, 40.

[558] I am not suggesting that those with right doctrine will automatically be able to successfully lead multicultural teams. Leading multicultural teams requires cultural intelligence, which takes work to develop. Leading multicultural teams requires a certain skill set that might not be possessed by all those who adhere to orthodox doctrine.

pragmatism. Team leaders should not become culturally intelligent simply to motivate their multicultural teams to perform at a high level. They should become culturally intelligent because God has called Christians to love their neighbors (Mark 12:31). Urban ministers should become culturally intelligent because Jesus modeled the self-sacrificial love of "The Other" (Phil. 2:1–11).

An approach such as this requires cultural humility. It means an individual must recognize that her culture might not have all the answers and that she might be blind to certain realities because of her cultural upbringing. An approach such as this requires listening to people from other cultures as well as learning from them. Above all, it requires proximity. One can only learn so much about other cultures from a book, podcast, or from Twitter. What is required of leaders is that they immerse themselves into the lives of their culturally "other" team members.[559]

When leaders embrace this path of vulnerability, they will be shaped and taught by the diverse "others." This is the long, never-ending path towards a biblically based cultural intelligence. The field of cultural intelligence has already been applied to various facets of Christian ministry, from short-term mission trips to preaching.[560] However, the most fertile realm of application probably lies in the field of urban missiology. Contemporary cities could benefit from diverse ministry teams that possess high levels of cultural intelligence.

---

[559] See Michael Emerson and George Yancey, *Transcending Racial Barriers: Towards a Mutual Obligations Approach* (New York: Oxford University Press, 2011), 73–90, for a discussion of the "Contact Hypothesis."

[560] David Livermore, *Serving with Eyes Wide Open: Doing Short-Term Missions with Cultural Intelligence* (Grand Rapids: Baker, 2013); Matthew Kim, *Preaching with Cultural Intelligence: Understanding the People Who Hear Our Sermons* (Grand Rapids: Baker, 2017).

Cultural Tension

Anyone who has led a ministry team knows that tension will inevitably surface.[561] It does not necessarily follow that the tension is ungodly. In team settings, various opinions, strategies, and agendas will be present. A team leader must work to marshal these various perspectives and strengths, unite the team, and launch it towards the agreed upon vision. In a multicultural team, the potential for tension between team members can be heightened. Elmer notes, "What is surprising is not that we have so many conflicts but that, given everyone's cultural centeredness, there are not more conflicts."[562]

In fact, as Silzer observes, we all develop culture-based judging systems (CbJS) based, in part, upon our upbringing.[563] She opines that "when you encounter different cultural ways of doing things, you decide (judge) that your preferred pattern is right and that other patterns are wrong."[564] Multiple culturally based judging systems will exist on a diverse ministry team, and this can lead to tension. For instance, different team members might have divergent approaches to decision-making, conflict resolution, spiritual warfare, and justice. The challenge for those who lead multicultural teams is to discern the appropriate response when tension emerges because of these various culturally based judging systems.

When considering this question, it is important to acknowledge that not all tension must be eliminated. If various team members have different perspectives based upon their cultural backgrounds, that does not mean this is unhealthy. Team leaders would be unwise if they sought

---

[561] See, for example, Jimmy Stallard, *Facing the Sons of Thunder: Biblical Principles for Conflict Resolution* (Huntsville, AL: Evangel Publications, 2007), for a discussion of peacemaking.

[562] Duane Elmer, *Cross-Cultural Conflict: Building Relationships for Effective Ministry* (Downers Grove, IL: IVP, 1993), 2.

[563] Sheryl Takagi Silzer, *Biblical Multicultural Teams: Applying Biblical Truth to Cultural Differences* (Pasadena: William Carey, 2011).

[564] Silzer, *Biblical Multicultural Teams*, 21.

to eliminate such tension. Instead, tension should be managed, and even embraced, when appropriate. In fact, much decision making on ministry teams could be enhanced through a frank but healthy exchange of various perspectives.

In an American presidential cabinet, the various leaders all provide their input to the team leader (President). They are not expected to articulate an identical perspective. Instead, each cabinet member usually brings something unique to the conversation. In a similar vein, those who lead diverse ministry teams should not attempt to flatten out differences of opinion (especially if they are culturally rooted perspectives). Instead, team leaders should embrace both the team and the process, recognizing that it is inherently challenging, but that it can present its own unique rewards.

Building upon the above foundation, I want to conclude with four recommended postures for those who seek to lead diverse teams through seasons of cultural tension. These recommended postures are derived from a reflection upon Scripture and my own experience leading a multicultural team in Brooklyn. The four postures are those of a servant, a student, a confessor, and an intercessor.

First, team leaders should develop the posture of a servant.[565] When writing to a church that experienced conflict (Phil. 4:2), Paul urged his readers to adopt humility. He held up the example of Christ Jesus, who existed in the form of God, yet did not exploit his power and majesty for his own sake (Phil. 2:6). Instead, Paul notes, Jesus went to the cross as a servant (Phil. 2:7). Humility is at the heart of a servant. Paul urges, "Do nothing out of selfish ambition or conceit, but in humility consider others as more important than yourselves. Everyone should look out not

---

[565] [565] See my mentor Taylor Field, *Upside Down Leadership: Rethinking Influence and Success,* (Birmingham: New Hope, 2012), for timeless lessons on servant leadership.

only for his own interests, but also for the interests of others" (Phil. 2:3–4).

If team leaders are going to successfully navigate the tensions that arise on multicultural teams, they must embrace their calling to serve others. They must be willing to lay aside their power. Lingenfelter notes that "people are more important than authority and control."[566] In multicultural contexts, this could include humbling oneself in order to help another team member save face.[567] It could also include a member of the majority culture intentionally laying aside her privilege in order to empower another team member from a minority culture. When team leaders and members view themselves as servants to their teammates who are culturally "other," it can foster a greater spirit of unity and love on a team. This will be essential to any team that seeks to navigate cultural tension.

Second, team leaders should develop the posture of a student. Based upon what we learned about cultural intelligence, it stands to reason that those who work hard to adapt to other cultures will oftentimes be more successful. The Lingenfelters argue that "to be effective in a new culture, we must learn a host of new behaviors that are not part of our way of life."[568] They make this assertion in the context of considerations of cross-cultural teaching. However, the principle also holds true for those who seek to minister in any cross-cultural capacity. Those who are a part of a diverse team (especially those who lead such a team) will need to permanently embrace the posture of a student.

The Scriptures imply that Paul adopted this posture, since he chose to "become all things to all people" (1 Cor. 9:22). To preach effectively

---

[566] Sherwood G. Lingenfelter, *Leading Cross-Culturally: Covenant Relationships for Effective Christian Leadership* (Grand Rapids: Baker, 2008), 111.

[567] Elmer, *Cross-Cultural Conflict*, 80–98.

[568] Judith E. Lingenfelter and Sherwood G. Lingenfelter, *Teaching Cross-Culturally: An Incarnational Model for Learning and Teaching* (Grand Rapids: Baker, 2003), 23.

cross-culturally, Paul had to learn about his various target cultures. Members of diverse teams could take this one step further by intentionally learning about the cultural perspectives, customs, and traditions of their teammates. Doing so will probably increase mutual appreciation and enhance ministry effectiveness.

Third, team leaders should develop the posture of a confessor. At times, members of a multicultural ministry team will probably commit a cultural faux pas. They might act upon implicit bias, might utter an insensitive remark, or might wrongly judge their team members. In times of tension, team leaders should foster an atmosphere of confession. This is first modeled by the team leader as she adopts the posture of a confessor. A confessor is someone who acknowledges their error, asks for forgiveness, and seeks reconciliation. Readers of Scripture are told to confess their sins to both God (1 John 1:9) and to other Christians (James 5:16).

The biblical emphasis upon turning from sin demonstrates the centrality of repentance for Christian ministry. Lee even asserts, "Unless repentance permeates the process of incarnational leadership, triumphalism poisons the whole enterprise."[569] When members of a multicultural ministry team hurt one another (whether by sinful choice or unconscious error),[570] it is an opportunity for the display of the grace that is at the heart of the gospel. Those who lead such teams should practice confession. They should acknowledge their own individual cultural biases, mistakes, and sins. They should, when appropriate, acknowledge their participation in ungodly systems and structures that have oppressed

---

[569] Kyuboem Lee, "Repentance and Bonding Dynamics Within Cross-Cultural Church Planting Teams," in *Globalization and Its Effects on Urban Ministry in the 21st Century,* ed. Susan Baker (Pasadena: William Carey, 2009), 199.

[570] See Eric H. F. Law, *The Wolf Shall Dwell with the Lamb: A Spirituality for Leadership in a Multicultural Community* (St. Louis: Chalice Press, 1993), ix–xi, for a poignant example of apologizing for an unintentional, culturally insensitive approach to worship ministry.

certain cultures.[571] In confession, guilty parties have a chance to acknowledge their sin against the wounded party. This gives the wounded party a chance to extend forgiveness. When team members humble themselves and practice confession before their culturally "other" teammates, it provides an opportunity for healing and unity.

Fourth, team leaders should develop the posture of an intercessor. At times, cultural tension on a diverse team will create difficult situations. Sometimes it will seem as if there is no way forward. Wise leaders and members of multicultural teams will adopt the posture of an intercessor by praying for one another. When team members pray, unity can become a reality as team members draw closer to both God and to one another. As Sosa notes, "Being in a right relationship with God will always give you a vision of what he wants you to be engaged in as you seek to enlarge his kingdom here on earth."[572]

Intercession is biblical. Paul writes, "For this reason also, since the day we heard this, we haven't stopped praying for you" (Col. 1:9). Paul was determined to pray for the Colossian Christians. When experiencing cultural tension, team leaders and members should adopt the posture of an intercessor. They should pray for one another and with one another. This tends to align one's heart with both God and one's teammates. Team leaders and members should pray for wisdom, for unity, and for forgiveness.

Cultural tension is inevitable on ministry teams. However, the discerning leader can foster an environment that manages the tension, instead of eliminating the tension. She will adopt the posture of a servant,

---

[571] Stefan Paas, *Pilgrims and Priests: Christian Mission in a Post-Christian Society* (London: SCM, 2019), provides examples of a missiology infused by humility. His is a missiology that acknowledges the errors of colonialism and is comfortable with working from the margins to reach secularized societies. A missiology from the margins will likely be comfortable with the tension inherent to a multicultural team.

[572] Manuel Sosa, "Church Planting in South America's Urban Centers," in *Globalization and Its Effects on Urban Ministry in the 21st Century,* ed. Susan Baker (Pasadena: William Carey, 2009), 236.

a student, a confessor, and an intercessor. These recommendations will not provide a guaranteed path to success. However, when you adopt these practices, I believe that your chances of successfully participating in a diverse team will considerably improve.

Conclusion

We set out to discover if the ancient approach to urban mission included the use of diverse teams in the Book of Acts. We also sought to discover if the models from Acts could be applied to ministry teams in urban contexts. Having studied the nine ministry teams in Acts, I can definitively state that diverse teams played a key role in the early Church's ancient approach to urban mission. This is especially true the further one reads in the Book of Acts.

Furthermore, we discovered a high degree of similarity between the cities of Acts and contemporary cities. So, I argued that ministries in urban contexts should strongly consider fostering multicultural teams. There are both challenges and opportunities for those who wish to embrace the challenge of deploying diverse teams. That is why leaders of diverse teams must reflect deeply upon cultural equity, cultural intelligence, and cultural tension.

While I have not been able to answer every question related to multicultural teams, I believe we have forged new ground in linking the ancient way of the disciples in the Book of Acts with the modern way of Christians in urban contexts. As contemporary Christians recover their ancient roots, the urban centers of the 21st century will undoubtedly serve as a fertile laboratory for the exploration of both new and old approaches to team-based ministry. By retrieving this ancient approach, we can build a bridge to Brooklyn, and beyond.

APPENDIX: Cultural Map of the Ministry Teams in the Book of Acts

Ministry Team	Cultural Designation
Jerusalem Team (Acts 2)	Monocultural
Antioch (Acts 13)	Multicultural
First Pauline Team (Acts 13)	Multicultural
Philippian Team (Acts 16)	Multicultural
Thessalonian Team (Acts 17)	Monocultural
Berean Team (Acts 17)	Bicultural
Corinthian Team (Acts 18)	Multicultural
Ephesian Team (Acts 19)	Multicultural
The Return Team (Acts 20–21)	Multicultural

BIBLIOGRAPHY

Adams, Sean. *The Genre of Acts and Collected Biography.* Cambridge: Cambridge University Press, 2013.

Alexander, Loveday C. A. *Acts in Its Ancient Literary Context: A Classicist Looks at the Acts of the Apostles.* London: T&T Clark, 2005.

Algera, John A. "The Ends of the Earth Have Come to New York: A Church Multiplication Movement in the NY Metro Area." In *Globalization and Its Effects on Urban Ministry in the 21st Century,* 177-192. Edited by Susan Baker. Pasadena: William Carey, 2009.

Allen, David. *Lukan Authorship of Hebrews.* Nashville: B&H, 2010.

Allen, Roland. *Missionary Methods: St. Paul's Or Ours?* Grand Rapids: Eerdmans, 1962.

Ang, Soon, Linn Van Dyne, Christine Koh, K. Yee Ng, Klaus J. Templer, Cheryl Tay, and N. Anand Chandrasekar. "Cultural Intelligence: Its Measurement and Effects on Cultural Judgment and Decision Making, Cultural Adaptation, and Task Performance." *MOR* 3 (2007): 335–371.

Ascough, Richard. *Lydia: Paul's Cosmopolitan Hostess.* Collegeville, MN: Liturgical Press, 2009.

Ashford, Bruce. "The Gospel and Culture." In *Theology and Practice of Mission: God, the Church, and the Nations*, 109-127. Edited by Bruce Riley Ashford. Nashville: B&H, 2011.

Ashford, Bruce Riley and Heath Thomas. *The Gospel Of Our King: Bible, Worldview, and the Mission of Every Christian.* Grand Rapids: Baker, 2019.

Baker, Cynthia. "'From Every Nation Under Heaven:' Jewish Ethnicities in the Greco-Roman World." In *Prejudice and Christian Beginnings: Investigating Race, Gender and Ethnicity in Early Christian Studies*, 79-100. Edited by Laura Nasrallah and Elisabeth Schüssler Fiorenza. Minneapolis: Fortress Press, 2010.

Baker, Susan. "Introduction: Globalization, Urbanization and Mission," in *Globalization and Its Effects on Urban Ministry in the 21st Century.* Edited by Susan Baker. Pasadena: William Carey, 2009.

Balch, David. "ΜΕΤΑΒΟΛΗ ΠΟΛΙΤΕΙΩΝ—Jesus as Founder of the Church in Luke-Acts: Form and Function." In *Contextualizing Acts: Lukan Narrative and Greco-Roman Discourse,* 139-188. Edited by

Todd Penner and Caroline Vander Stichele. Leiden, The Netherlands: Brill, 2004.

Bale, Alan. *Genre and Narrative Coherence in the Acts of the Apostles.* London: Bloomsbury, 2015.

Barclay, John M. G. *Jews in the Mediterranean Diaspora: From Alexander to Trajan (323 BCE–117 CE).* Berkley: University of California Press, 1996.

———. *Pauline Churches and Diaspora Jews.* Grand Rapids: Eerdmans, 2011.

———. "Poverty in Pauline Studies: A Response to Steven Friesen." *Journal for the Study of the New Testament* 26 no. 3 (2004): 363–366.

Baretto, Eric. *Ethnic Negotiations: The Function of Race and Ethnicity in Acts 16.* Tübingen: Mohr Siebeck, 2010.

Baur, Ferdinand Christian. *Paul the Apostle of Jesus Christ: His Life and Works, His Epistles and Teaching;* 1845; repr., Grand Rapids: Baker, 2010.

Bauckham, Richard. "Paul and Other Jews with Latin Names in the New Testament." Pages 202–220 in *Paul, Luke, and the Graeco-Roman World.* Edited by Alf Christopherson, Carsten Claussen, Jörg Frey, and Bruce Longenecker. New York: Sheffield Academic Press, 2002.

Bergquist, Linda and Michael Crane. *City Shaped Churches: Planting Churches in the Global Era.* Portland: Urban Loft, 2018.

Bird, Michael. *An Anomalous Jew: Paul Among Jews, Greeks, and Romans.* Grand Rapids: Eerdmans, 2016.

———. "Paul's Religious and Historical Milieu." In *Paul's Missionary Methods: In His Time and Ours,* 17-28. Edited by Robert Plummer and John Mark Terry. Downers Grove, IL: IVP, 2012.

Bock, Darrell. *Acts.* Baker Exegetical New Testament Commentary. Grand Rapids: Baker, 2007.

Bond, Gilbert. *Paul and the Religious Experience of Reconciliation.* Louisville: Westminster John Knox Press, 2005.

Breckenridge, James and Lillian Breckenridge. *What Color Is Your God? Multicultural Education in the Church.* Grand Rapids: Baker, 1995.

Brooks, William. "A Biblical Understanding of the Diversity of Paul's Missionary Coworkers." In *Reflecting God's Glory Together: Diversity in Evangelical Mission,* 209-225. Edited by A. Scott Moreau and Beth Snodderly. Pasadena: William Carey, 2011.

Brouwer, Douglas J. *How to Become a Multicultural Church.* Grand Rapids: Eerdmans, 2017.

Bruce, F. F. *Acts.* NICNT. Grand Rapids: Eerdmans, 1976.

———. *Paul Apostle of the Heart Set Free.* Grand Rapids: Eerdmans, 1981.

———. *The Pauline Circle.* Eugene, OR: Wipf & Stock, 1985.

Buell, Denise Kimber. *Why This New Race: Ethnic Reasoning in Early Christianity.* New York: Columbia University Press, 2005.

Burridge, Richard. "The Genre of Acts—Revisited." In *Reading Acts Today: Essays in Honour of Loveday C. A. Alexander*, 3-28. Edited by Steve Walton, Thomas E. Phillips, Lloyd Pietersen, and F. Scott Spencer. London: T&T Clark, 2011.

Cacciola, Scott and Marc Stein. *Kevin Durant to Join Nets in N.B.A. Free Agency.* https://www.nytimes.com/2019/06//30/sports/kevin-durant-nets.html.

Cadbury, Henry. *The Book of Acts in History.* New York: Harper & Brother, 1955.

Carson, D. A. *Christ and Culture Revisited.* Grand Rapids: Eerdmans, 2008.

———. "Paul's Mission and Prayer." In *The Gospel to the Nations: Perspectives on Paul's Mission*, 175-184. Edited by Peter Bolt and Mark Thompson. Downers Grove, IL: IVP, 2000.

———. *The Gagging of God: Christianity Confronts Pluralism.* Grand Rapids: Zondervan, 1996.

Centers for Disease Control and Prevention. *About Refugees.* https://www.cdc.gov/immigrantrefugeehealth/about-refugees.html.

Centers for Disease Control and Prevention. *The Public Health Approach to Violence Prevention.* https://www.cdc.gov/violenceprevention/publichealthissue/publichealthapproach.html?CDC_AA_refVal=https%3A%2F%2Fwww.cdc.gov%2Fviolenceprevention%2Foverview%2Fpublichealthapproach.html.

Charles, Mark a nd Soong Chan Rah. *Unsettling Truths: The Ongoing, Dehumanizing Legacy of the Doctrine of Discovery.* Downers Grove, IL: IVP, 2019.

Chrysostom, St. John. *The Homilies on the Acts of the Apostles.* Rome: Veritatis Splendor Publications, 2012.

Clayman, Chris and Meredith Lee. *ethNYcity: The Nations, Tongues, and Faiths of Metropolitan New York.* New York: MNYBA, 2010.

Cohen, Shaye. *The Beginnings of Jewishness: Boundaries, Varieties, Uncertainties.* Berkley: University of California Press, 1999.

———. "The Origins of the Matrilineal Principle in Rabbinic Law." *AJS Review* 10, no. 1 (1985): 19–53.

———. "Was Timothy Jewish (Acts 16:1–3)? Patristic Exegesis, Rabbinic Law, and Matrilineal Descent." *Journal of Biblical Literature* 105, no. 2 (1986): 251–268.

Collins, John. *Between Athens and Jerusalem: Jewish Identity in the Hellenistic Diaspora.* Grand Rapids: Eerdmans, 2000.

Community District 8. *Community District 8 Brooklyn Neighborhood Report.* https://issuu.com/studybrooklyn/docs/community-district-8-brooklyn-neighborhood-report.

Conn, Harvie and Manuel Ortiz. *Urban Ministry: The Kingdom, the City & the People of God.* Downers Grove, IL: IVP, 2001.

Copeland, E. Luther. "Church Growth in Acts." *Missiology: An International Review* 4, no. 1 (1976): 13–26.

Crane, Michael. *Sowing Seeds of Change: Cultivating Transformation in the City.* Portland: Urban Loft, 2015.

Cranfield, C. E. B. *Romans: A Shorter Commentary.* Grand Rapids: Eerdmans, 1985.

Crowe, Jerome. *From Jerusalem to Antioch: The Gospel Across Cultures.* Collegeville, MN: Liturgical Press, 1997.

Danker, Frederick William. *A Greek-English Lexicon of the New Testament and Other Early Christian Literature,* 3rd edition (BDAG). Chicago: University of Chicago Press, 2000.

Davis, Kenneth. "Designing a Church Planting Internship for Seminarians That Is Mentor Led and Is Local Church Based." DMin diss., Trinity Evangelical Divinity School, 2013.

DeYmaz, Mark. *Building a Healthy Multiethnic Church.* San Francisco: Jossey-Bass, 2007.

DeYoung, Curtiss Paul, Michael Emerson, George Yancey, and Karen Chai Kim. *United By Faith: The Multiracial Congregation as an Answer to the Problem of Race.* Oxford: Oxford University Press, 2003.

"Lucius of Cyrene." In *Dictionary of African Christian Biography.* https://dacb.org/stories/libya/lucius/.

Dollar, Harold. *St. Luke's Methodology: A Cross-Cultural Challenge.* Pasadena: William Carey, 1996.

Donne, John. *A Sermon Upon the Eighth Verse of the First Chapter of The Acts of the Apostles: Preached to the Honourable Company of the Virginia Plantation, November 30th, 1622.*

https://www.biblestudytools.com/classics/the-works-of-john-donne-vol-6-/sermon-clvi.html.

Downey, Glanville. *A History of Antioch in Syria: From Seleucus to the Arab Conquest.* Princeton: Princeton University Press, 1961.

Duddridge, Natalie. *'He Asked Me Why He Can't Feel His Legs': 11-Year Old Struck By Stray Bullet May Be Paralyzed From the Waist Down."* https://newyork.cbslocal.com/2019/06//24/jayden-grant-stray-bullet-shooting/.

Earley, P. Christopher and Soon Ang. *Cultural Intelligence: Individual Interactions Across Cultures.* Stanford: Stanford University Press, 2003.

Ehrensperger, Kathy. *Paul and the Dynamics of Power: Communication and Interaction in the Early Christ-Movement.* London: T&T Clark, 2007.

———. *Paul at the Crossroads of Cultures: Theologizing in the Space Between.* London: Bloomsbury, 2015.

Ellis, E. Earle. "Paul's and His Co-workers." *New Testament Studies* 17, no. 4 (1971): 437–452.

Elmer, Duane. *Cross-Cultural Conflict: Building Relationships for Effective Ministry.* Downers Grove, IL: IVP, 1993.

Emerson, Michal and George Yancey. *Transcending Racial Barriers: Towards a Mutual Obligations Approach.* New York: Oxford University Press, 2011.

Fee, Gordon and Douglas Stuart. *How To Read The Bible For All Its Worth.* Grand Rapids: Zondervan, 2014.

Feinberg, John S., ed. *Continuity and Discontinuity: Perspectives on the Relationship Between the Old and New Testaments.* Westchester, IL: Crossway, 1988.

Fellows, Richard. "Name Giving by Paul and the Destination of Acts." *Tyndale Bulletin* 67, no. 2 (2016): 247–268.

Fiensy, David A. "The Composition of the Jerusalem Church." In *The Book of Acts in Its Palestinian Setting*, 213-236. Edited by Richard Bauckham. Vol 4 of *The Book of Acts in Its First Century Setting,* ed. Bruce Winter and Andrew Clarke. Grand Rapids: Eerdmans, 1993.

Flaherty, Jane. "The Effects of Cultural Intelligence on Team Member Acceptance and Integration in Multinational Teams." In *Handbook of Cultural Intelligence: Theory, Measurement, and Application*, 192-205. Edited by Soon Ang and Linn Van Dyne. New York: Routledge, 2008.

Flemming, Dean. *Contextualization in the New Testament: Patterns for Theology and Mission.* Downers Grove, IL: IVP, 2005.

Friesen, Steven J. "Poverty in Pauline Studies: Beyond the So-called New Consensus." *Journal for the Study of the New Testament* 26, no. 3 (2004): 323–361.

———. "The Wrong Erastus: Ideology, Archaeology, and Exegesis." In *Corinth in Context: Comparative Studies on Religion and Society*, 231-256. Edited by Steven J. Friesen, Daniel N. Schowalter, and James Walters. Leiden: Brill, 2010.

Gallagher, Robert. "Missionary Methods: St. Paul's, St. Roland's, or Ours?" In *Missionary Methods: Research, Reflections, and Realities*, 3-22. Edited by Craig Ott and J. D. Payne. Pasadena: William Carey, 2013.

Gill, Brad. "Beyond Groupism: Refining Our Analysis of Ethnicity and Groups." *International Journal of Frontier Mission* 35, no. 4 (2018): 179–184.

Glaeser, Edward. *Triumph of the City: How Our Greatest Invention Makes Us Richer, Smarter, Greener, Healthier, and Happier.* New York: Penguin, 2011.

Goheen, Michael. *A Light to the Nations: The Missional Church and the Biblical Story.* Grand Rapids: Baker 2011.

———. *Introducing Christian Mission Today: Scripture, History and Issues.* Downers Grove, IL: IVP, 2014.

Goldschmidt, Henry. *Race and Religion Among the Chosen Peoples of Crown Heights.* New Brunswick, NJ: Rutgers University Press, 2006.

Gonzalez, Justo. *Acts: The Gospel of the Spirit.* Maryknoll, NY: Orbis, 2001.

———. *The Mestizo Augustine: A Theologian Between Two Cultures.* Downers Grove, IL: IVP, 2016.

———. *Luke.* BTCB. Louisville: Westminster John Knox Press, 2010.

Goodrich, John K. "Erastus, Quaestor of Corinth: The Administrative Rank of ὁ οἰκονόμος τῆς πόλεως (Rom 16.23) in an Achaean Colony." *New Testament Studies* 56 (2009): 90–115.

Goudzwaard, Bob and Craig Bartholomew. *Beyond the Modern Age: An Archaeology of Contemporary Culture.* Downers Grove, IL: IVP, 2017.

Green, Joel B. "Luke-Acts, or Luke and Acts?" In *Reading Acts Today: Essays in Honour of Loveday C. A. Alexander*, 101-119. Edited by

Steve Walton, Thomas E. Phillips, Lloyd Pietersen, and F. Scott Spencer. London: T&T Clark, 2011.

Gruca-Macaulay, Alexandra. *Lydia as a Rhetorical Construct in Acts.* Atlanta: SBL Press, 2016.

Gruen, Erich. *Heritage and Hellenism: The Reinvention of the Jewish Tradition.* Berkley: University of California Press, 1998.

Guest, Kenneth. *Cultural Anthropology: A Toolkit for a Global Age.* New York: W. W. Norton & Company, 2014.

Haley, Shelley. "Be Not Afraid of the Dark: Critical Race Theory and Classical Studies." In *Prejudice and Christian Beginnings: Investigating Race, Gender and Ethnicity in Early Christian Studies*, 27-49. Edited by Laura Nasrallah and Elisabeth Schüssler Fiorenza. Minneapolis: Fortress Press, 2010.

Hall, Jonathan. *Hellenicity: Between Ethnicity and Culture.* Chicago: University of Chicago Press, 2002.

Hansen, Bruce. 'All of You are One:' The Social Vision of Gal 3:28, 1 Cor 12:13 and Col 3:11. New York: T&T Clark, 2010.

Harland, Philip. *Dynamics of Identity in the World of the Early Christians.* New York: T&T Clark, 2009.

Hays, J. Daniel. *From Every People and Nation: A Biblical Theology of Race.* Downers Grove, IL: IVP, 2003.

Herodotus. *The Histories.* www.perseus.uchicago.edu/perseus-cgi/citequery3.pl?dbname=GreekFeb2011&query=Hdt.%208.144.2&getid=1.

Hertig, Paul. "The Magical Mystery Tour: Philip Encounters Magic and Materialism in Samaria." In *Mission in Acts: Ancient Narratives in Contemporary Context*, 103-113. Edited by Robert L. Gallagher and Paul Hertig. Maryknoll, NY: Orbis 2004.

Hiebert, Paul. *Anthropological Insights for Missionaries.* Grand Rapids: Baker, 1985.

———. *Cultural Anthropology.* Grand Rapids: Baker, 1983.

———. *Constants in Human Context: Anthropological Explorations for Contemporary Missions.* Grand Rapids: Baker, 2009.

———. *The Missiological Implications of Epistemological Shifts: Affirming Truth in a Modern/Postmodern World.* Harrisburg, PA: Trinity Press, 1999.

———. *Transforming Worldviews: An Anthropological Understanding of How People Change.* Grand Rapids: Baker, 2008.

Hiebert, Paul and Eloise Hiebert Meneses. *Incarnational Ministry: Planting Churches in Band, Tribal, Peasant, and Urban Societies.* Grand Rapids: Baker, 1995.

Hill, Craig. *Hellenists and Hebrews: Reappraising Division Within the Earliest Church.* Minneapolis: Fortress Press, 1992.

Hill, Daniel. "Just Power: Ten Principles for Building Intercultural Leadership Teams." In *Intercultural Ministry: Hope for a Changing World*, 111-123. Edited by Grace Ji-Sun Kim and Jann Aldredge-Clanton. Valley Forge, PA: Judson Press, 2017.

Hodge, Caroline Johnson. *If Sons, Then Heirs: A Study of Kinship and Ethnicity in the Letters of Paul.* Oxford: Oxford University Press, 2007.

Hong, Angie. "Equals at the Table." In *Intercultural Ministry: Hope for a Changing World*, 124-133. Edited by Grace Ji-Sun Kim and Jann Aldredge-Clanton. Valley Forge, PA: Judson Press, 2017.

Howell, Brian M. and Jenell Paris. *Introducing Cultural Anthropology: A Christian Perspective,* 2nd edition. Grand Rapids: Baker, 2019.

International Mission Board. *PeopleGroups.info.* https://www.peoplegroups.info/.

Jackson, Kenneth and John Manbeck. *The Neighborhoods of Brooklyn.* New Haven, CT: Yale University Press, 2004.

Jennings, Willie. *Acts.* BTCB. Louisville: Westminster John Knox Press, 2017.

———. *The Christian Imagination: Theology and the Origins of Race.* New Haven, CT: Yale University Press, 2010.

Josephus. *Antiquities of the Jews.*www.sacred-texts-.com/jud/josephus/ant-20.htm.

Kasinitz, Philip. *Caribbean New York: Black Immigrants and the Politics of Race.* Ithaca, NY: Cornell University Press, 1992.

Keathley, Kenneth. "The Work of God: Salvation." In *A Theology for the Church*, 686-784. Edited by Daniel Akin. Nashville: B&H, 2007.

Keener, Craig. *Acts: An Exegetical Commentary.* 4 vols. Grand Rapids: Baker, 2012–2015.

Kim, Grace Ji-Sun and Graham Hill. *Healing Our Broken Humanity: Practices for Revitalizing the Church and Renewing the World.* Downers Grove, IL: IVP, 2018.

Kim, Luther Jeom O. *Doing Diaspora Missiology Toward "Diaspora Mission Church."* Eugene, OR: Wipf & Stock, 2016.

Kim, Matthew. *Preaching with Cultural Intelligence: Understanding the People Who Hear Our Sermons.* Grand Rapids: Baker, 2017.

Kotkin, Joel. *The City: A Global History.* New York: Random, 2005.

K. R. "Growing Up A Third Culture Kid: A Sociological Self-Exploration." *Human Architecture: Journal of the Sociology of Self-Knowledge* 9, no. 1 (2011): 29–42.

Kuecker, Aaron. *The Spirit and the 'Other': Social Identity, Ethnicity and Intergroup Reconciliation in Luke-Acts.* London: T&T Clark, 2011.

Kumbi, Hirpo. *The Culturally Intelligent Leader: Developing Multi-ethnic Communities in a Multicultural Age.* Watford, England: Instant Apostle, 2017.

Ladd, George Eldon. "Paul's Friends in Colossians 4:7–16." *Review and Expositor* 70, no. 4 (1973): 507–514.

Law, Eric H. F. *The Wolf Shall Dwell with the Lamb: A Spirituality for Leadership in a Multicultural Community.* St. Louis: Chalice Press, 1993.

Le Donne, Anthony. "Complicating the Category of Ethnos Toward Poliscentrism: A Possible Way Forward Within Second Temple Ethnography." In *The Urban World and the First Christians*, 3-19. Edited by Steve Walton, Paul Treblico, and David Gill. Grand Rapids: Eerdmans, 2017.

Lee, Kyuboem. "Repentance and Bonding Dynamics Within Cross-Cultural Church Planting Teams." In *Globalization and Its Effects on Urban Ministry in the 21st Century*, 193-211. Edited by Susan Baker. Pasadena: William Carey, 2009.

Lee, Peter and James Sung-Hwan Park. "Beyond People Group Thinking: A Critical Reevaluation of Unreached People Groups." *Missiology* 46, no. 3 (2018): 212–225.

Leonhardt-Balzer, Jutta. "Diaspora Jewish Attitudes to Metropoleis: Philo and Paul on Balanced Personalities, Split Loyalties, Jerusalem, and Rome." Pages 86–98 in *The Urban World and the First Christians.* Edited by Steve Walton, Paul Treblico, and David Gill. Grand Rapids: Eerdmans, 2017.

Levinskaya, Irina. *The Book of Acts in Its Diaspora Setting,* vol 5 of *The Book of Acts in Its First Century Setting,* ed. Bruce Winter and Andrew Clarke. Grand Rapids: Eerdmans, 1996.

Li, David K. *Garden Wilting at No. 2 as Barclays Center named highest-grossing venue in US.* https://nypost.com/2013/07/24/garden-wilting-at-no-2-as-barclays-center-named-highest-grossing-venue-in-us/.

Lightfoot, J. B. *The Acts of the Apostles: A Newly Discovered Commentary.* Edited by Ben Witherington III and Todd Still. Downers Grove, IL: IVP, 2014.

Lingenfelter, Judith and Sherwood G. Lingenfelter. *Teaching Cross-Culturally: An Incarnational Model.* Grand Rapids: Baker, 2003.

Lingenfelter, Sherwood G. *Leading Cross-Culturally: Covenant Relationships for Effective Christian Leadership.* Grand Rapids: Baker, 2008.

Little, Christopher. *Mission in the Way of Paul: Biblical Mission for the Church in the Twenty-First Century.* New York: Peter Lang, 2005.

Livermore, David. *Cultural Intelligence: Improving Your CQ to Engage Our Multicultural World.* Grand Rapids: Baker, 2009.

———. *Leading with Cultural Intelligence.* New York: AMACOM, 2015.

———. *Serving with Eyes Wide Open: Doing Short-Term Missions with Cultural Intelligence.* Grand Rapids: Baker, 2013.

Lucius of Samosata. *Life of Demonax.* https://lucianofsamosata.info/Demonax.html.

Martin, Francis. *Acts.* ACCS. Downers Grove, IL: IVP, 2006.

Matisyahu. www.matisyahuworld.com.

———. "King Without a Crown." https://www.youtube.com/watch?v=ChV5BZ8SmS0.

Matthews, Kenneth and M. Sydney Park. *The Post-Racial Church: A Biblical Framework for Multiethnic Reconciliation.* Grand Rapids: Kregel, 2011.

McCarty, V. K. "Lydia in Acts 16: 'The Lord Opened Her Heart.'" *ICJ* 13, no. 1 (2014): 13–30.

———. "Prisca-Fellow Tent-maker and Fellow Missionary of Paul: Acts 18.2–3, 18, 26; Romans 16.3–4; 1 Corinthians 16.19; 2 Timothy 4.19.'" *ICJ* 11, no. 2 (2012): 44–60.

McCoskey, Denise Eileen. *Race: Antiquity and Its Legacy.* Oxford: Oxford University Press, 2012.

McGavran, Donald. *The Bridges of God: A Study in the Strategy of Missions.* Eugene, OR: Wipf & Stock, 2005.

McKnight, Scot. *The King Jesus Gospel: The Original Good News Revisited.* Grand Rapids: Zondervan, 2011.

———. *The Letter to the Colossians.* NICNT. Grand Rapids: Eerdmans, 2018.

McRoberts, Omar. *Streets of Glory: Church and Community in a Black Urban Neighborhood.* Chicago: University of Chicago Press, 2003.

Mead, Margaret. *Coming of Age in Samoa: A Psychological Study of Primitive Youth for Western Civilization.* New York: HarperCollins, 2001.

Meeks, Wayne. *The First Urban Christians: The Social World of the Apostle Paul.* New Haven, CT: Yale University Press, 2003.

Merkle, Benjamin. *40 Questions About Elders and Deacons.* Grand Rapids: Kregel, 2008.

Meriam-Webster. *Equity.* https://www.merriam-webster.com/dictionary/equity.

Merkle, Benjamin L. "Paul's Ecclesiology." In *Paul's Missionary Methods: In His Time and Ours*, 56-73. Edited by Robert Plummer and John Mark Terry. Downers Grove, IL: IVP, 2012.

Metzger, Bruce. "Antioch-on-the-Orontes." *The Biblical Archaeologist.* 11, no. 4 (1948): 70–88.

———. *A Textual Commentary on the Greek New Testament*, 2nd edition. New York: UBS, 1994.

Moy, Russell. "Biculturalism, Race, and the Bible." *Religious Education* 88, no. 3 (1993): 415–433.

Murray, George. "Paul's Corporate Evangelism in the Book of Acts." *Bibliotheca Sacra* 155 (1998): 189–200.

Nasrallah, Laura. "'You Were Bought with a Price': Freedpersons and Things in 1 Corinthians." In *Corinth in Contrast: Studies in Inequality*, 54-73. Edited by Steven J. Friesen, Sarah James, and Daniel N. Schowalter. Leiden: Brill, 2014.

Neighbors in Action. www.neighborsinaction.org/sos.

Niebuhr, H. Richard. *Christ and Culture.* New York: Harper & Row, 1951.

Niessen, Johannes. *New Testament and Mission: Historical and Hermeneutical Perspectives.* New York: Peter Lang, 2007.

Oakes, Peter. "Constructing Poverty Scales for Graeco-Roman Society: A Response to Steven Friesen's 'Poverty in Pauline Studies.'" *Journal for the Study of the New Testament* 26, no. 3 (2004): 367–371.

Oden, Thomas. "A Libyan History Awaiting Discovery." *Bibliotheca Sacra* 167 (2010): 3–16.

———. *Early Libyan Christianity: Uncovering a North African Tradition.* Downers Grove, IL: IVP, 2011.

———. *The African Memory of Mark.* Downers Grove, IL: IVP, 2011.

Olson, C. Gordon. *What in the World Is God Doing?* Cedar Knolls, NJ: Global Gospel Publishers, 2003.

Orsi, Robert. *Gods of the City: Religion and the American Urban Landscape.* Indianapolis: Indiana University Press, 1999.

———. "The Religious Boundaries of an In-Between People: Street *Feste* and the Problem of the Dark-Skinned Other in Italian Harlem." In *Gods of the City: Religion and the American Urban Landscape*, 257-288. Edited by Robert Orsi. Indianapolis: Indiana University Press, 1999.

Osborne, Grant. *The Hermeneutical Spiral: A Comprehensive Introduction to Biblical Interpretation,* Revised and Expanded edition. Downers Grove, IL: IVP, 2006.

Osman, Suleiman. *The Invention of Brownstone Brooklyn: Gentrification and the Search for Authenticity in Postwar New York.* Oxford: Oxford University Press, 2011.

Ott, Craig and Gene Wilson. *Global Church Planting: Biblical Principles and Best Practices for Multiplication.* Grand Rapids: Baker, 2011.

Ott, Craig and J. D. Payne. *Missionary Methods: Research, Reflections, and Realities.* Pasadena: William Carey, 2013.

Paas, Stefan. *Pilgrims and Priests: Christian Mission in a Post-Christian Society.* London: SCM, 2019.

Padilla, Osvaldo. *The Acts of the Apostles: Interpretation, History and Theology.* Downers Grove, IL: IVP, 2016.

Padilla, René. "El Reino de dios y la Historia en la Teologia Latinoamericana." *Cuadernos de Teologia* 7, no. 1 (1985): 5–12.

———. "The Unity of the Church and the Homogenous Unit Principle." *International Bulletin of Missionary Research* 6, no. 1 (1982): 23–30.

Palmer, Daryl. "Acts and the Ancient Historical Monograph." In *The Book of Acts in Its Ancient Literary Setting*, 1-30. Vol 1 of *The Book of Acts in Its First Century Setting,* ed. Bruce Winter and Andrew Clarke. Grand Rapids: Eerdmans, 1993.

Parsons, Mikeal C. *Body and Character in Luke and Acts: The Subversion of Physiognomy in Early Christianity.* Grand Rapids: Baker, 2006.

Parsons, Mikeal and Joseph Tyson, eds. *Cadbury, Knox, and Talbert: American Contributions to the Study of Acts.* Atlanta: Scholars Press, 1992.

Penner, Todd. *In Paise of Christian Origins: Stephen and the Hellenists in Lukan Apologetic Historiography.* New York: T&T Clark, 2004.

Peterson, David G. *The Acts of the Apostles.* PCNT. Grand Rapids: Eerdmans, 2009.

Pilch, John. *Stephen: Paul and the Hellenist Israelites.* Collegeville, MN: Liturgical Press, 2008.

Pitts, Andrew and Joshua Walker. "The Authorship of Hebrews: A Further Development in the Luke-Paul Relationship." In *Paul and His Social Relations*, 143-184. Edited by Stanley Porter and Christopher Land. Boston: Brill, 2013.

Phillips, Thomas. "Paul as a Role Model in Acts: The 'We'-Passages in Acts 16 and Beyond." In *Acts and Ethics*, 49-63. Edited by Thomas Phillips. Sheffield, England: Sheffield Phoenix Press, 2005.

———. *Paul, His Letters, and Acts.* Peabody, MA: Hendrickson, 2009.

Philo. *Flaccus 45–46.* www.earlychristianwritings.com/yonge/book36.html.

Plummer, Robert and John Mark Terry. *Paul's Missionary Methods: In His Time and Ours.* Downers Grove, IL: IVP, 2012.

Polhill, John B. *Acts.* NAC. Nashville: B&H, 1992.

———. "The Hellenist Breakthrough: Acts 6–12." *Review and Expositor* 71, no. 4 (1974): 475–486.

Porter, Stanley. "The Genre of Acts and the Ethics of Discourse." In *Acts and Ethics*, 1-15. Edited by Thomas Phillips. Sheffield, England: Sheffield Phoenix Press, 2005.

———. "How Do We Define Pauline Social Relations?" In *Paul and His Social Relations*, 7-33. Edited by Stanley Porter and Christopher Land. Boston: Brill, 2013.

Rabens, Volker. "Paul's Mission Strategy in the Urban Landscape of the First-Century Roman Empire." In *The Urban World and the First Christians*, 99-122. Edited by Steve Walton, Paul Treblico, and David Gill. Grand Rapids: Eerdmans, 2017.

Rah, Soong-Chan. *Many Colors: Cultural Intelligence for a Changing Church.* Chicago: Moody Press, 2010.

Ramsay, William. *St. Paul the Traveler and Roman Citizen,* Full-Color Updated & Revised Edition. Grand Rapids: Kregel, 2001.

Robinson, Thomas. *Ignatius of Antioch and the Parting of the Ways: Early Jewish-Christian Relations.* Peabody, MA: Hendrickson, 2009.

Rockstuhl, Thomas and Kok-Yee Ng. "The Effects of Cultural Intelligence on Interpersonal Trust in Multicultural Teams." In *Handbook of Cultural Intelligence: Theory, Measurement, and Application*, 206-220. Edited by Soon Ang and Linn Van Dyne. New York: Routledge, 2008.

Roediger, David. *Working Towards Whiteness: How America's Immigrants Became White.* New York: Basic, 2018.

Roembke, Lisa. *Building Credible Multicultural Teams.* Pasadena: William Carey, 2000.

Rolston, Holmes and Clovis Chappell. *Personalities Around Paul: Men and Women Who Helped or Hindered the Apostle Paul.* Richmond: John Knox Press, 1954.

Rose, Tamara. *Raising Brooklyn: Nannies, Childcare, and Caribbeans Creating Community.* New York: NYU Press, 2011.

Rowe, C. Kavin. *World Upside Down: Reading Acts in the Graeco-Roman Age.* Oxford: Oxford University Press, 2009.

Rynkiewich, Michael. *Cultures and Languages of Papua New Guinea: The Story of the Origins, Migrations and Settlements of Melanesian Peoples, Languages and Cultures.* Goroka, Papua New Guinea: Melanesian Institute 2004.

———. *Soul, Self, and Society: A Postmodern Anthropology for Mission in a Postcolonial World.* Eugene, OR: Cascade Books, 2001.

Sanchez, Leopoldo A. "Can Anything Good Come Out Of ____ ? Come and See! Faithful Witness in Marginality and Hospitality." *Concordia Journal* 41, no. 2 (2015): 111–123.

Sciorra, Joseph. "'We Go Where the Italians Live': Religious Processions as Ethnic and Territorial Markers in a Multi-ethnic Brooklyn Neighborhood." In *Gods of the City: Religion and the American Urban Landscape*, 310-340. Edited by Robert Orsi. Indianapolis: Indiana University Press, 1999.

Schnabel, Eckhard. *Acts.* ZECNT. Grand Rapids: Zondervan, 2012.

———. *Early Christian Mission.* 2 vols. Downers Grove, IL: IVP, 2004.

Sechrest, Love. *A Former Jew: Paul and the Dialectics of Race.* London: T&T Clark, 2010.

Shively, Elizabeth. "Recognizing Penguins: Audience Expectation, Cognitive Genre Theory, and the Ending of Mark's Gospel." *CBQ* 80, no. 2 (2018): 273–292.

Silzer, Sheryl Takagi. *Biblical Multicultural Teams: Applying Biblical Truth to Cultural Differences.* Pasadena: William Carey, 2011.

Sire, James. *The Universe Next Door.* Downers Grove, IL: IVP, 2009.

Skinner, Matthew. *Intrusive God, Disruptive Gospel: Encountering the Divine in the Book of Acts.* Grand Rapids: Brazos, 2015.

Sleeman, Matthew. "Paul, Pentecost, and the Nomosphere: The Final Return to Jerusalem in the Acts of the Apostles." In *The Urban World and the First Christians*, 20-41. Edited by Steve Walton, Paul Treblico, and David Gill. Grand Rapids: Eerdmans, 2017.

Sosa, Manuel. "Church Planting in South America's Urban Centers." In *Globalization and Its Effects on Urban Ministry in the 21st Century*, 225-240. Edited by Susan Baker. Pasadena: William Carey, 2009.

Spradley, James and Michael Rynkiewich. *The Nacirema: Readings on American Culture*. New York: Little Brown & Company, 1975.

———. *Ethics and Anthropology: Dilemmas in Fieldwork*. Indianapolis: Wiley, 1976.

Spencer, F. Scott. *The Portrait of Philip in Acts: A Study of Roles and Relations*. Sheffield, England: Sheffield Academic Press, 1992.

Stacy, Robert Wayne. "Colossians 4:11 and the Ethnic Identity of Luke." *Eruditio Ardescens* 2, no. 1 (2015): 1–15.

Stallard, Jimmy. *Facing the Sons of Thunder: Biblical Principles for Conflict Resolution*. Huntsville, AL: Evangel Publications, 2007.

Stallard, Mike. "A Proposal for Theological Method: Systematic Theology as Model Building." http://our-hope.org/blog/wp-content/uploads/2009/09/Method2.pdf.

———. *First & Second Thessalonians: Looking for Christ's Return*. Chattanooga: AMG, 2009.

Stallard, Stephen. "Placemaking in the City: A Theological Vision for Church Planters in Brooklyn's Gentrifying Neighborhoods." *International Journal of Urban Transformation* 4 (2019): 47–59.

———. "Voices in the Violence: How Black Churches in Brooklyn Can Help us Find our Voice as we Minister in Violent Contexts," *Journal of Urban Mission*. 6 (2020).

Stark, Rodney. *Cities of God: The Real Story of How Christianity Became an Urban Movement and Conquered Rome*. New York: HarperSanFrancisco, 2006.

———. *The Rise of Christianity*. New York: HarperCollins, 1996.

Sternberg, Meir. *The Poetics of Biblical Narrative: Ideological Literature and the Drama of Reading*. Bloomington, IN: Indiana University Press, 1987.

Strauss, Stephen. "The Significance of Acts 11:26 for the Church at Antioch and Today." *Bibliotheca Sacra* 168 (2011): 283–300.

Talbert, Charles. *Literary Patterns, Theological Themes and the Genre of Luke-Acts*. Missoula, MT: Scholars Press, 1974.

Taber, Charles. *To Understand the World to Save the World: The Interface Between Missiology and the Social Sciences*. Harrisburg, PA: Trinity Press, 2000.

Taylor, Charles. *A Secular Age*. Cambridge: Belknap Press, 2007.

Taylor, Clarence. *The Black Churches of Brooklyn.* New York: Columbia University Press, 1994.
Tennent, Timothy. *Invitation to World Missions: A Trinitarian Missiology for the Twenty-first Century.* Grand Rapids: Kregel, 2010.
Thompson James. *The Church According to Paul: Rediscovering the Community Conformed to Christ.* Grand Rapids: Baker, 2014.
Thompson, Richard. *Keeping the Church In Its Place: The Church as Narrative Character in Acts.* New York: T&T Clark, 2006.
Thompson, Robin. "Diaspora Jewish Freedmen: Stephen's Deadly Opponents." *Bibliotheca Sacra* 173 (2016): 166–181.
Tweed, Thomas. "Diasporic Nationalism and Urban Landscape: Cuban Immigrants at a Catholic Shrine in Miami." In *Gods of the City: Religion and the American Urban Landscape*, 131-154. Edited by Robert Orsi. Indianapolis: Indiana University Press, 1999.
Van Til, Henry R. *The Calvinistic Concept of Culture.* Grand Rapids: Baker, 2001.
Vanhoozer, Kevin, Charles Anderson, and Michael Sleasman, eds. *Everyday Theology: How To Read Cultural Texts and Interpret Trends.* Grand Rapids: Baker, 2007.
Walls, Andrew. *Crossing Cultural Frontiers: Studies in the History of World Christianity.* Maryknoll, NY: Orbis, 2017.
———. *The Cross-Cultural Process in Christian History.* Edinburgh: T&T Clark, 2002.
Wan, Enoch and Anthony Casey. *Church Planting Among Immigrants in US Urban Centers: The "Where", "Why", and "How" of Diaspora Missiology in Action.* Portland: Institute of Diaspora Studies, 2014.
Wellborn, L. L. "'Inequality in Roman Corinth: Evidences from Diverse Sources Evaluated by a Neo-Ricardian Model." In *Roman Corinth*, 47-84. Edited by James R. Harrison and L. L. Wellborn. Vol. 2 of *The First Urban Churches.* Atlanta: SBL, 2016.
Whitman, Walt. *Crossing Brooklyn Ferry.* https://www.poetryfoundation.org/poems/45470/crossing-brooklyn-ferry.
Williams, Jarvis. *One New Man: The Cross and Racial Reconciliation in Pauline Theology.* Nashville: B&H, 2010.
Williamson, Darryl. "Word and Witness: Church Leadership for Twenty-First Century Gospel Missions." In *All Are Welcome: Toward a Multi-Everything Church*, 209-226. USA: White Blackbird, 2018.
Witherington III, Ben. *The Acts of the Apostles: A Socio-Rhetorical Commentary.* Grand Rapids: Eerdmans, 1998.

Woo, Rodney. *The Color of Church: A Biblical and Practical Paradigm for Multiracial Churches*. Nashville: B&H, 2009.

World Population Review. "Brooklyn Population 2019." *World Population Review*. worldpopulationreview.com/boroughs/brooklyn-population/.

Wright, N. T. *Paul and the Faithfulness of God*. Minneapolis: Fortress Press, 2013.

———. N. T. *Scripture and the Authority of God: How to Read the Bible Today*. New York: HarperOne, 2011.

Wright, N. T. and Michael Bird. *The New Testament in Its World*. Grand Rapids: Zondervan, 2019.

Wrogemann, Henning. *Intercultural Theology, Volume One: Intercultural Hermeneutics*. Downers Grove, IL: IVP, 2016.

Wytsma, Ken. *The Myth of Equality: Uncovering the Roots of Injustice and Privilege*. Downers Grove, IL: IVP, 2017.

Yancey, George. *One Body, One Spirit: Principles of Successful Multiracial Churches*. Downers Grove, IL: IVP, 2003.

Young, Robert. *Postcolonialism: A Very Short Introduction*. Oxford: Oxford University Press, 2003.

Yuckman, Colin. "Mission and the Book of Acts in a Pluralist Society." *Missiology* 47, no. 2 (2019): 104–120.

Zetterholm, Magnus. *The Formation of Christianity in Antioch: A Social-Scientific Approach to the Separation Between Judaism and Christianity*. New York: Routledge, 2003.

Zukin, Sharon. *Naked City: The Death and Life of Authentic Urban Spaces*. Oxford: Oxford University Press, 2010.

www.ingramcontent.com/pod-product-compliance
Lightning Source LLC
Chambersburg PA
CBHW050243170426
43202CB00015B/2894